John Lewis and the Challenge of "Real" Black Music

JAZZ PERSPECTIVES

Eric Porter and John Szwed, Series Editors
Lewis Porter, Founding Editor

Head Hunters: *The Making of Jazz's First Platinum Album*
By Steven F. Pond

Lester Young By Lewis Porter

The Last Miles: The Music of Miles Davis, 1980–1991
By George Cole

The André Hodeir Jazz Reader
By André Hodeir Edited by Jean-Louis Pautrot

Someone to Watch Over Me: The Life and Music of Ben Webster
By Frank Büchmann-Møller

Rhythm Is Our Business: Jimmie Lunceford and the Harlem Express
By Eddy Determeyer

Lennie Tristano: His Life in Music By Eunmi Shim

Lee Konitz: Conversations on the Improviser's Art By Andy Hamilton

Delightfulee: The Life and Music of Lee Morgan
By Jeffery S. McMillan

"Ellington Uptown": Duke Ellington, James P. Johnson, and the Birth of Concert Jazz By John Howland

New Orleans Style and the Writing of American Jazz History
By Bruce Boyd Raeburn

The Music of Django Reinhardt By Benjamin Givan

Music Is My Life: Louis Armstrong, Autobiography, and American Jazz
By Daniel Stein

Dameronia: The Life and Music of Tadd Dameron By Paul Combs

Jazz and Machine-Age Imperialism: Music, "Race," and Intellectuals in France, 1918–1945 By Jeremy F. Lane

After Django: Making Jazz in Postwar France By Tom Perchard

John Lewis and the Challenge of "Real" Black Music
By Christopher Coady

John Lewis and the Challenge of "Real" Black Music

Christopher Coady

University of Michigan Press

Ann Arbor

Published in the United States of America by the
University of Michigan Press
Manufactured in the United States of America
⊗ Printed on acid-free paper

2019 2018 2017 2016 4 3 2 1

A CIP catalog record for this book is available from the British Library.

Library of Congress Cataloging-in-Publication Data

Names: Coady, Christopher, 1980- author.
Title: John Lewis and the challenge of "real" black music / Christopher Coady.
Description: Ann Arbor : University of Michigan Press, [2016] |
Series: Jazz perspectives | Includes bibliographical references, filmography, and index.
Identifiers: LCCN 2016027223| ISBN 9780472053209 (pbk. : alk. paper) |
ISBN 9780472073207 (hardcover : alk. paper) | ISBN 9780472122264 (ebook)
Subjects: LCSH: Lewis, John, 1920–2001—Criticism and interpretation. | Modern Jazz Quartet. | Third stream (Music)—History and criticism. | Jazz—1941–1950—History and criticism. | Jazz—1951–1960—History and criticism. | Music and race—United States—History—20th century.
Classification: LCC ML410.L6245 C5 2016 | DDC 781.65092—dc23
LC record available at https://lccn.loc.gov/2016027223

for Caitlin

Acknowledgments

This book would not have been possible without the support of the following people and organizations. First and foremost I would like to thank my colleagues at the University of Sydney for their ongoing encouragement and interest in this project and for contributing to what I see as the extraordinary intellectual culture of the Sydney Conservatorium of Music. It is in this environment that the core arguments of this book were forged and I am grateful to all those who provided feedback during their formation. In particular, I would like to thank Charles Fairchild of the University of Sydney and Gabriel Solis of the University of Illinois for reading draft chapters and offering advice that truly helped shape my thinking around such a complicated topic. The manuscript has been greatly improved by their advice. Any deficiencies in the work that remain are well and truly of my own making. I also extend thanks to my colleagues at the University of New South Wales Dorottya Fabian and John Napier for helping set things off in the right direction many years ago, as well as to Nicholas Gebhardt of Birmingham City University and Walter Van de Leur of the University of Amsterdam for advice provided during this project's initial stages.

I am indebted to Christopher Hebert, editor-at-large for popular music and jazz at the University of Michigan Press, for helping me navigate the submission of my first monograph and the Sydney Conservatorium of Music Research Unit for the award of an Early Career Researcher grant that helped carve out the time necessary to finish this project. Throughout the years I've spent working on this book, the collegiality and advice provided by the Musicology Colloquium Series at the University of Sydney in Australia and the Rhythm Changes research conferences in Europe have helped keep me both motivated and on track, and for this I am also thankful. Finally, I'm sure I cannot thank enough my family, friends, and wife, Caitlin, for their patience and encouragement during several years in which writing time invariably crept into the time we normally spend together. Their support is woven through every page that follows.

Fontessa
By John Lewis
Copyright (c) 1956 (Renewed 1984) by MJQ Music, Inc.
This arrangement Copyright (c) 2015 by MJQ Music, Inc.
All Rights Administered by Hal Leonard - Milwin Music Corp.
International Copyright Secured All Rights Reserved
Reprinted by permission of Hal Leonard Corporation

Harlequin
By John Lewis
Copyright (c) 1958 (Renewed 1986) by MJQ Music, Inc.
This arrangement Copyright (c) 2015 by MJQ Music, Inc.
All Rights Administered by Hal Leonard - Milwin Music Corp.
International Copyright Secured All Rights Reserved
Reprinted by permission of Hal Leonard Corporation

The Queen's Fancy
By John Lewis
Copyright (c) 1954 (Renewed 1982) by MJQ Music, Inc.
This arrangement Copyright (c) 2015 by MJQ Music, Inc.
All Rights Administered by Hal Leonard - Milwin Music Corp.
International Copyright Secured All Rights Reserved
Reprinted by permission of Hal Leonard Corporation

Three Little Feelings
By John Lewis
Copyright (c) 1957 (Renewed 1985) by MJQ Music, Inc.
This arrangement Copyright (c) 2015 by MJQ Music, Inc.
All Rights Administered by Hal Leonard - Milwin Music Corp.
International Copyright Secured All Rights Reserved
Reprinted by permission of Hal Leonard Corporation

Sketch For Double Quartet
By John Lewis
Copyright (c) 1960 (Renewed 1988) by MJQ Music, Inc.
This arrangement Copyright (c) 2015 by MJQ Music, Inc.
All Rights Administered by Hal Leonard - Milwin Music Corp.

Versailles
By John Lewis

Sections of this work have been published previously and appear here with the following permissions:

Chapter 5 from: Coady, C. (2012). AfroModernist Subversion of Film Noir Conventions in John Lewis' Scores to *Sait-on Jamais* (1957) and *Odds Against Tomorrow* (1959). *Musicology Australia*, 34(1), 1–31. *Reprinted by permission of the publisher (Taylor & Francis Ltd, http://www.tandfonline.com).*

Contents

Introduction

In February 1957 the pianist and composer John Lewis sat down with Nat Hentoff of *Down Beat* magazine to discuss, among other things, the public perception of Lewis's music. This was not the first time Hentoff had taken an interest in Lewis and his group the Modern Jazz Quartet (MJQ). He had already published two Counterpoint columns between December 1953* and January 1954 charting the extent of Western art music influence on the MJQ's inaugural LP for the record label Prestige. In October 1954 he riffed on a similar theme about works performed by the group at a Birdland concert in New York. These public analyses of the group's engagement with Western art music tropes were undeniably supportive. Hentoff even went so far as to refer to the resultant music as "the epitome of modern jazz" (1955b, 14). Yet by the time of the 1957 interview, suspicion had begun to creep into the journalist's tone. Lewis was asked to respond to criticism that the MJQ "wasn't funky enough," that it had "too limited a range of expression," and that it relied "too much on fugal structures." A parallel line of questioning emerged about why Lewis preferred to remain entirely in jazz—the subtext being that his musical innovations seemed to indicate an inevitable genre shift. This part of the interview did not go particularly well. In Hentoff's words, Lewis was "incredulous," shooting back: "This is where I have to be. . . . I have no desire to be any place else. There has never been any question in my mind about it" (1957b, 15).

The central mystery of this interview—and the focus of this book—is how we might reconcile such divergent interpretations of Lewis's musical trajectory. Indeed, from the very outset, Lewis's participation in the New York jazz scene was characterized by a unique approach to composition that seemed to denote, more often than not, the influence of Western art music. Replacing pianist Thelonious Monk in 1946, Lewis first gained prominence as a pianist and arranger for Dizzy Gillespie's big band. His through-composed work "Tocatta for Trumpet" (1947), premiered by Gillespie at a 1947 Carnegie Hall concert, stood in stark contrast to the group's riff-driven Afro-Cuban numbers and signaled Lewis's arrival in the popular press as "a man to be watched in the writing field" (Levin 1947, 1). His following collaboration with the Miles Davis Nonet between 1949 and 1950 on what would eventually be termed the *Birth of the Cool* recordings in turn resulted in "modal harmony and polyphony" applied to the group in a way that mimicked the conventions of French impressionism (Van de Leur 2001, 19). This outward-looking compositional style continued to drive many of the works Lewis would write for his own group, the MJQ, beginning in 1952. Within this collection, perhaps the most overt are the fugal pieces "Vendome" (1952), "Concorde" (1955), and "Versailles" (1957).

Given such an apparent compositional bent, it is easy to understand why Hentoff might have asked a question or two regarding genre affiliation. Yet Lewis's response to Hentoff's query not only refutes the suggestion that Lewis may have been moving away from the jazz realm through the composition of these syncretic works, it appears to put forth the idea that even Lewis's most Western-sounding pieces have the potential to be read as genuine jazz products. The reader of the *Down Beat* piece is then left to wonder, Is there, in fact, a way of hearing the critiqued works as being grounded in the jazz tradition, as Lewis suggests? Or do these works cross an essential sonic "line in the sand," precluding them from a jazz-oriented analysis?

To be clear, these are familiar questions in jazz discourse. Works from the diverse oeuvres of Duke Ellington, Miles Davis, and Charles Mingus (to name just the tip of the iceberg) have at one time or another been subject to criticism for straying too far from ingredients perceived as essential to the jazz sound. Yet through careful study of the historical worlds from which these works emerged, jazz scholars have come to an understanding of their syncretic nature in terms of a musical strategy aimed at keeping alive particular African American musical tropes in an environment hostile to their presence (see Howland 2009; Magee 2007; Porter 2002). The cultural significance of Lewis's music remains less certain. Certainly there is a willingness in jazz discourse to view Lewis's works as part of the modern jazz movement of the 1950s (see, for example, Floyd 1995; Joyner 2000; Lopes 2002), yet a spectrum of views persist regarding how we might best interpret Lewis's particular modernist bent. Is the fusion inherent in Lewis's approach, for instance, an attempt to resolve in jazz "significant shortcomings in the eyes of the classical music community" (Joyner 2000, 80)? Or might it better be understood as an approach aimed at "rescu[ing] jazz from the banality of the endless solo" (Balliett 1971, 161)? In turn, does Lewis's embrace of Western art music conventions work to assert "jazz as a colorblind art," as Paul Lopes suggests (2002, 255), or does such fusion pose a "musical, social, and cultural threat to 'real' black music," as others have claimed (Floyd 1995, 167)?

This book aims to wrestle with and bring some measure of clarity to this spectrum of ideas by, for the first time, unpacking Lewis's music through the lens of what Scott DeVeaux refers to as "moments of historical particularity" (1991, 553). Writing in the 1990s, DeVeaux produced two groundbreaking works of scholarship that threw into question traditional methods of jazz analysis. The first of these, an article titled "Constructing the Jazz Tradition" (1991), put forth the argument that the acceptance of jazz as art music in the United States between 1940 and 1950 was inextricably linked to perceptions of the music as being evolutionary in nature. Jazz scholars seeking to put forth a taxonomy of the genre's development, then, naturally did so in positivistic terms, aligning their work with the disciplinary norms of 1950s musicology. DeVeaux believes that continued reliance on such a methodology forced oversimplifications and mythological constructs to develop in relation to the stories told about the emergence of different jazz styles. His book *The Birth of Bebop*, published in 1997, set out to rectify this issue by providing a more nuanced and historically informed reading of one of these movements. Over the course of the work, DeVeaux demonstrates that commonplace readings of bebop as a "revolutionary" musical response to the commercialization of swing music could be challenged by linking the economic and social pressures experienced by the movement's practitioners with the musical and professional decisions they made. By telling the story of bebop's emergence through an analysis of how musicians negotiated a morphing wartime and postwar music industry, DeVeaux demonstrated that the "revolutionary" narrative of bebop's emergence was overstated, debunking one of the more powerful myths of the jazz canon.

One goal of this book is to contextualize Lewis's work in a similar vein. To this end, it begins by detailing shifts in the jazz marketplace following the 1940s big band decline and then surveys the ways in which New York and West Coast musicians recruited and initiated new patrons in order to maintain their livelihoods amid a changed professional landscape. One particular strategy utilized in this context was a compositional approach that managed to conjure European compositional conventions through the innovative deployment of what have traditionally been perceived to be African American vernacular tropes. The clearest example of this double-voiced construct is the use of independent improvised counterpoint—a defining element of traditional New Orleans jazz—as a way of meeting the relevant polyphonic requirements of fugal episodes and expositions in Lewis's pieces "Vendome," "Concorde," and "Versailles," although a plethora of additional compositional strategies similarly conceived can be identified both across Lewis's oeuvre and in the works of his contemporaries Miles Davis, Dave Brubeck, and Charles Mingus.

Yet unpacking Lewis's engagement with Western art music constructs exclusively within an economic frame effectively circumvents dealing with some of the trickier aspects of Lewis's character. After all, this was a man who spoke fondly of his "classical" training as a child ("MJQ Views" 1987, 28), pursued a bachelor's degree from the Manhattan School of Music decades before the school had a jazz program (Lalo 1991, 22), often expressed a fascination with the commedia dell'arte theatrical form (writing several pieces inspired by its characters), and, during the second half of his career, set about recording both Bach's *Goldberg Variations* and his *Well-Tempered Clavier*. While such interests undoubtedly positioned Lewis on the edge of the jazz world, I argue in this book that they do not necessarily cast him beyond the parameters of "'real' black music" when one considers the wider African American musical world. Through a survey of middle- and upper-class African American musical practices extending from the antebellum era through the 1950s, I demonstrate how, for many African Americans, Western art music lay at the center of their musical lives. The musical works produced by this demographic—notably those of the spiritual arranger

Robert Nathaniel Dett and the symphonic composer William Grant Still—celebrate a history of African American experience in the United States connected with folk practice yet simultaneously more expansive. The politics driving such engagement were undoubtedly rooted in an assimilationist goal, yet in the minds of many middle- and upper-class African Americans during the 1940s and 1950s, they had clearly yielded something different: a particular conception of being African American that overlapped but did not graph neatly onto identity constructs of the white hegemony. Reading Lewis's music in relation to this mind-set enables a paradigm shift to occur in which we are able to understand its European sound in relation to a unique African American experience linked strongly to social class.

Still, even this approach can seem, at times, a little forced. Indeed, to approach Lewis's works as artifacts of a realized racial identity essentially prioritizes race over other contributing factors in the development of his unique aesthetic approach. In particular, focusing on racial identity issues crowds out discussion of developments in jazz "thought" that worked to obliterate claims of musical authenticity grounded in racial ideas—paradigms that inevitably resulted in expanded parameters around what jazz could potentially sound like. Some of the more liberal of these philosophies developed overseas. In France following World War II, for example, "skepticism towards . . . dogmatic or purist cultural criticism" very much defined the intellectual landscape (Jordan 2010, 236). But even in settings like postwar Germany, where African American musical ability was still harshly stereotyped, the desire of local musicians to participate in the production of jazz led to an erosion of racial prerequisites and an expansion of musical approaches to the form. Indeed, the expansiveness of European-based jazz concepts after the war coupled with an ongoing European fascination with American jazz musicians seems to have paved the way for Lewis's positive reception on the Continent. This reception in turn appears to have affected both Lewis's confidence *in* and his selection *of* artistic projects both at home and abroad during the late 1950s and early 1960s.

These three ways of thinking about Lewis's music highlight for me both the usefulness and the challenge of answering DeVeaux's call to examine jazz music within "moments of historical particularity." Indeed, while such a methodology yields much useful data that informs our understanding of why Lewis may have composed the way he did, it fails to give us a definitive answer to the question of intent. If anything, the more one charts out the complexity of a historic moment, the harder it becomes to tell a story about that moment that might convincingly come across as complete and absolute. In other words, the more paradoxes or contradictions one reveals to a set of readers, the more difficult it becomes for both readers and author alike to settle on definitive meanings related to the use of particular musical tropes or compositional devices. From this viewpoint, my phrase "the challenge of 'real' black music" might be best understood as speaking to the difficulty involved in telling a story about an artist's involvement with something that many people experience as a very real thing but conceive of differently.

I have therefore focused mainly in this monograph on charting out how Lewis's works might have ticked the "authenticity" box for an array of different listeners, without attempting to distill any specific underlying truth about their musical pedigree. Yet at the same time I do not shy away from the fact that I am most interested in undertaking arguments that challenge the idea that Lewis's music somehow evinced an abdication of African American identity. Given all of the stories we could potentially tell about Lewis, it is particularly revealing to me that the dominant theme of his reception history—as I chart out in chapter 2—is that of an abandonment of African American culture. I believe such an understanding emerges from the persistent tendency of the trade press to decipher and write about African and African American music as inherently rhythmic, effusive, mystical, and naïve. The analyses I provide throughout the second half of this book seek to break free from such discourse by offering new ways of thinking about what it might mean to produce music reflective of the African American experience once we've accepted that such an experience is in no way monolithic.

Decoding the "Double-Voiced": Minstrel Masks and Signifyin(g)

Although the central argument of this book is for a consideration of diversity within the African American cultural experience, there can be little doubt that parallels between Lewis's double-voiced approach and metatropes of African American artistic expression do exist. In particular, the playful reinvention of hegemonic conventions through the deployment of polyphonic improvisation that I describe in relation to Lewis's fugal works above can be linked in no uncertain terms to what many have considered a preeminent preservation strategy within African American culture—the "masking" of vernacular tropes. Houston Baker's *Blues, Ideology and Afro-American Literature* (1984) and *Modernism and the Harlem Renaissance* (1987) detail similar practices in the literary and discursive realms, documenting how African American spokesmen of the late nineteenth century appropriated rhetorical devices from outside the African American cultural set as a means of preserving the African American voice in an environment hostile to African American progress. Perhaps the most well-known figure of Baker's *Modernism* study is the somewhat controversial educator and civil rights champion Booker T. Washington—a man whose life work is often summed up as equal parts racial advancement (most visible in his involvement with the Tuskegee Institute) and accommodation to white interests, evident in his Atlanta Exposition (or Atlanta "Compromise") speech and the self-deprecatory tone of his autobiography *Up from Slavery* ([1901] 2010).

Baker's analysis of Washington's autobiography, however, argues for a different conception of its supposedly accommodationist tone. Engaging rather than pushing to the side the plethora of African American stereotypes present in the work, Baker demonstrates how the offensive serves as a veil or "minstrel mask" through which more radical agendas could be subversively articulated to a resistant audience. Such stereotypes are not difficult to find in the work; Baker points, for example, to Washington's story about how his mother stole chickens as a slave and to Washington's admission of the difficulties involved in explaining to a "heathen" people the benefits of education (1987, 27–28)—conceptions of African American morality and intelligence not uncommon in the target audience for Washington's work. Yet Baker views the intent of these stories as going beyond increasing the mere commercial palpability of Washington's autobiography in white circles. He views their inclusion as a necessary framing device through which Washington is able to articulate conceptions of African American identity *unfamiliar* to the white hegemony. By beginning with stereotypes but then telling a story of advancement that frames white paternalism as a central gear in the mechanics of racial uplift, Washington is able to make something potentially threatening to white audiences—the intellectual and political empowerment associated with the Tuskegee Institute, for instance—into something unthreatening and apparently organic within the ideology of white supremacy (Baker 1987, 33). In other words, Baker endeavors to show that Washington and others adopted a conscious rhetorical approach in which they were ostensibly able to say two things at once about African American identity.

The findings of Baker's study can be seen to have had a dramatic impact on the development of both African American literary and African American musical theory in the following years. In particular, Baker's findings form the foundation of Henry Louis Gates's (1988) theory of African American literary criticism and his promotion of the "Signifyin(g)" rhetorical trope as a primary lens for reading African American cultural production.[1] *Signifyin(g)*, in Gates's study, refers to a mode of vernacular discourse long acknowledged by African American sociologists and linguists in which multiple semantic relationships emerge through the playful deployment of seemingly unrelated terms (1988, 49–52). Simply put, as with Baker's theory, it is the act of saying one thing and meaning another, usually in a humorous way, and while many have pointed out that such semantic play is not unique to African American discourse (Myers 1990; Fenstermaker 2008), Gates (1988, 21) does convincingly demonstrate its dominant function in the myths and storytelling of the African diaspora.

As a result, both Baker and Gates were used as central theorists throughout the early 1990s in a body of cross-disciplinary scholarship aimed at illuminating syncretic strategies employed to political and social ends across the spectrum of African American expressive culture (Murphy 1990; Tomlinson 1991; Brackett 1992; Walser 1993; Floyd 1995). In the musical realm, this "masking" principle proved particularly influential in the reassessment of dismissed syncretic works produced by African American artists. Indeed, it forms the primary analytical lens of Samuel Floyd's *The Power of Black Music* (1995), in which African American orchestral composers such as William Grant Still and Robert Nathaniel Dett are rehabilitated as genuine crafters of African American cultural products through the revelation of their "double-voiced" strategies.[2] This approach, according to Floyd, imbued works with the "semantic value" of both African American and European musical traditions—but realized a more Afrocentric political aim in its expansion of the African American voice into nominally white spaces, such as the concert hall (1995, 110).

In recent years, similar applications of the Baker-Gates paradigm have taken on new life in the analysis of symphonic pieces written by Duke Ellington (Burrows 2007; Howland 2009) and assessments of the disparate oeuvre of Miles Davis (Magee 2007). These studies demonstrate how compositional elements once viewed as working against vernacular elements in jazz can alternatively be understood as providing a platform for their promotion. Within this set of analyses, the accounts of George Burrows and John Howland prove most convincing, as they take the additional step of detailing the historically specific social and economic pressures that led to the use of a "masking" approach in Ellington's pieces. In both investigations, attitudes regarding the social value of jazz are shown to have stymied broad promotion of the music, and Ellington's symphonic approach is framed as an initiative aimed at winning over a reluctant demographic. In the view of Burrows and Howland, the strength of the Ellington enterprise across diverse quarters of the music industry during the 1940s and 1950s stands, in part, as a testament to the effectiveness of this strategy.

Given this current state of play, a Signifyin(g) or "masking" analysis of John Lewis's music certainly seems overdue. The MJQ recording of the "La Ronde Suite" in 1955, for instance, shouts out to Europe in its title and multimovement structure. Contrapuntal interplay drawing heavily on the composed theme weaves a thread through each individual movement, and Lewis's planing of coloristic chords at the end of the first is hard to read as anything but a direct reference to French impressionism. Yet these movements are simultaneously filled with improvisation, each serving as a showcase for a particular instrument in the quartet. In turn, the content of these improvisations is unambiguously "bluesy"—they are chock full of pendular thirds, flat sevenths, and flat fifths, and each movement contains an open passage based on a twelve-bar blues form. When we then shift our focus from the sonorities of the work to its historic context, we can in turn see a set of circumstances that seem to confirm the political aims of the "masking" approach. Specifically, the work was recorded while Lewis was embarking on a quest to find new venues and new audiences for his music. He had formed the Modern Jazz Society in New York in 1955 and had actively reached out to patrons of "modern music" by including in his first program Luigi Nono's *Polifonica, Monodia, Ritmica.* Lewis was also poised to bring the MJQ to Europe for the first time, a successful economic endeavor that many have made sense of in terms of the fusion of musical aesthetics outlined above.[3]

Baker's "masking" concept helps us read this interplay of context and sound within a "jazz" rather than a "classical" music framework. In other words, instead of seeing a work like the "La Ronde Suite" as evidence of Lewis stepping toward Western art music, we can conceive of it as operating in the interest of jazz by opening up new markets and providing a pathway toward jazz appreciation for new consumers. It might even be seen in this light as a didactic work, in that it teaches appreciation for jazz by eliding contrapuntal and formal concepts from two different musical cultures. Such an understanding appears to reconcile the paradox of Lewis's orientation outlined in the opening pages of this book while carving out a space for it in the body of "'real' black music."

Heritage, Class, and the Idea of the "Negro Gentleman"

Or not. Certainly this would have been an easier book to write if all of John Lewis's syncretic works could be explained away in such terms—if his work could somehow be reconceptualized in toto under the banners of "Signifyin(g)" or the "minstrel mask." Yet the way Western art music tends to be valued in double-voiced analyses—as a vehicle suitable for the delivery of vernacular tropes only—does not seem to fit with what we know about Lewis's interests in and appreciation of the European cultural products that I described earlier.

Many have interpreted such interests as indicative of what jazz critic Bill Coss referred to as a "sociological trend" during the 1950s (1956, 50). Believers in this trend saw African American involvement with what were traditionally held to be European cultural forms as a purposeful assimilation project in which participants moved away from their folk roots and into a sort of amorphous white American cultural milieu. The terms "black bourgeoisie" (Frazier 1957) and "black Anglo-Saxons" (Hare 1965) were introduced during this period by sociologists E. Franklin Frazier and Nathan

Hare as a way of encapsulating the economic, political, and identity issues tied up in what they viewed as increasing mimicry of white society among African Americans. Yet others, particularly those driving commentary in the African American newspapers the *Chicago Defender* and the *New York Age*, held an opposing view on the nature of what appeared to Frazier and Hare as blatant cultural abandonment. In the eyes of this group, the phenomenon of the "black bourgeoisie" was evidence not of a rejection but of a recommitment to African American values. As the editors of the *New York Age* put it, it demonstrated the resilient "heritage" of what they termed the "Negro gentleman" ("These Two Leave" 1953, 10). Unsurprisingly, when it came to assessments of Lewis's interests in European cultural products, the idea that Lewis was actively abandoning his cultural "heritage" failed to hold water with members of this camp, and it was in their publications that he was loudly applauded for taking "jazz out of the 'type' category and set[ting] it into international orbiting" (Pulley 1960, A17).

One way we can understand how such different views about the possibilities or limits of African American identity could emerge so forcefully in the 1950s is to break down the notion that the social experience of African Americans throughout the history of the United States has been somehow entirely uniform. In many ways, despite its combative tone, the first half of Frazier's *The Black Bourgeoisie* provides us the tools to start such a project in that it details what at the time was a largely under-researched topic in American history—the cultural legacy of wealthy African American families. Frazier notes that many in this elite class could trace their lineage to African Americans who "were free before the Civil War, or those who had enjoyed the advantages of having served in the houses of their masters" and places this group's assimilation of traditions practiced by the "slaveholding aristocracy" front and center in discussions of how members of the elite maintained their (albeit limited) political power (1957, 112–14). Frazier loosely defines these traditions as the celebration of European literature and music, affiliation with the "Episcopal, Congregational, Presbyterian, and . . . Catholic Churches," the use of a particular set of social codes (what Frazier calls "manners"), and the valuation of a "professional education" (1957, 113–15). Yet while Frazier notes that economic and political integration correlated to some degree with the cooptation of these practices, he points out that social integration remained perpetually elusive for the African American elite. Such a state of affairs had the ironic result of causing the "African-American aristocracy" (as Frazier sometimes refers to it) to become an increasingly insulated social group, cordoned off from both lower-class African Americans as well as from the wealthy white classes whose traditions they had borrowed (1957, 113–14).

This isolation allowed the adopted traditions of the "slaveholding aristocracy" to take on new meaning for many in the elite class and for those who would later aspire to its ranks via education and the accumulation of capital. Davarian Baldwin's work on the great migration in Chicago is particularly enlightening in this regard. He describes the manner in which values linked to Frazier's "genteel" tradition, such as "temperance, bodily restraint, and functional modesty in dress," coalesced into an ideology of African American identity held by upper-class African Americans during the 1920s. Initially, those who promoted this identity publicly did so as a way of presenting a "unified and positive public image of the [African American] race [in order] to counteract the cultural assumptions of white supremacy" (Baldwin 2007, 29). In her study of women activists in the black Baptist Church at the turn of the century, Evelyn Brooks Higginbotham points to a similar phenomenon and coins the term "the politics of respectability" as a way of explaining the pursuit of racial uplift via the adoption of hegemonic behavior (1993, 188). As the mouthpiece of the African American elite, urban African American newspapers in turn frequently endorsed such respectability politics by making comparisons between the "white" world and the accomplishments of the African American world as a way of demonstrating the facts of racial equality.[4] Yet these comparisons were almost always caged in the language of competing spheres. In other words, even though the sort of cultural development prized by the African American elite ran a parallel course to what they viewed as "white" cultural development, the reality of segregation made it difficult for those thinking about these issues to discuss them in unified terms.

Thus the framing of African American "genteel" behavior as a cultural project separate from other cultural changes occurring in the United States allowed it to garner the weight of a bona-fide African American tradition—a concept frequently articulated in the pages of the African American press during the 1940s and 1950s. Publications such as the *Chicago Defender*, the *New York Age*, the *Pittsburgh Courier*, and the *Cleveland Gazette*, among other African American newspapers, routinely presented features and editorials that either implicitly or explicitly lay claim to refinement, artistic sensibility, Christian morality, and education as part of what they viewed as an African American cultural legacy. As consumerism and liberalism in turn became increasingly part of the ether of white middle-class America (a societal change charted deftly in Elizabeth Fraterrigo's *Playboy and the Making of the Good Life in Modern America* [2009]), these media outlets used this legacy to articulate what they saw as a growing rift between the values of AfroAmerica and the American cultural mainstream.

Therefore, from the perspective of the African American elite, the oft-cited formal behavior and dress of the Modern Jazz Quartet—along with the group's apparent interest in Western art music—did not signal, as it did to Coss (1956), a move away from African American culture. To the contrary, it appeared to be the realization of a long-awaited style of jazz that could effectively showcase folk elements while simultaneously rejecting liberal values of "rebelliousness" and "emotional abandonment" ("Modern Jazz Quartet Top Unit" 1963, 29). The tools Lewis used to craft such a product—his deployment of what one journalist at the *Chicago Defender* referred to as "lapidarian construction" techniques but what might more simply be referred to as an emphasis on preplanning and composition—did not wipe out "jazz's inspiration and spontaneity," it simply "disciplined and directed" it ("Modern Jazz Quartet Top Unit" 1963, 29). The point here is merely to highlight the fact that although critics in the African American press were not necessarily reporting on the music of the group in terms different from those used in publications like the *New York Times* or the trade magazines *Down Beat* and *Metronome*, the terms themselves carried different meanings depending on the orientation of the press within which they appeared.

When the cultural frame of the "Negro Gentleman" is used to read the works of John Lewis, Lewis's embrace of Western art music conventions can be seen to take on a decidedly different tone. To return to the example of the "La Ronde Suite," nods to French impressionism mentioned earlier need not be understood in this alternate paradigm as some sort of marketing trick—or at least not solely in those terms. They can also be read as celebrating a specific type of conservative musicality stemming from one particular conception of African American identity. Lewis's upbringing in a middle-class New Mexico suburb (Lalo 1991, 9), his pursuit of a degree in music theory, and his general interest in European cultural products certainly helps us place him in this world. But we can make an even stronger claim to affinity with the bourgeois mind-set by considering Lewis's comments about strengthening jazz "with structure" (Hentoff 1953a, 8) alongside his diatribes against those who would assume jazz necessarily correlates with bad behavior (Hentoff 1957b, 16). Reading Lewis's music through this lens is no less political than a Signifyin(g) assessment, but it does accomplish a different sort of "cultural work" (to use Guthrie Ramsey's [2001] phase) by keeping the door open in the field of jazz studies for all sorts of sonorities that might be considered "traditional" in assessments of African American cultural presence.

Lewis and the European Encounter

Yet examining class-based ideological differences between African American communities is not the only way we can chart out an increasingly expansive view during the 1950s related to what jazz might sound like. In the U.S. context, acceptance of increasingly modernist jazz products aligned neatly with rising interest in jazz from the university sector and the publication of a range of musicological texts that celebrated the pursuit of new sonic frontiers, including George Russell's *Lydian Chromatic Concept of Tonal Organization* ([1953] 1959) and André Hodeir's *Jazz: Its Evolution and Essence* (1956a). Lewis's directorship of the Lenox School of Jazz from 1957 to 1960 in turn oversaw the recruitment of jazz pedagogues with decidedly modernist mind-sets (such as Russell, Lennie Tristano, Bill Russo, and Jimmy Giuffre) and the endorsement of a jazz curriculum aimed at pushing the limits of existing musical boundaries. Yet Lewis's confidence that this approach was, in fact, the right approach to teaching students new to the industry seems at odds with the MJQ's frustrating early tours of jazz clubs in the United States, detailed in chapter 1 of this book—tours in which audience indifference occasionally forced the group to abandon the stage. Indeed, as I will show, such confidence seems to have instead arisen out of Lewis's experiences in Europe during the mid-1950s and his exposure to markets in both

France and Germany that enthusiastically embraced syncretic jazz forms and boundary-pushing jazz works.

In considering the French context first, it is important to note that an expansive view regarding the sonic possibilities of jazz music very much defined the French encounter with the genre even before the existentialist turn that followed World War II. There is of course no denying the fact that extensions of the "noble savage" Enlightenment motif—specifically the idea that unique musical ability resided in the biology of African descendants—typified French jazz critiques during the interwar period (Jackson 2002, 154). Yet at the same time it needs to be understood that alternate and more pluralistic understandings of how one might authentically contribute to the form were almost always simultaneously in play. For instance, Matthew Jordan details how several interwar French jazz critics pointed to the music's origin in New Orleans—a city with deep French cultural ties—as a way of arguing that the French had just as much right to claim ownership of the new musical genre as those who were viewed as stewarding its "African" components (2011, 512–14). The success of groups like the piano duo Wiéner and Doucet during the 1920s and Ray Ventura et Ses Collégians during the 1930s inextricably linked with this conception of an authentic French jazz grounded in the audibility of nationalistic tropes: Wiéner and Doucet, for instance, were applauded for tapping into what was seen as jazz's roots in "the French romantic song" tradition (Delage 1926, 19), while Ray Ventura was heralded for jazzing up French folk songs (Jackson 2002, 160).

Most discussion of postwar jazz in France has focused on the debate between those who endorsed pluralistic concepts of jazz practice—of which the nationalist school was just one version—and the leaders of the New Orleans revivalist movement, famously headed by the French jazz critic Hugh Panassié (Jackson 2002; Perchard 2011). Yet focusing on this debate, in my mind, carries with it the potential to obscure the extent to which French audiences welcomed and in fact expected to encounter sonic shifts in the jazz world. Such an orientation is evident in even just a cursory look at Lewis's reception in France during the 1950s. Indeed, while to many American critics Lewis's style of composition signaled movement toward a new musical genre, or the formation of what Gunther Schuller referred to as a "Third Stream" of music (Schuller 1986, 120), French critics outside the influence of Panassié weren't so sure that the parameters of jazz had been breached. Following the MJQ's first tour of Europe in 1956 with the Birdland All-Stars, the Parisian publication *Jazz Magazine* came out in full support of the music audiences had heard, stating, "Ultimately, these concerts marked an important victory for the 'modern sound' in our country and French fans could see firsthand that jazz has never been better" ("Sous le signe du 'Birdland'" 1956, 19).[5] In the same year, the English translation of André Hodeir's *Jazz: Its Evolution and Essence* was published, including an expanded section on "the state of jazz at the death of Charlie Parker" (Hodeir 1956a), in which Hodeir applauded Lewis's innovations for pointing the way forward to a music that had lost its way. Hodeir writes of Lewis, "He deserves unreserved praise for having faced up to the problem of the relationship between theme, arrangement, and solo, which is the most critical and the most formidable problem the modern jazz-man has to solve. In fact, it may be the problem on which the whole future of jazz depends" (1956a, 278).[6]

Such resistance to purist jazz ideology seems to have in turn enabled greater interdisciplinary use of Lewis's music across the French cultural landscape. The French filmmaker Roger Vadim, for instance, boldly approached Lewis in 1957 with the idea that he provide a score for Vadim's 1957 "noir" film *Sait-on jamais* (1957). While the use of a jazz score in film noir was not without precedent (see Butler 2002), Vadim's offer did mark Lewis's first encounter with the form and resulted in an incredibly innovative musical track in which improvisation was used to explore a variety of narrative themes. Furthermore, it was in Paris in 1960 that Lewis began his dalliance with writing for ballet, collaborating with choreographer Louis Johnson on a work that saw dancers improvise in counterpoint to improvised music played by the MJQ ("Precious Asset" 1960, 9). It is difficult to avoid comparing these projects with their American counterparts: Lewis's score to the Robert Wise film *Odds against Tomorrow*, released in 1959, and his score for the ballet *Original Sin*, performed by the San Francisco Ballet company in 1961. Indeed, as I explore in depth in chapter 4, acceptance of Lewis's innovative vision within the French context seems to have encouraged Lewis's pursuit of similar projects in works later performed on American soil.

Yet it was not only Lewis's time in France that seems to have encouraged commitment to his modernist project. Lewis's encounter with the German jazz scene in turn can be seen to have endorsed aspects of his compositional style that had met less friendly reception in the American sphere. Unlike in France, postwar attitudes toward jazz in Germany remained firmly grounded in myths about African American primitivism and intellectual inferiority (Hurley 2009, 20). The majority of jazz assessments that did occur in print, at least those written immediately after the war, tended to be negative and to depict the music as a continued threat to German society, evincing, as Andrew Hurley has put it, "an ideological hangover from National Socialist anti-jazz indoctrination" (2009, 20). German jazz advocates in the postwar period were therefore required to find ways of challenging this ideology covertly—in that their primary aim was to convert, not alienate, the German public. Jazz critic Joachim-Ernst Berendt deserves credit for leading this assault, pursuing both musical and written projects bent on illuminating for the German populace ways in which jazz could be compared favorably to *ernste Musik* (serious music) (Hurley 2009, 24–25). In particular, Berendt was interested in promoting the idea that *alte Musik* (early music) shared an affinity with jazz that could not be denied. Toward this end, he instigated a lecture tour in 1956 involving the music historian Joseph Tröller and a jazz combo lead by Wolfgang Lauth—a tour that involved the discussion and performance not only of the music of J. S. Bach but also that of the MJQ (Hurley 2009, 27).

Indeed, for Berendt, the music of the MJQ highlighted a very plausible route to changing German minds about the value of jazz, and accordingly, he sought to promote the group widely during the 1950s. In addition to his role in supporting the Tröller-Lauth tour and Lauth's performance of Lewis's fugal work "Vendome" ("Jazz und Alte Musik" 1957), Berendt worked to call attention to the MJQ's embrace of Western art music conventions in the pages of *Melos*, describing in detail Lewis's use of fugal processes before concluding, "The connection between Jazz and European music is something many white Americans have experimented with, but John Lewis so gratifyingly actualized—without an experimental phase—in his Modern Jazz Quartet" (1955, 350).[7] Furthermore, Berendt played an instrumental role in organizing the German leg of the group's first European tour in 1956, arranging its appearance at "a Freiburg concert celebrating the SWF's [southwestern German public broadcasting station's] one-thousandth jazz program" and introducing the group to the DJF (German Jazz Federation), which scheduled a national tour following the Freiburg concert (Hurley 2009, 26). This promotional blitz culminated in the MJQ's performance at the Donaueschingen Festival in 1957—a festival devoted to the promotion of "new" art music and at which Igor Stravinsky served as guest conductor in the same year (G. Lewis 2008, 248).

Given the context of Germany's rediscovery of jazz and Berendt's framing of the MJQ's importance, it is unsurprising to see that when musical opportunities arose for Lewis in Germany beyond those offered to his quartet, they carried with them a decidedly *ernste Musik* bent. For instance, Lewis's work with the Süddeutscher Rundfunk Sinfonie-Orchester in Stuttgart in February 1958 marked a new milestone for him in terms of engagement with the European musical tradition. The orchestra was the first Lewis had ever written for and the first, but not the last, he would ever conduct. In his own words, it provided an opportunity to finally make use "of everything I studied at Manhattan [School of Music]," yielding an album that in Nat Hentoff's view went far beyond earlier experiments in jazz string scoring, in which arrangers used orchestras solely as "inert cushion[s] for . . . other instrumental lines." Lewis's compositions instead drew on what Hentoff framed as a European style of string writing consisteing of both "logical" theme development and overt counterpoint (1958, 1).

While the effect of such an experience is difficult to prove in empirical terms, there is little doubt that Lewis's time with the Süddeutscher Rundfunk Sinfonie-Orchester precipitated an era of experimentation with larger ensembles. In 1959 Lewis would write the work "Sketch," scored for both the MJQ and the Beaux Arts String Quartet, and perform it in New York at Town Hall. He would also write and record the work "Exposure" (1959), performed by the MJQ and a small ensemble consisting of bassoon, cello, harp, and French horn. In 1960 he would rework several earlier pieces into a multimovement work titled *Excerpts from "The Comedy,"* scored for a large brass ensemble comprising four trumpets, four French horns, two trombones, and a tuba in addition to piano, bass, and drums.

When a consideration of Lewis's ambiguous reception in American jazz clubs prior to his European tours is taken into account, it seems likely that encounters with jazz scenes on the Continent played at least some role in encouraging Lewis to stay the course. The idea that such an encounter can have an effect on one's artistic mind-set is of course not a novel concept.

Even in the realm of jazz, this is fairly well trodden territory. Tyler Stovall's *Paris Noir*, for instance, demonstrates the liberating effect an environment devoid of racism had on the artistic ambitions of the first MJQ drummer, Kenny Clarke, who moved to Paris permanently in 1956 (1996, 178). Annegret Fauser in turn has discussed the "transformative effects of the French gaze"—an eloquent aphorism for pedagogue Nadia Boulanger's ideas about what American music could be—on the music of Aaron Copland (2006, 526). The argument I'm making here is not so different. Lewis's extensive touring of the Continent, his positive reception, and his endorsement by European modernists such as André Hodeir and Joachim-Ernst Berendt make a strong case for reading works performed in the wake of his European tours as somehow influenced by the European gaze. Furthermore, exploring this aspect of Lewis's experience in the story of his musical development allows us to engage with the very real power jazz held as a global phenomenon during this particular historical moment, an important methodological shift with serious ramifications for future investigations of this period

Challenges and Choices in Storytelling

In an attempt to set up a wide enough frame for weaving these somewhat disparate themes together, I begin this book with a general overview of the "how" and some "whys" behind the emergence of jazz-classical fusion works during the 1950s. Leaving aesthetic motivations temporarily to the side, in chapter 1 I examine how these works helped shore up a struggling postwar jazz industry decimated by the 1940s big band decline. In particular, I demonstrate how many jazz composers endeavored to relocate their music into new performance spaces, both appropriated and created, with the intent of indoctrinating and winning over uninitiated patrons. While these ventures often involved the direct appropriation of Western art music conventions, I demonstrate in this chapter that many times the musical approach employed was far more subversive, involving the deployment of jazz conventions in a manner that conjured—rather than drew upon—European musical aesthetics. Lewis's embrace of "double-voiced" or Signifyin(g) devices during this period is therefore framed as not being exceptionally different from the syncretic approaches embraced by his contemporaries (Duke Ellington, Miles Davis, and Charles Mingus, among many others).

Yet there is no doubt that Lewis's music was received as exceptionally different. In chapter 2 I explain this reception in terms of internalized biases in the popular press around both what jazz should sound like and what jazz musicians should look like. Surveying a history of essentialist rhetoric regarding African and African American musical production, I demonstrate a pervasive emphasis on rhythm in assessments of African American musical authenticity. In the second half of the chapter I analyze discussion of Lewis's music in the popular press in light of this history, questioning the veracity of essentialist readings and illuminating how the "double-voiced" aspects of his work crowded out discussion of rhythm in favor of commentary regarding "European" parity.

Furthermore, I demonstrate how the group's physical presentation—that is, their use of suits and tuxedos—was made to seem out of the ordinary, when it in fact was not, in order to set the stage for discussions about the cultural value inherent in Lewis's music. Lewis's response to such criticism—also discussed in chapter 2—would of course evince a clear frustration. In 1957, for instance, he would argue that "there's nothing remarkable" about "conducting ourselves as grown men" (Hentoff 1957b, 16), and in 1987 he would claim, "I'm not the one to say whether we've added distinction to jazz—or whether that's important or not, even. Why *not* present a smart appearance and polished music?" (MJQ Views 1987, 28). Yet despite such pushback, references to the group's appearance can be seen to have continued to serve as a consistent opening device for critics keen to interrogate the ways in which the MJQ appeared to be abandoning African American traditions through its affiliation with the Western art music world.

In chapter 3 I challenge the assumptions of the trade press discussed in chapter 2 by charting out the cultural world of middle- and upper-class African Americans during the 1950s, with a particular focus on the role Western art music played in affirming class boundaries and articulating class values. While I argue that editorials and feature articles in the African American press serve as a useful window into this world, I also include a discussion of how African American community orchestras and church-sponsored Western art music concerts, along with other social initiatives, reified the views of the elite in African American urban centers. This discussion helps illuminate the importance of Western art music within certain constructs of African American identity while in turn countering 1950s popular press assertions regarding what African American cultural production might entail. I end this chapter by examining Lewis's positive reception in this world along with comments regarding his perceived suitability to its ideals.

I then turn in chapter 4 to a discussion of Lewis's musical output produced between 1952 and 1962. An argument for the temporal parameters of this study based on ideological shifts related to the emergence of the Black Arts movement during the 1960s is put forth in the beginning of this chapter. In particular, I argue that the ideological energy of "Black Nationalist" thought reshaped conceptions of authenticity within the jazz world to such an extent that tracing the ways in which race, class, and sound are bound up in Lewis's post-1950s works would effectively require a book-length study of its own. Certainly many fascinating projects are omitted as a result of this choice. Lewis's involvement with Orchestra U.S.A. during the mid-1960s, his scores for television programs during the 1970s, and his rendering of Bach's *Well-Tempered Clavier* during the 1980s are, unfortunately, left unaddressed in this account. Yet it should be noted that the aim of this monograph is not, primarily, biographical. To the contrary, my intent is to examine the ways in which historical energies constellate in the music for which John Lewis is most renowned and to postulate how reading these works through different modes of emphasis might expand our understanding of the "cultural work" with which they are engaged.

Chapter 4 therefore proceeds by examining the compositional design of works Lewis produced in association with the MJQ as well as with other collaborators both at home and abroad during his first decade of productivity. This analysis is used to illuminate how the compositional ambiguities inherent in Lewis's music that had caused such a stir in the jazz press were able to engage a range of different audiences, each with their own unique set of aesthetic expectations and musical ideologies. Much of the music from this period, for instance, can be understood as deploying "double-voiced" tropes such as the innovative reshaping of blues forms, riffs, and improvised counterpoint in a way that manifested or "shouted out" to

Western art music aesthetics. Yet I also discuss in this chapter how some of Lewis's works appear to be less subversive in terms of their engagement with Western art music—or more genuine, depending on one's orientation. This is evident in his work with European orchestras, ballet companies, large brass ensembles, and string quartets, together with his increasing focus on extended works during the late 1950s—interests that indicate in their scope something beyond the use of European or Western art culture as a mere veneer or "mask" for the vernacular. Given my discussion of middle- and upper-class African American music practices in chapter 3, I frequently make the point in this discussion that such engagement should not be read as cultural abandonment.

Lewis's penchant for manipulating genre boundaries is further explored in chapter 5 in relation to his scores for the noir films *Sait-on jamais* (1957) and *Odds against Tomorrow* (1959). Building on the work of David Butler (2002, 2009), I begin this chapter with a discussion of how shifts in the cultural meaning of jazz led to the erosion of its use as a deviance trigger in film noir, enabling more varied deployment of jazz across the film genre. In teasing out this idea, I demonstrate that this shift was felt primarily in relation to the composed score, with improvisation remaining tied for the most part to darker thematic strains. I then argue that Lewis's use of improvisation in connection with a variety of narrative strains in *Sait-on jamais* (1957) and *Odds against Tomorrow* (1959) worked to push the boundaries of jazz's potential role in film noir in a manner similar to the way in which his syncretic musical works chipped away at the sonic parameters of the jazz genre. In other words, I conceive of Lewis's work in film as part of a larger aesthetic concept aimed at delivering musical innovation in dialogue with established hegemonic conventions.

In my final chapter I discuss the broader implications of the reassessment of Lewis put forth in this book. I begin by reiterating that rather than assimilating into European culture, many of Lewis's syncretic projects during the 1950s and early 1960s might be better understood as evidence of a more complicated aesthetic agenda—an agenda informed by various ideologies about what African American music could and should sound like, woven together in different ways across the contexts of particular historical moments. I then use this observation as a springboard for a discussion about what it means to produce African American music, exploring the question of whether or not a piece of music can uphold African American cultural values even if its content challenges prominent ideas about what "real" African American music sounds like.

In discussing Lewis's music in this manner, I hope to endorse a methodology for jazz studies that is more honest in terms of what we, as researchers, can actually do. Much to our chagrin, we cannot mind-read. But we can embrace complexity and tell stories that force the public to question long-held beliefs about much-loved music. In doing so, we can strip monolithic paradigms of their power and bring to light a variety of competing opinions, orientations, and approaches that have been unnecessarily silenced by well-meaning but all too often narrow-minded "constructors of the jazz tradition." We don't make the narrative game easier for ourselves by throwing these gates open, but we are able to better depict the spirit, if not the infinite complexity, of artistic process when we adopt such an approach.

1 • Branching Out

The Great Era of Venue Creation

When John Lewis moved to New York to pursue a music career in 1945, he entered an industry on the precipice of collapse. Prior to World War II, swing bands had led popular music sales in the United States, permeated nightclubs and ballrooms, held hefty contracts with recording companies, and occasionally been welcomed into venues normally reserved for the performance of Western art music. They were, in many respects, the largest part of the jazz industry, and the war years were to be no less kind. Although many talented musicians were taken out of the market and conscripted into military service, those who remained were faced with increasing demand for their services and the latitude—due to a lack of competition—to experiment with the formal and harmonic elements of the swing genre (Stowe 1994, 184).

Yet the end of World War II carried perilous repercussions for those making their living in the swing market. The postwar recession affected the entertainment budgets of swing supporters, setting off a chain reaction that began with promoters losing money on guarantees, followed by band leaders lowering payroll costs to assist promoters, then band leaders decreasing the size of their ensembles to remain economically viable, and eventually the dissolution of bands in their entirety (Stowe 1994, 192). Simultaneously, recording companies began to embrace a more efficient model of popular music production by promoting singers over bands (Lopes 2002, 225). This new approach enabled labels like Columbia and RCA Victor to draw on the newly saturated talent pool of instrumental musicians returned from war, employing them for what was essentially "session" work and thereby circumventing the more expensive payroll demands of bandleaders who preferred working with consistent lineups.

There exists a long tradition in jazz historiography of pointing to the bebop movement as a foreshadowing response to this market shift. Scott DeVeaux (1997, 273–74), for instance, discusses the "centripetal pull" of increasingly poor working conditions on jazz musicians during the early 1940s—a phenomenon that forced jazz practitioners to the periphery of the music business but in turn provided the opportunity for a less corporate musical aesthetic to develop. Paul Lopes (2002, 213) in turn makes the argument in *Rise of the Jazz Art World* that the bebop genre's new chromatic language effectively reconceptualized jazz in the public eye as an art music replete with its own base of "hipster" supporters, laying the foundation for a new sort of jazz market. Yet despite such reshaping of the industry, the bebop movement was ultimately unsuccessful in reconstructing a workspace comparable to that of the heights of the Swing Era, and by the early 1950s many jazz artists were again pressured to seek out alternative paths toward financial stability.

Three broad performance options seemed to have been considered at this point. The first was for jazz musicians to continue down the path of bebop, utilizing increasingly smaller ensembles and capitalizing on individual reputation in the hope of cornering the "hipster" market. Dizzy Gillespie's move from an ensemble of seventeen members in 1949 to a sextet in 1951 and a quintet in 1953, all marketed under his name, provides just one example of an artist utilizing this approach. The second option was to move the jazz genre back toward popular music by embracing the rhythm and blues (R&B) style, "a kind of shuffle-boogie . . . that employed both swing and blues elements" (Floyd 1995, 143). Initially there was a great deal of interaction between the bebop and R&B worlds. Samuel Floyd (1995) points to Paul Williams's 1949 revision of Charlie Parker's 1944 hit "Now's the Time" as evidence of dialogue between the genres, and John Gennari (2006, 72) writes of jazz saxophonist John Coltrane playing R&B gigs during his tenure at the Granoff School of Music in Philadelphia. Yet those committed to the idea that the stability of the jazz world rested on developing jazz's art music credentials saw little potential in R&B for advancing their goals. While many of these artists remained convinced that given time, the innovations of the bebop movement would suitably carve out a sustainable market niche, other musicians appeared less certain. It is this latter group that can be seen to have pursued yet another strategy—one in which bebop chromaticism, African American blues elements, and sonic effects seemingly derived from European compositional conventions were fused into musical works that expanded the reach of jazz by tapping into a parallel art music world. Initially this approach was referred to as "Cool Jazz," but variation within the camp would lead to what is currently referred to as "Third Stream" music.

In the following pages I provide an overview of the emergence of these styles and discuss their effectiveness in ushering in renewed interest in jazz during the 1950s. I also make the more provocative point that many Cool and Third Stream works deployed jazz improvisational practices and organizational tropes in a manner that resulted in music that sounded like European classical music while not in fact employing European compositional conventions per se. Both approaches can be read as the enactment of a double-voiced compositional agenda that enabled Cool and Third Stream practitioners to expand both the parameters of the jazz world and their own economic power by relocating jazz practices into spaces where unfamiliar audiences could be introduced to jazz tropes surreptitiously. In the early 1950s advances in jazz tertiary education opened up American universities to such endeavors, and by the mid-1950s jazz artists were creating performance spaces themselves where jazz conventions were brought to the uninitiated through the guise of "modern music." Central to this story is Lewis's journey from arranger to small-group leader during the first half of the decade—and his emergence as what many would call an "assimilationist" during the second half.

"Double-voiced" Roots of 1950s "Modern" Jazz

It is of course necessary to point out that by the early 1950s, the potential benefits of alluding to Western art music as a way of reaching out to new audience demographics was not a novel concept to jazz musicians. Prior to the big band decline, several artists had already nodded or "shouted out" to the European tradition in the design or framing of their work, including Duke Ellington, whose multimovement programmatic piece

"Black and Tan Fantasy" (1927) prefigured the structural arc of his later work *Black, Brown and Beige* (1943), and Paul Whiteman, who famously commissioned George Gershwin's *Rhapsody in Blue* (1924) for the concert billed as "An Experiment in Modern Music" at Carnegie Hall (Schiff 1997, 2).

It is therefore perhaps more the scope than the general intent of syncretic projects undertaken in the wake of the big band decline that makes this musical period stand out. Certainly classical-jazz fusion began to gather force during the late 1940s as a guiding aesthetic principle, surpassing its previous role as an occasional curio effect. Indeed, as demand for swing bands decreased, a virtual explosion of new musical approaches rippled through the jazz industry—often in aid of what appears to have been a two-tiered promotional approach in which artists sought to both sustain remaining jazz supporters while simultaneously recruiting uninitiated patrons from the art music realm.

For instance, during the 1940s orchestra leaders Claude Thornhill and Stan Kenton embraced what seemed to be, on the surface, a dance band format while pushing the sonic boundaries of the jazz genre through the use of extended harmonies, the application of more diverse instrumental pallets, and in the case of Kenton, the use of atonal melodic figures (Noss 1948, 414–15). Small jazz groups in turn played a part in reshaping the jazz landscape. Pianist Lennie Tristano notably broke with the idea of preplanned form in his free jazz works *Intuition* (1949) and *Digression* (1949), attracting the interest of the American avant-garde (Shim 2007, 72). John Lewis's arrangement of works for the Miles Davis Nonet in 1948 applied a coloristic approach to chordal writing that—as stated earlier—shouted out to fans of French impressionism (Van de Leur 2001, 19). Such diversity in approaches (to which we might add Lewis's later interest in baroque fugal processes) set in place a strong foundation for the eventual acceptance of "modern" jazz as a diverse field of expression capable of satisfying a variety of tastes. Yet during the waning years of the 1940s, many in this camp struggled to find a way of framing their works in a manner truly capable of connecting with the uninitiated.

The syncretic works of Duke Ellington and Billy Strayhorn stand in partial contrast to this overall trend. While many of these pieces were initially received with some ambiguity, the vast majority of their efforts contributed to the strength of the Ellington organization over the course of the 1940s. It is certainly true that the dressing up of jazz in European garb met with criticism from some Ellington supporters, as noted plainly in Barry Ulanov's ([1946] 1975, 253) account of Ellington's Carnegie Hall debut, yet the resultant buzz around Ellington's syncretic approach appears to have ensured repeated access to concert halls (Howland 2009, 247), setting in place a promotional system that worked to lead at least some sectors of the Western art music audience into an appreciation of African American vernacular music.

Such a system was clearly at work during Ellington's famous January 23, 1943, Carnegie Hall concert. Ellington's framing of the Strayhorn work "Dirge" (1943) on the program, for instance, presents solid evidence of an attempt to lead listeners from an appreciation of one musical genre to the appreciation of another. In terms of the music itself, Walter Van de Leur has identified intense chromaticism as a constant theme in Strayhorn's writing, linking it in some cases to Ernö Lendvai's (1971) axis system and in others to the use of chords as discrete coloristic units typical of French impressionism (Van de Leur 2001, 28, 22). This penchant for chromaticism can be seen to fuse with African American vernacular music in "Dirge" through the pairing of "dissonant chords" with a "free-flowing trombone melody . . . that draws on the blues scale" (Van de Leur 2002, 90).

Yet Ellington was quick to dismiss the idea that the piece shared progeny with the European realm, introducing it as the work of "a young man who has really contributed so much to *our* recently acquired music" (1943; emphasis added). Following its performance, and that of a second Strayhorn piece, "Stomp" (which Van de Leur identifies as the already recorded "Johnny Come Lately" [1942]), Ellington (1943) set out again to make the audience understand that Strayhorn, as an artist, was grounded in African American musical practice, claiming,

> We feel that these two numbers selected in the Strayhorn group are somewhat related. As we find it in the picture of the early jazz days, when a jazz band, or rather a small band, was picked to play at a funeral, they played the dirge—something like that—and then on their way back from the funeral we find the dirge resembling something like Strayhorn's *Stomp*.

Ellington's promotion of Strayhorn's work as part of the African American expressive realm, while subtle, indicates an attempt to shift the sonic parameters of what the Carnegie Hall audience might have considered African American music in the early 1940s. Such an approach would have allowed Ellington to recruit support for his music, and jazz in general, by drawing in patrons of Western art music by way of sonorities and compositional devices familiar to that demographic. As the January 23 performance led to a series of more or less regular appearances at Carnegie Hall over the following eight years, the goals of recruitment and financial success embedded in Ellington's approach appear in part to have been realized through this process.

Arrangements performed by the Claude Thornhill band during the late 1940s utilized a similar compositional strategy, albeit toward less effective ends. While Thornhill's arranger, Gil Evans, was not trained in Western art music composition, his work for the ensemble incorporated the dissonance of bebop and its related art music connotations. The fusion of this sonic element with Thornhill's expanded ensemble, a big band containing French horns and tuba, distinguished the group from big band predecessors like Benny Goodman. Yet improvisation continued to play a key role in works performed by the group, occasionally echoing back to the polyphonic improvisation of the New Orleans jazz style (consider, for example, the interweaving lines of improvised call-and-response between tenor saxophonist Mickey Folus and clarinettist Danny Polo on the 1948 recording of "Robbin's Nest").[1]

Thornhill's indeterminate approach to marketing, however, hampered the success of his syncretic ensemble. Avoiding both popular music alignment and what Gil Evans refers to as "concert orchestra" alignment (Crosby 1971, 9), Thornhill played an increasingly marginalized role in the 1940s jazz world. Although he produced several "sweet" music recordings in the mid-1940s, Thornhill frequently chose to perform his more modern works in dance halls, "baffle[ing] the dancers" who had come to hear the commercial ballads (Crease 2002, 156). Ambiguity regarding the framing of these modern works is identified as having been a key barrier to economic success (Crosby 1971; Van de Leur 2001). Indeed, the demographic through which Thornhill sought financial reward was not one in which "modern" effects would have held a good deal of interest. Yet Thornhill's sonic concept remains important in a discussion of 1950s Cool and Third Stream works, as Miles Davis and John Lewis would employ it as part of their own uplift strategy in collaboration with Thornhill arrangers during the late 1940s.

The *Birth of the Cool* album released in 1957 comprises recordings made between 1949 and 1950 and is conventionally held to have emerged from group discussions on the future of jazz hosted by Gil Evans and Miles Davis at Evans's New York apartment. While most historical accounts depict these sessions as debates over aesthetics, it is fair to say that a degree of professional networking and financial problem solving were at play as well. Both Evans and apartment regular Gerry Mulligan spent time on the Thornhill payroll in the late 1940s, and the band's financial instability had long undermined their ability to earn steady wages. In March 1947 Thornhill was forced to disband his group and then hire back musicians at reduced rates in order to cover expenses for performances at the Glen Island Casino ("Thornhill Ork on 3-Week Vacation" 1947, 1). A year later he disbanded for a two-month "vacation," leaving his musicians without pay while he worked on new compositions ("Claude Thornhill to Disband Ork" 1948, 1). Davis, the project organizer, faced equally insecure economic circumstances. Personality conflicts with his 1948 partner, Charlie Parker, foreshadowed a split between the two (Davis 1989, 115), and his reputation had not yet lead to a leadership position on a commercial recording. In addition, his improvisatory style remained quite similar to those of his bebop peers. By collaborating with Mulligan and Evans on arrangements but remaining the lead improvisatory voice, Davis was able to negotiate a sonic space that set him apart from the bebop realm while not requiring the development of a new improvisatory style. In turn, Mulligan and Evans were able to bridge an employment gap.

Such financial and professional benefits were not without their artistic frustrations. Tension between a modernist drive for structure and the promotion of improvisatory elements came to typify arguments between Davis and his arrangers. In the end, membership in the latter group expanded to include Lewis and an additional Thornhill staffer, Johnny Carisi. Mulligan, for instance, believed that the new style of jazz did not lend itself to the extensive soloing of the bebop era. He felt extended solos caused "the composed parts [to] lose their continuity . . . their connection with each other" and that this negatively affected the structural innovations of the music. Davis, in turn, remained focused on extended improvisation during the workshop period of the project, improvising for "more and more choruses" in performances of the arrangements at the Royal Roost (Mulligan 1995, 16). Mulligan recalled Lewis's shared frustration with this approach, stating, "Lewis used to get really mad at him because he wouldn't assume the responsibility and wouldn't consider the band—because the band was a unique thing. It's not like going into the club with a sextet" (1995, 16).

The limits of 78-rpm recordings in part forced a compromise between emphasis on structure and emphasis on improvisation. The two singles immediately released from this collaboration, "Move" (1949) and "Budo" (1949), both arranged by Lewis, are each under three minutes in length and contain only one thirty-two-measure chorus by Davis each. The Royal Roost recordings of "Move," in contrast, are longer, with Davis soloing for three choruses on both the September 4, 1948, and September 18, 1948, club dates.[2] Arrangements, however, are not lost in these club recordings. To the contrary, written passages come across as far more rehearsed than any of the improvisations. Unease with the chord changes on "Move," for instance, is apparent in trombonist Mike Zwerin's September 4 performance and saxophonist Lee Konitz's September 18 performance, but both recordings demonstrate close to perfect execution of the head and composed coda. Importantly, it was these composed sections that held the most immediate repercussions for Davis as a professional musician.

Presentation of the *Birth of the Cool* arrangements at the Royal Roost can be clearly linked to Davis's first leadership contract. According to Stephanie Crease (2002, 160), Capitol had been searching for a way to develop its jazz resources but held a general "antipathy" toward the bebop style. Since its formation in 1942, the label had made the bulk of its money by recording popular vocalists and had largely focused on building audiences outside "race music" demographics. Yet the label's success with Stan Kenton between 1943 and 1947 indicated the potential for engagement with jazz audiences, albeit through an appeal to more modern tastes, and Davis's embrace of Thornhill-sounding syncretism provided Capitol a means of expanding the momentum it had built with Kenton while entering the bebop market at the same time.

Despite the immediate professional benefits for Davis, from a financial perspective, the project was a failure. Crease writes,

> After the Royal Roost engagement, the Nonet had no gigs and, as the fall of 1948 wore on, no prospects of any kind. Meanwhile, the Thornhill band started up again and reclaimed some of its personnel, while John Lewis and other Nonet musicians and colleagues landed other gigs . . . Equally remarkable was the fact that these recordings . . . sold dismally when initially released as singles. (2002, 160)

The responsibility for a lack of follow-up gigs must at least partially lie with Davis. Like Thornhill, Davis had embraced an ambiguous style of promotion. He chose the Royal Roost as a venue because he had worked there throughout 1948 with Tadd Dameron and because he had established some credibility with the management. Yet the Royal Roost was synonymous with the promotion of bebop, drawing heavily from bebop artists in its lineup and broadcasting their performances live on Friday nights. This near-exclusive focus had even garnered the venue the nickname "[the] Metropolitan Bopera House" (Crease 2002, 158). The audiences at the Royal Roost—the same that had embraced Davis as part of Parker and Dameron's group—were not part of the demographic that needed to be drawn into jazz through new twists in its presentation. This new demographic existed outside the jazz club scene.

Yet Capitol's marketing of the *Birth of the Cool* singles also failed to reach beyond the confines of Davis's established audience. Using the credit line "Miles Davis and His Orchestra" on the singles "Move" and "Budo," Capitol neglected to push the "arrangement" focus of the recordings, an approach that may have resulted in better alignment with the Stan Kenton audience already tapped by the label. The 1950 release of the nonet's *Venus de Milo* recording does evince a slight change in approach, with Mulligan given credit as arranger before Davis and his orchestra, but the shift seems to have come too late. The earlier singles had already been critically received as Capitol's first bebop recordings ("Record Review: Miles Davis" 1949a, 14; "Record Review: Miles Davis" 1949b, 14; "Record Review: Miles Davis" 1949c, 15), and their arrangements would not be given considerable focus until the 1957 release of the *Birth of the Cool* album (Hentoff 1957a, 15).

This failure stands in contrast to Ellington's success and can be best understood as the result of poor venue choice and ambiguous promotional vision. Like Thornhill, Davis attempted to engage a new audience by way of sound alone, but by remaining locked into established jazz domains, he put the onus of expansion on those uninitiated. In other words, the success of this strategy relied on the curiosity of a demographic located outside the Royal Roost, a group Davis made little effort to reach. Ellington, on the other hand, sought out the uninitiated within their own space, recruiting outsiders through sonorities familiar to them while simultaneously exposing them to African American blues and improvisatory tropes. Familiarity with Ellington's success, and with Davis's and Thornhill's failures, would drive future jazz artists to pursue syncretic projects in venues outside the jazz realm as they searched for economic security.

Expanding the Jazz Market: Jazz Goes to College

While the concert hall had served as an obvious venue choice in efforts to reach new audiences a decade earlier, by the late 1940s the concept of the jazz concert had become more or less normalized. Eddie Ronan illuminates this shift in a 1947 issue of *Down Beat*:

> With big band business still in a hazardous state, many sidemen today are turning to the concert hall to keep in cakes and drapes. More jazz concerts are being planned or held here at the present time than at any other era of the biz. And local sidemen are enjoying them financially as well as musically. It's a chance to keep their wallets out of an anemic condition and their lips in form at the same time. (Ronan 1947, 1)

The concerts Ronan cites as evidence include the Jazz at the Philharmonic tours produced by Norman Granz and the Eddie Condon series of concerts performed at Carnegie Hall. Other examples would include Charlie Parker's and Dizzy Gillespie's Carnegie Hall debuts in 1947 and the bebop-heavy tribute to Charlie Parker after his death in 1955. Such performances demonstrate the successful appropriation of these spaces as locales where jazz could be performed for large, informed, and appreciative audiences. New spaces were therefore required in order to tap a truly fresh market, and advances in tertiary jazz education in the late 1940s and early 1950s made the college campus an ideal domain for such growth.

The introduction of jazz lectures into American universities very pointedly foreshadowed the formalistic approaches to jazz scholarship that Scott DeVeaux critiques in "Constructing the Jazz Tradition." Central to this orientation was an acceptance of the linear evolution of jazz as championed by jazz pedagogue Marshall Stearns. Stearns earned a PhD in English at Yale in 1942 and began promoting the formation of university jazz clubs as a Cornell University faculty member in 1947. The Cornell Rhythm Club may have been the first of these, instituting a concert and lecture series overseen by Stearns along with projects cataloging old periodicals and rare records ("Stearns Starts Club" 1947, 4). Other early projects with Stearns at the head included the 1950s courses Perspectives in Jazz and Giants in Jazz, delivered at New York University ("NYU to Conduct Jazz Course" 1950, 1; "Jazz Course at NYU" 1950, 1), and the now well-known roundtable discussions at Music Inn in Lenox, Massachusetts, beginning in 1951. Each of these projects conceived of jazz as an evolving music in which stylistic shifts revolved around the fusion of established conventions and new compositional devices. As John Gennari indicates in *Blowin' Hot and Cool*, the evolutionary narrative of these lectures was often well received by participants active in jazz performance, demonstrating for many both the usability of the past and an impetus on future invention (2006, 217).

Acceptance of the evolutionary model in universities challenged definitions of authenticity tied to early performance practice and helped solidify a modernist theoretical perspective regarding the music in academic circles. It must be noted that while Stearns was at the forefront of this movement, he was not the only advocate working within the modernist paradigm. John Lucas's series of talks delivered at Carleton College in 1948 evince a similar approach, tracing the development of jazz through five one-hour lecture and music-sharing programs, covering "Folk song," "Blues," "Ragtime," "Jazz," and "Swing" periods (Hoefer 1948, 11). Chicago promoter Joe Segal's 1951 lecture comparing Dixie and modern groups at Roosevelt College again put forth an evolutionary narrative ("Tristano Returns to Chi" 1951, 6). Further evidence can be found in a 1952 Union College series featuring "dixie" performances by Rex Stewart and a "modern" performance by Billy Taylor ("Jazz Experiment" 1952, 8). By ending with a discussion of "modern" jazz, these lecture-concerts legitimized syncretism as a key element of the jazz tradition and primed college audiences for the acceptance of new jazz products.

Yet like initial entry into the concert hall, access to these venues required a circumvention of perceptions of jazz as a musical practice linked to deviant behavior. As Lopes writes, the jazz deviance trope, "whether romantic or derogatory," was well entrenched in the popular imagination by the 1940s (2002, 145). As a barrier to university entrance, the ramifications of this stereotype are evident in the example of the University of Kentucky's 1951 ban on jazz music. In laying out its reasoning, the university issued the following statement:

> A story on the front page of *The Leader* of Feb. 19 might give the erroneous impression that the music department of the university has been won over by the advocates of jazz or bop and is encouraging wider and more generous acceptance in cultural circles of this strange malady. . . . 'Jazz' music has no part in the university program. . . . It is [the university's] duty . . . to attempt to elevate the tastes of its students and the people of the commonwealth. . . . No member of the music faculty plays in any "jazz" band or has ever played in any bar or orchestra. Furthermore, the university has never approved the assembling of its students in any taproom or bar in this or other cities. ("Jazz Is Barred" 1951, 16)

Interestingly, the University of Kentucky ban seemed targeted at the type of jazz played in clubs and pubs as opposed to the style performed in dance halls and hotel ballrooms. The link between jazz and alcohol is mentioned twice at the end of the passage, and in both instances it is framed as an almost integral part of jazz culture. This is only a slightly veiled dig at the bebop genre, as jazz in the form of swing had much earlier moved from the "taproom" into more morally sound venues, evident in its frequent use at college dances throughout the 1940s and 1950s

("School Dance Contest" 1953, 1). The deviance associated with bebop, on the other hand, kept permutations of jazz associated with African American performers from expanding beyond established domains, despite its art music status. Eric Porter describes this paradox:

> Even as the practitioners of bebop were cast as artists and intellectuals, they could still be objects of the primitivist fascination that had long characterized the jazz discourse. The perception of musicians as social deviants was by no means inconsistent with the construction of jazz as avant-garde expression. . . . Ronald Radano discusses the development of a "primitive/intellectual homology" used to comprehend the character of black jazz musicians in the post-war United States. White observers frequently saw "contrasting images of respectability and degeneracy, of noble romanticism and black bestiality" as they sought to understand the jazz artist. (2002, 92)

As Porter indicates, despite the art music status of bebop, the deviance associated with its practitioners impeded its expansion. As a result, performance priority was given in tertiary settings to either white-dominated jazz genres such as swing or, less often, simply to white jazz modernists.[3]

Two early examples of this expansion, Stan Kenton's performance at the University of Minnesota in 1951 and Lennie Tristano's performance at Brandeis University in 1952, were delivered as part of performance-lectures similar to the Stearns model ("Kenton Lectures" 1951, 7; "Brandeis Arts Festival" 1952, 5). Other performances shed the lecturing component but remained largely focused on the presentation of "modern" pieces. Chet Baker's appearance at an inaugural University of California Los Angeles jazz concert in 1954 ("New Approach" 1954, 12) and the MJQ's performance at Oberlin College in 1955 ("MJQ to Storyville" 1955, 6) are indicative of this later approach.[4] Yet no jazz musician capitalized more effectively on this new space than pianist Dave Brubeck.

During the early 1950s, Brubeck and four members of his octet toured college campuses extensively throughout the United States. By his own recollection, the group played up to ninety colleges per four-month tour, building up a list of impressive venues that eventually included the University of California–Berkeley and Oberlin College (Garcia 2001, 39). Stylistically, the quartet sound was well suited to the university campus. As in Davis's *Birth of the Cool* recordings, the group was able to "mask" improvisation and jazz rhythmic effects with composed arrangements. Gioia's description of Brubeck's style in the early 1950s details the variety of devices employed toward this end:

> Many of his devices would become standard Brubeck fare in later years, but in 1949 few jazz fans were conversant with compositional techniques such as polytonality, unexpected modulations from major to minor (listen to "Blue Moon," where bassist Ron Crotty holds on to the original changes while Brubeck's harmonies take off into the stratosphere); the jolting switch from twentieth-century to eighteenth-century harmony at the close of "Indiana"; the rumbling, dissonant block chords that transformed "Laura" and "Tea for Two" into biting Bartókian vignettes. (1992, 86)

This list of devices is then tied inextricably to the group's reliance on a repetitive, syncopated "ground beat," a device Gioia locates in the African American realm. He writes,

> The group's sense of ground rhythm owes more to Basie and McShann than it does to Bartók and Milhaud. . . . The band's rhythmic experimentations, at their best, were often superimposed on this steady ground beat rather than replacements for it. . . . It was perhaps the underlying rhythmic conservatism of his music that allowed Brubeck to incorporate elements of modernism into his work without alienating—indeed while attracting—a large audience. (1992, 91)

As Gioia indicates, this pairing of tropes worked to Brubeck's financial advantage as well as to the benefit of jazz dissemination. Not only was his band allowed access to college campuses, his brand of modern jazz sold well in these venues. Brubeck's college tours led to his contract with Columbia in 1954, and his first album for the label was compiled from recordings of his 1953 Oberlin performance, released as *Jazz Goes to College*.[5]

Brubeck's comments regarding the intent or spirit of his fusion enable us to read such success in the context of a double-voiced expressive paradigm. Admittedly, examining Brubeck in these terms—terms developed for the study of African American expressive culture—might be viewed by some as problematic. His tertiary training in Western art music at the University of the Pacific and his association with Darius Milhaud at Mills College initially paint him as operating outside African American expressive culture (along with the fact that he was, in fact, a white artist). Yet such aspects of Brubeck's background do not alter the fact that Brubeck himself viewed his compositional approach as being grounded in an African American sensibility. While the degree of Brubeck's cultural orientation, whether toward Western art music or African American vernacular music, may never be known (if such a thing is knowable with any musician), certainly his desire to work from an African American foundation and to promote its core elements is made clear in his early statements to interviewers, as evinced in a description of the future of American music composition that he provided in 1950:

> Since jazz is not provincial, regional, nor chauvinistic, but as much an expression of our people as our language, it is the natural idiom for the American composer. I firmly believe that the composer who will most successfully typify America will have been born into jazz, will have absorbed it in his early years unconsciously, and will probably be an active participant in shaping its future course. (Brubeck 1950, 18)

Brubeck's focus on uniting American culture with jazz culture in this statement is at odds with Gates's (1988) pan-African nationalistic readings of African American cultural products but nonetheless demonstrates a personal connection to the processes believed to drive African American music. While Brubeck strips jazz of African American ownership in this passage, he does not fully move it into the "white" or European musical realm. Instead he chooses to realign it as a uniquely American, multiracial phenomenon. This context allows Brubeck to put forth the argument that the promotion of jazz vernacular elements is in fact a promotion of core American musical elements: "Most of the contemporary composers, including most of the 12-tone system writers, are getting too far from the roots of our culture. And for American composers, our roots should be in jazz" (qtd. in Hentoff 1954c, 2).

Brubeck might be seen as working from these roots most overtly in his use of rhythm or what Gioia (1992) refers to as his reliance on the "ground beat." Devices such as chromatic harmonizations, modal shifting, polytonality, and polyrhythm are then added on top of this foundation. This combination of elements, designed to engage a new market while holding central the tenets of vernacular jazz rhythm, function to the same double-voiced ends as Ellington's, Strayhorn's, and Davis's projects. To exclude Brubeck from this paradigm based on perceptions of his outsider status would therefore ignore both his familiarity and facility with double-voiced compositional processes.

Yet Brubeck's work is more often than not subsumed under the "Cool" label (Gioia 1992; Lopes 2002; Meadows 2003), the definitions of which mirror in technical terms but not in intent the syncretic "masking" processes discussed above. Lopes, for example, defines "Cool" as "a reserved soft version of the swing ensemble with influences from bop and European classical harmony and timbre used by progressive big bands" (2002, 243). Meadows in turn summarizes the musical facets of the genre as an "emphasis on written arrangements, interesting orchestrations, melodic counterpoint, less use of higher ranges on melodic instruments, use of conjunct melodies and straight tone qualities, and a preference for ballads" (2003, 262). While these two definitions are certainly accurate as general descriptions, they evince a tendency to avoid discussion of stylistic particularities, such as Brubeck's use of the "ground-beat" and Davis's emphasis on improvisation. As demonstrated thus far, the presence of these musical elements takes on increasing import when each work is contextualized in terms of the "cultural work" with which it is engaged, both economic and social.

Expanding the Jazz Market: The Creation of "Modern" Music Venues

A tendency to ignore the presence of improvisation, jazz rhythmic effects, and blues sonorities is even more prevalent in discussion of works labeled "Third Stream." The term *Third Stream*, first introduced into the music lexicon by Gunther Schuller at a Brandeis University lecture in 1957, has been defined in retrospect as "improvisation or written composition or both" that "synthesizes the essential characteristics and techniques of contemporary Western art music and various ethnic or vernacular musics" (Schuller 1986, 377). Historically the term can be seen to have gained initial traction as a label only for works meeting this definition and played by ensembles with instrumentation greater than that of standard small group or big band setups. Smaller jazz ensembles utilizing a similar pairing of "Western" and "non-Western" musical conventions were lumped into the West Coast or Cool camps. Retrospective assessments have, however, cast a slightly wider net, incorporating the mid-1950s jazz quartet works of John Lewis into the Third Stream fold (Floyd 1995, 167; Joyner 2000, 79). This problematic labeling is discussed further in chapter 4 but is introduced here in order to argue that, to a large extent, the promotion of what would come to be known as Third Stream works mirrored the attempts of Cool Jazz modernists like Dave Brubeck to expand the jazz audience.

Composer-bassist Charles Mingus articulated a promotional strategy conceived along these lines in a letter to *Down Beat* published in June 1951—six years before he wrote his now-lauded Third Stream work "Revelations" (1957). Elaborating on comments from an earlier *Down Beat* interview, Mingus wrote of learning from "every score of the great composers, old and modern," and of the practicality of viewing jazz and classical streams as "all one music" (Gleason 1951, 7). Such an orientation, he assumed, would result in wider appeal for his own projects. As Eric Porter writes in reflection, "He was convinced that the lines between classical music and jazz were not immutable, and he saw composition as a means of moving outside the marketing categories imposed upon jazz" (2002, 105). Yet Mingus did not view this approach as an abandonment of African American musical culture. To the contrary, Porter indicates that Mingus's mid-1950s works utilized this approach as a means to an end regarding the promotion of African American musical elements. By casting rhythmic drive and blues tonalities within composed forms, Mingus was able to both promote vernacular tropes and expand his commercial reach beyond the existing parameters of the jazz market (Porter 2002, 117). His concerts of "modern jazz composition" presented throughout New York in the mid-1950s in turn demonstrate the importance of branding in achieving these goals.

Unable to enter the college market as directly as white modernists, Mingus chose instead to take part in a project that aimed to reinvent established jazz spaces in a manner that might attract Western art music listeners. This was largely accomplished through the promotion of his works under the banner of "modern jazz composition." While linkage between the terms "jazz" and "composition" had been occurring in jazz since the 1930s, even quite overtly, as in the promotion of Ellington's Carnegie Hall performances, these early associations used the performer, not the composition, as their main focus. Ellington's 1943 concert at Carnegie Hall, for instance, received a good deal of attention related to his composition *Black, Brown and Beige*, yet the performance was marketed to patrons under the name "Duke Ellington and His Orchestra" (Tucker 1993, 161). Dizzy Gillespie's 1947 Carnegie Hall debut, in turn, despite its importance in showcasing modern bebop innovation and John Lewis's arrangements, was marketed under Gillespie's name (Levin 1947, 1). The promotion of Mingus's 1950s performances, in contrast, switched the focus from "performer" to "composition."

Initially this was realized through Mingus's 1954 collaboration with the Jazz Composers Workshop, a collective that included Max Roach, Thelonious Monk, Art Blakey, Kenny Clarke, John Lewis, Teo Macero, and John LaPorta (Porter 2002, 116). Performances of works composed by group members were set up at both Carnegie Recital Hall in January and the Museum of Modern Art in May, the former demonstrating reliance on an established domain and the latter, a shift in venue. The compositions themselves, and not the performers, were made the focal point of these events and were given considerable coverage in the popular press. Such focus, it should be noted, was not always beneficial. The works presented at the January concert served as fodder for the group's first review in *Down Beat*, which referred to them as "uniformly disappointing" in terms of "structure, thematic content and rhythmic interest" ("Jazz Composers Workshop" 1954, 21). George Simon's review of the May performance, published in *Metronome*, was again mixed, referring to Mingus's work "Background for Thought" as "an involved bit of writing, far too confusing to be digested at one hearing, and even intricate enough to call for a halt by Mingus and then a fresh start" (qtd. in Priestley 1982, 57). Yet the group steadily progressed, and by 1955 follow-up performances had been scheduled at Carnegie Recital Hall and the YMHA on Lexington Avenue ("New Series" 1955, 16). Utilizing the series title "Developments in Modern Jazz," these concerts mirrored the format of Stearns's lecture series. Audience members were encouraged to ask questions after the performance of each work, and in at least one instance debate surrounding compositional intent erupted between performers on the stage ("New Series" 1955, 16). The audience outreach goals of such a format were quite obvious. Speaking on behalf of the musicians at a January 1955 performance, Bill Coss told *Down Beat*, "Jazz is now at a point where it must make some forward steps to meet its potential audiences," a point to which the journalist responded, "These concerts are an excellent and commendatory example of one of the best ways for musicians to make those steps" ("New Series" 1955, 16).

While Mingus's relationship with the Jazz Composers Workshop helped accomplish his goal of reaching a new audience, his compositions for the group capitalized on this access by utilizing musical material and performance conventions from the jazz realm to activate what would appear to many to be Western art music sonic concepts. This is most evident in his arrangement of "Tea for Two," released on the 1955 album *Jazz Composers Workshop*. Here Mingus utilizes the standard thirty-two-bar form of the title work but pairs the "Tea for Two" melody in counterpoint with the melodies of jazz standards "Perdido" and "Body and Soul" (Priestley 1982, 58). The resulting polyphony Signifies on Western art music contrapuntal practices, in effect presenting the work as derived from European processes to one set of listeners while acknowledging its debt to jazz history for others. His original composition "Purple Heart," released on the same album, utilizes improvised counterpoint to a similar end. In the context of the "Developments in Modern Jazz" series, the interweaving lines of clarinettist John LaPorta and baritone saxophonist George Barrow would have likely appeared to be the jazz practice of polyphonic improvisation to one group of listeners and an effect derived from European contrapuntal practices to the Western art music cohort.

Further evidence of Mingus's double-voiced approach can be heard in his work "Revelations" (1957), presented at the Brandeis University jazz festival in June 1957. Mingus's access to the university in this instance can be understood as a result of both gradual advances during the early civil rights movement and the normalization of modern jazz performances at universities during the early 1950s. Yet it must also be noted that this was not a "Mingus" concert. The focus of the festival lay in the promotion of composition, similar to the "Developments in Modern Jazz" series. "Revelations" was a commissioned work, as were the works by other festival participants Jimmy Giuffre, George Russell, Harold Shapero, Milton Babbitt, and Gunther Schuller. Such compositional focus likely aided Mingus's inclusion in the program while casting a wide net in terms of potential audience members.

Certainly Babbitt's participation would have contributed to the success of the latter cause. Babbitt had established himself in the late 1940s and early 1950s as a composer who synthesized and expanded on "Schoenbergian and Webernian practices" (Mead 1994, 54). The work Babbitt would present, "All Set" (1957), built on the twelve-tone compositional procedures he had advanced during the first part of his career while incorporating jazz improvisational and formal gestures (Wintle 1976, 121). As the work marked Babbitt's first interaction with jazz, it seems reasonable to assume that some of his supporters would have been less familiar with the genre than those who had long supported Mingus and the other composers on the program, all of whom maintained at least some connection with the jazz art world.

While Mingus's awareness of Babbit's involvement was likely, given the early announcement of the festival participants ("Six Works" 1957, 11), it is difficult to say with certainty that "Revelations" was designed with his participation in mind. Still, the work Signifies on the atonality of the Second Viennese School in a manner that would have engaged Babbit's supporters. This can be heard in the work's opening section, which begins with a theme performed in unison by the baritone saxophone, bassoon, horn, trombone, harp, and bass.

While not strictly a twelve-tone row, the opening theme is highly chromatic and presents eleven out of twelve possible pitches in quick succession (A♭/G# is missing and some notes are repeated). This passage then progresses through three interweaving composed solos, one for French horn, one for trumpet, and one for trombone, all utilizing similar nondiatonic pitch collections before the theme returns in its original orchestration. An ostinato on the pitch B♭ begins the following section, played by the baritone sax, bassoon, harp, guitar, and bass parts, accompanying a fanfare played by the alto saxophone, French horn, trumpet, and trombone. This section climaxes in the juxtapositioning of an A-major chord (spelled A–D♭–E) against the B♭ ostinato and the lyric "oh yes, my LORD!" sung by the percussionist.

It is the incorporation of this latter element that demands the most attention in a Signifyin(g) analysis. Mingus made clear his intention to evoke the vernacular in this moment, writing in his performance notes,

> The singing shout "Oh, yes, my Lord" can be delivered by a performer other than the drummer, or optionally by several players. Finally, if no one is able to produce this shout in authentic "black church" style, a brief improvised "shout" by, for example, the alto saxophone could be substituted. (1976, 2)

This reference to the black church links the lyric to the "testifying" trope of African American religious services in which vocal shouts are used as a means of affirming preached content. One level of Signifyin(g) can therefore be seen when the shout is viewed as a comment on the strictures of notated performance. Mingus's dissonant opening pushes the limits of traditionally notated music, freeing his melody from the confines of diatonicism by embracing atonal concepts. The shout comes at the climax of this section, confirming or praising the preceding material while in turn pointing to additional or alternate freedoms found in vernacular practices.

This commentary is advanced further in Mingus's section of "open" improvisation. Located between the work's quasi-atonal opening and ending, this section draws on a slight variation of the blues scale in the creation of a dissonant group improvisation. The structural components employed toward this end are a two-measure repeated vamp and two sets of "blowing scales," written in the trumpet part. The same scales are provided earlier in the score for the other instruments directed to improvise during this section. The first scale, located in measure 169, is the B♭ harmonic minor scale with an added raised fourth degree. This pitch is blues derived (an enharmonic equivalent of the flat fifth) and presents again in the second scale, played over E♭7. Mirroring the first scale, this second pitch collection includes another addition, a raised sixth degree, allowing the performer access to pendular thirds over the E♭7 harmony. The two-measure section includes the directions "Repeat ad libitum, build to climax," and the 1957 recording demonstrates an interpretation of this requirement: the performers steadily increase both the length and volume of their improvised statements until a high degree of dissonance has been reached. This section is then followed by a restatement of the work's initial theme.

Where Mingus's shout confirms the use of notation in freeing music from diatonic restrictions and points to alternate paths toward musical freedom, the design of Mingus's open section demonstrates the capacity for blues-based polyphonic improvisation to achieve similar sonic goals. The parallel between the approaches is made overt in the transition from the "open" section to the (nearly) twelve-tone theme that follows, thus framing polyphonic improvisation as an equal partner in tonal liberation. In the Mingus examples cited thus far, it is important to note that African American musical elements are utilized as the core building blocks of Western art music sonic effects. Instead of using jazz (or Western art music practices) as a veneer, Mingus manipulates the vernacular directly, forcing it to speak the double-voiced utterances required by the Signifyin(g) trope.

In terms of audience expansion, these compositional processes met with mixed success. Gunther Schuller recognized the potential of Mingus's compositions in what would become the Third Stream market and collaborated with him on the 1960 project *Pre-Bird*, realizing jazz standards and syncretic Mingus originals through an expanded jazz orchestra that included flute, oboe, and tuba (in addition to the traditional trumpets, trombones, saxes, and rhythm section). Development of the album was supported by Mercury Records, yet its release marked Mingus's first and last project with the label. The work "Revelations," in turn, would become increasingly aligned with the Third Stream genre while the composer moved more aggressively toward blues-based projects. "Revelations" was released with other syncretic works, including Lewis's "Three Little Feelings" (1956), on a 1964 album titled *Outstanding Jazz Compositions of the 20th Century* and has been referred to in retrospect as one of the earliest commissioned Third Stream works (Joyner 2000, 78) as well as a hallmark of the "classical jazz modernist" approach (Lopes 2002, 244). The bulk of Mingus's post-"Revelations" pieces, in contrast, are described by Porter as follows:

> Whether it was based on a fear of being marginalized by black reformulations of the idiom, the influence of Charlie Parker and other bebop architects, the expectations of record labels and audiences, the political moment, an artistic impasse, or, more likely, a combination of factors, Mingus changed his approach to composition and bandleading. He began working with original compositions that included more African-American vernacular musical elements (for example, gospel and blues inflections), and he allowed musicians greater leeway in creating the melodic (if not harmonic) structure of each performance of these compositions. (2002, 124)

The 1959 albums *Blues and Roots* and *Mingus Ah Um* are indicative of this vernacular-heavy approach. While continuing to tease and manipulate the blues, these albums showcase vernacular elements such as "open fourths and fifths, rhythmic vamps that shuffled back and forth for extended periods, gospel cries of enthusiasm from the band stand [and] melodies that traded the snaky chromatics of bebop for simpler repeated blues statements" (Saul 2003, 195) in a more overt manner than Mingus's works for the Jazz Composers Workshop and the Brandeis Jazz Festival. This approach was encouraged by Atlantic Records producer Nesuhi Ertegun (Saul 2003, 195) and can be seen to permeate the popular 1961 album *Mingus Oh, Yeah!* Such alignment moved Mingus's compositions closer to the R&B and popular music audience. As Saul notes, "The mainstream youth market" was already embracing blues-heavy syncretic works by vocalists Sam Cooke and Paul Anka, and while Mingus rejected popular music alignment in interviews, his late-1950s success is at least partially tied to the interests of this demographic (2003, 195).

Lewis and the Search for a Third Stream Audience

Despite such a shift, Mingus's participation in a project that had sought to bring into the fold followers of Western art music instilled some lasting promotional models in the jazz world. John Lewis in particular can be seen to have continued to utilize the "modern music" banner during his work with both the Modern Jazz Society and the Jazz and Classical Music Society between 1955 and 1957. Alignment between the goals of the two composers in terms of audience outreach is apparent in Lewis's statements regarding a modernist agenda, put forth in a 1953 *Down Beat* interview with Nat Hentoff. Echoing Mingus's call for the expansion of the jazz audience, Lewis vented frustration with bebop-style improvisation and his perception of its alienating effects, stating,

> If solos go on for chorus after chorus, it's hard enough for the musician to remember what he's constructing. It must be even more difficult for the listener . . . The audience for jazz can be widened if we strengthen our work with structure. If there is more of a reason for what's going on, there'll be more overall sense, and, therefore, more interest for the listener. (Hentoff 1953a, 8)

These comments parallel Mulligan's recollection of Lewis's attitude during the *Birth of the Cool* sessions and have a tendency to be used in discussions of Lewis's appropriation of European compositional conventions (F. Davis 1983; Bourne 1992). Yet Lewis was quick to champion familiar jazz conventions in the same article, pointing to the rhythmic interplay of New Orleans–style improvisation as a solution to what he perceived as "rhythmic dullness" in contemporary jazz and to the primacy of swing in creating "meaningful rhythmic sense" in a work (qtd. in Hentoff 1953a, 26). Indeed, balance between both the old and the new in jazz works was paramount in Lewis's vision, a sentiment made clear in his concluding statement: "It must be possible to hear all of the music or else . . . these other aspects lose their impact" (qtd. in Hentoff 1953a, 26). Yet as with Mingus, such an agenda would prove problematic to implement within the confines of established jazz domains.

Lewis's experience with Davis's nonet had demonstrated the futility of syncretic pursuits in existing jazz venues. Like Davis, the arrangers and collaborators on the *Birth of the Cool* had felt the pain of a lack of follow-up performances and the general disinterest by jazz consumers toward their experiments. Lewis's subsequent projects, in response, demonstrated a shift away from the syncretic sound of the nonet back toward the earlier bebop style. Examples from this period include a 1951 recording with Davis released as *Miles Davis and Horns* and four separate recordings made as part of the Milt Jackson Quartet between 1951 and 1952.[6] Yet Lewis struggled in a style where pianistic virtuosity was paramount to success. As Davis realigned with the bebop sound in the early 1950s, he dropped Lewis and replaced him with pianists more capable of performing bebop lines, a list that eventually included, among others, Kenny Drew and Walter Bishop. As Martin Williams would later point out, Lewis's strength as a pianist did "not include obvious finger dexterity" and he frequently avoided "the percussively delivered chord patterns . . . typical [of] modern jazz pianist[s]," instead choosing to "offer complementary countermelodies behind . . . soloist[s]" (Williams 1970, 158–59). While this approach apparently met Jackson's approval (evident in his reliance on Lewis as an accompanist), it left little room for Lewis to maneuver outside his role as sideman. Leadership success would instead need to be pursued through Lewis's strengths in arrangement and composition, embraced in a new permutation of the Milt Jackson Quartet, this time with Lewis at the head.

Lewis articulated his strategy for the "new" ensemble—the Modern Jazz Quartet—to bassist Percy Heath and vibraphonist Jackson in 1952, and Heath remembered it in the following terms:

> John's vision for the group was to change the music from just a jam session, or rhythm section and soloist idea, to something more. We were all equal members, and the dress, the wearing of tuxedos, and trying to perform in concert rather than always in nightclubs, was part of what he envisioned to change the whole attitude about the music. (Heath qtd. in Giddins 1998, 382)

Central to this strategy was the exploration of new performance spaces. Yet despite a desire to play more "concert" settings, the MJQ initially struggled to gain access to venues apart from nightclubs. Continuing to trade primarily under vibraphonist Milt Jackson's name, the group toured jazz clubs along the East Coast during 1953 and 1954, enduring a paradox of critical praise and audience disinterest. Evidence of the latter can be seen in Heath's recollection of a three-week residency at Birdland in 1954:

> We had a hard time getting people to quiet down and listen. At that time in nightclubs, people were talking about hanging out. In order

> to break that down, instead of trying to play over the conversation, we'd use reverse psychology and play softer. Suddenly, they knew we were up there and realized the conversation was louder than the music. Of course, it if got too loud, we'd come off—just stop playing and walk off. It didn't take long for them to realize they were wasting their time because we weren't going to entertain them in that sense. (Heath qtd. in Giddins 1998, 384)

Critical reception of the Birdland performances, in contrast, demonstrated excitement over the group's musical approach. Nat Hentoff, the journalist who had given Lewis a platform for articulating his modernist strategy in 1953, echoed back Lewis's comments regarding the balance of more traditional jazz elements and modern structural elements in his review of the performance:

> One new work that *is* now in the book is a warmly lyrical new Lewis original, *Django*, and a pungent *True Blues*. These numbers, like almost all of the Quartet's book, combine careful but fluid form with space for free improvisation. Thereby, the jazz improvisation becomes more meaningful within the added musical challenges provided by the imaginative form. Equally important is the fact that by working within intelligently flexible form, the Modern Jazz Quartet's number mean more as a whole than the book of any other current jazz small unit. There is thereby less inconsistency of performance from night to night by the unit as a unit than occurs with groups that are based almost entirely on the solo flights of its members with only tenuous ensemble interconnections between those solos. (Hentoff 1954a, 32)

Hentoff's praise offered support for Lewis's syncretic style, but Heath's recollections of club performances demonstrate its ill-fittedness for the jazz scene. These club dates failed additionally in meeting the recruitment priorities put forth in Lewis's 1953 interview. Fortunately, his involvement with the Jazz Composers Workshop in the early 1950s had modeled a way of addressing both of these issues.

Lewis endeavored to create his own new performance space under the label of the Modern Jazz Society in 1955. Like Mingus, Lewis strove to establish a setting in which composition could serve as the main vehicle for audience attraction. Teaming up with the French horn player and composer Gunther Schuller, Lewis assembled a program of works showcasing a range of ensembles, including the MJQ and a chamber ensemble consisting of flute, harp, bassoon, and French horn as well as more traditional big band units. Importantly, the Modern Jazz Society's emphasis on composition expanded beyond the jazz realm, evident in the inclusion of Italian composer Luigi Nono's *Polifonica, Monodia, Ritmica*. This performance marked Nono's first appearance in the United States, and his reputation abroad as an "an unusually important modern composer" formed part of the inaugural concert promotion (Hentoff 1955b, 14). Like Babbitt's later inclusion in the 1957 Brandeis Jazz Festival, Nono's inclusion on the Modern Jazz Society program would have ensured a broader audience demographic than had Lewis and the MJQ attempted to promote the performance on their own. In addition, while the group utilized an established jazz domain, Town Hall, the space was claimed early on in the name of composition as opposed to "jazz." An announcement for the concert reads, "A unique concert in Town Hall Nov. 19 will be the first venture of the new Modern Jazz Society, a nonprofit organization for providing a wider hearing for contemporary music and musicians" ("Jazz Society Spots MJQ" 1955, 52). Such "unique" aspects of this performance in effect created a new musical space in which Lewis's expansionist agenda could be more efficiently realized.

Indeed, the music itself appears custom built to intrigue both the Western art music listener and the modern jazz connoisseur to which the Modern Jazz Society's program was marketed. Lewis's "Concorde," performed at Birdland on January 23 and January 30, 1955, as well as at the Modern Jazz Society concert, stands out in this regard as a result of its Signifyin(g) treatment of fugal processes. As Owens (1976) shows in an early analysis of the work, the initial theme is treated in the manner of a fugal subject, traded between the bass, piano, and vibraphone over the course of a twenty-five-measure exposition. Yet the theme itself is composed largely of call-response tropes (example 1.1).

The opening two bars form a "call," employing the vernacular convention of pendular thirds, B moving to C, in transition to the A♭ harmony.

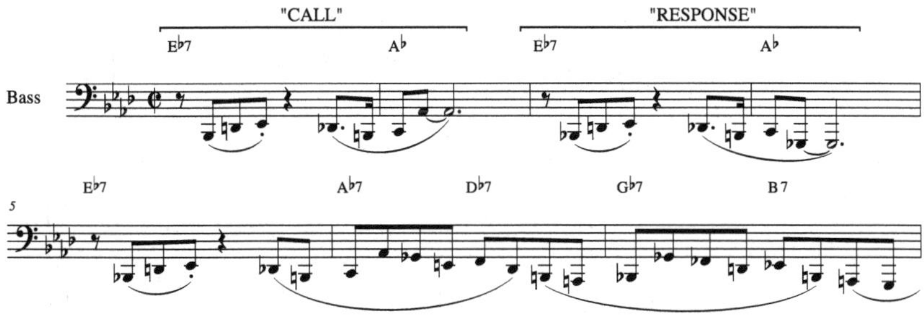

Example 1.1. "Concorde" (1954), "Fugal Subject," bass, mm. 1–7. Published score (reduced and set in Finale).

The "response" that follows in bars 3–4 again employs pendular thirds but embellishes the initial statement by adding yet another blues sonority, the flat seventh over the tonic harmony on the upbeat of beat 1 in bar 4. Signifyin(g) can then be seen to take place as the call-response statement reenters, first in the piano and then in the vibraphone. The dovetailing of these statements evokes the layered thematic construction of fugal compositions while simultaneously reiterating, again and again, the core blues components of the "fugal" subject. To a jazz audience, the repeated statements inherent to the fugal process may have signified an additional layer of blues-derived call-response structure, while to others they would have likely appeared linked to the canon of Western art music. Performing this work in front of a diverse audience would have therefore allowed Lewis to potentially entertain those "in the know" while simultaneously recruiting those uninitiated.

A similar strategy is employed in Lewis's work "Three Little Feelings" (1956), written for the Jazz and Classical Music Society (JCMS) in 1956. The JCMS was an outgrowth of the Modern Jazz Society, designed with the intent of encouraging the performance of contemporary music, especially works "written by composers in the jazz field who would not otherwise have an opportunity for their less-conventional work to be presented" (Avakian 1957, 1). The term *less-conventional* does not in and of itself strip African American alignment from these works, yet the JCMS went further than any previous space-creation project in targeting an audience of Western art music patrons. Not only did the group include the term *Classical Music* in their title, they recruited New York Philharmonic conductor Dmitri Mitropoulos's participation in their inaugural concert, seeking to capitalize on the reputation of a well-known Western art music figure ("Jazz, Classical Music Society" 1956, 9). While this performance was first delayed and then ultimately cancelled, early publicity paved the way for the marketing of an album of works in which Mitropoulos participated, sharing conducting credit with Schuller, and issued under the title *The Jazz and Classical Music Society Presents a Program of Music for Brass*.

"Three Little Feelings" again employs the call-response trope as a key structural device, seen most clearly in its first movement. The initial thematic statement, the "call," is stated in unison by two trombones and two French horns before being concluded in unison by two French horns and two trumpets (example 1.2). The blues-derived flat fifth features prominently in the second measure and the blues-derived flat third forms an integral part of the second half of the thematic figure seen in measure 4. The second thematic statement, or the "response," revises the first part of the theme while maintaining the second. Again, the flat fifth plays a significant role in the identity of the primary figure, falling to an F natural in measure 8 and thus paralleling measure 2 of the example; yet Lewis draws additional attention to the blues inflection by requiring semitonal movement between the pitch and scale degree 5 twice in measure 7 as opposed to just once in measure 1.

Repetition of these two sets of thematic material makes up the vast majority of written music during the first movement, the details of which are outlined in figure 1.1. The result is a riff-driven work in which nearly all composed material can be linked back to the initial thematic statement. The pairing of this material with improvisation in turn establishes its jazz sensibilities even more convincingly (see figure 1.1).

The Signifyin(g) aspects of the first movement of "Three Little Feelings" therefore have less to do with its compositional design than its choice of instrumentation and selection of presentation space. The addition of French horns, baritone horns, and tuba evoke associations with musical styles separate from African American vernacular music, and its location on an album with works conducted by Mitropoulos aligns it, at least in terms of marketing, more with Western art music than with the jazz art world. The extent to which the work's riff-driven design was successfully hidden by Lewis's selection of instruments and the paratextual frame of the album is evident in popular press reviews. Ray Ellsworth, for example, places it outside the jazz realm with the exception of its improvised passages, stating,

> The standout composition here for me is John Lewis' *Three Little Feelings* . . . I guess Lewis has the patent on this kind of writing, the formal structure on a three-part invention written out in some complexity with holes for blowing to provide the jazz feeling. (1957, 34)

Schuller concurs with Ellsworth's assessment, stating that Lewis had, "in a very simple, unspectacular way," combined "the romantic and the classical in a judicious blending" (1957, 1). John Wilson, writing for the *New York Times*, further contributes to the consensus, noting that "Three Little Feelings" indicates there could be "jazz composition based on the same kind of form and structure used in the composition of 'serious' music" (1957, 97), while Dom De Micheal and Pete Welding note that the work and Jimmy Giuffre's "Pharaoh," both included on the 1964 rerelease of *Music for Brass*, "show clearly the influence of classical composition on the composers" (1964, 25). While such assessments would have been crucial in meeting the expansionist agenda inherent in works that utilize the "minstrel mask," too much success along these lines would work to separate the piece in popular imagination from the realm of African American expressive culture.

Indeed, regardless of what these reviewers describe as a double-voiced design, the lack of jazz listeners willing or able to hear the music as double-voiced commentary is evident in Lewis's increasing marginalization from the jazz world, as surveyed in the following chapter. Part of this issue arises from the fact that "Three Little Feelings" was not a work easily performed outside of the newly created "modern music" venue and therefore was in many ways limited to the expansion and not the maintenance part of the double-voiced agenda. Another factor at play was the perceived subtlety of its blues components. Yet debate over how much "masking" is too much has constantly surrounded the reception of double-voiced texts. As dis-

Example 1.2. "Three Little Feelings" (1956), theme, mm. 1–5. Published score (set in Finale).

cussed in the introduction to this book, Baker (1987) uses as his primary "masking" example the speeches of Booker T. Washington, despite the fact that the strategies employed in these speeches were frequently challenged by those who favored more direct engagement with the African American voice. Washington's most notable critic, W. E. B. Du Bois, called out the "masking" trope in his essay "Of Mr. Booker T. Washington and Others," claiming that Washington "represents in Negro thought the old attitude of

Example 1.2 (continued). "Three Little Feelings" (1956), theme, mm. 6–11. Published score (set in Finale).

adjustment and submission" and that "in failing thus to state plainly and unequivocally the legitimate demands of their people, even at the cost of opposing an honored leader, the thinking classes of American Negroes . . . shirk a heavy responsibility" ([1903] 2007, 42). Du Bois's critique makes an appeal for clarity and demonstrates a desire for more direct action but does not criticize the intent of Washington's strategy. Later critics would be less

M.	Section	Length (mm.)	Key	Description
1	Introduction	12	Cmin	Unison thematic entrance in horns and trombone develops into harmonized thematic passage across the brass.
13	Composed trombone solo	8	Cmin	Horns play theme in counterpoint to trombone solo; drums and bass accompany.
21	Composed trumpet solo (theme paraphrase)	8	Cmin	Call-and-response between composed trumpet line and horn backing figures derived from mm. 1–2; drums and bass accompany.
29	Improvised trumpet solo	32	Cmin	One-measure horn, trombone, and baritone backing figure derived from mm. 1–2 accompanies first sixteen measures; tympani and drums accompany first fifteen measures; tympani, drums, bass accompany last seventeen measures.
61	Interlude	9	Eb	Full brass harmonization of thematic material from mm. 4–5; piano, tympani, drums, bass accompany.
70	Tuba solo (exact theme)	9	Cmin	Tuba thematic statement accompanied by tympani and drums transitions to unison horns, trombones, baritones, and tuba for second half of theme.
79	Improvised trumpet solo	7	Cmin	Call-and-response between improvised trumpet and theme played by the remaining trumpet section. Horns, trombones, baritones and tuba provide chordal accompaniment. Drums accompany.
86	Truncated theme and cadence	6	Cmin	Unison truncated theme played by the trumpets ending on unison G followed by three one-measure Cmin chords with added scale degrees 9 and 11, formed across the brass.

Fig. 1.1. Formal outline of John Lewis's "Three Little Feelings" (1956), movement 1.

kind, aligning Washington with Uncle Tomism and the persistence of African American disfranchisement (Norrell 2009, 15). As I will show, a similar trend persists in the evaluation of Lewis's musical works. Yet by placing them in the context of uplift strategies embraced following the 1940s big band decline, it is possible to come away with a sense that the works do in some way add up to more than the sum of their parts.

Such an interpretation would at first seem to confirm arguments put forth by Samuel Floyd (1995, 164) regarding the intent of syncretic jazz strategies deployed during the 1950s. Floyd bases this argument on Gary

Tomlinson's observation that pairing Western art music tropes with vernacular elements during this period allowed for communal affirmation of a "wide-ranging variety of African-American perceptions" (Tomlinson 1991, 256). This agenda accorded with the tenets of dominant civil rights perspectives during the era in which "race-thinking" was viewed as working against equality (Omi & Winant 1994, 96–100) while simultaneously recognizing the need to recruit audience members not yet initiated in African American expressive culture. In other words, it advanced African American social and economic presence by capitalizing on the idea that blackness was not monolithic—that while vernacular musical tropes were essential to African American music making, the assembly of these tropes could result in aural effects far different from consensus surrounding what "real" African American music sounded like. It is from this foundation that Floyd claims syncretic musicians in the 1950s "play[ed] on the verges, exploring the crossroads where African-American and European myth and ritual meet" while producing cultural works "the Harlem Renaissance thinkers would have embraced" (1995, 164).

Yet Floyd does not defend all 1950s syncretic compositions along these lines and in some cases takes Lewis to task for giving up too much of the vernacular in favor of Western art music alignment (1995, 166–67). In making this assessment, Floyd relies on the criteria of sonic "balance," failing to read how the aggregate of musical tropes functioned in an historic context. This is apparent in his description of the MJQ's version of the Charlie Parker piece "Now's the Time":

> The musicians of the cool and Third Stream schools tended to discard ring values, diluting the powerful expressions of Call-Response. An example of this dilution is the MJQ's ineffective 1957 version of Parker's "Now's the Time," in which, after a shaky start, the performers get into a cool groove but do not tell much of a story because of their too subtle treatment of the ring tropes they employ . . . For those who were emotionally and ideologically committed to the African-American side of the musical mix, many of the products of the cool/Third Stream trend were viewed either as vapid cultural irrelevances or as musical, social, and cultural threats to "real" black music. (Floyd 1995, 167)

Here Floyd refers to Sterling Stuckey's (1987) research on the early African American musical practice of the "Ring Shout" as a means of referencing a catalog of sonorities he views as essential to African American music making.[7] The use of such criteria in an assessment of Lewis's alignment with African American expressive culture, however, demonstrates an inconsistency in Floyd's methodology. His reading of William Grant Still's *Afro-American Symphony* as well as the *Birth of the Cool* recordings focuses on historical intent rather than a cataloging of sonorities. The MJQ's recording of "Now's the Time," in contrast, is left to float in the ether of an ill-defined historical space—approached from the angle of its primary sonic impression with no attempts made at hermeneutical analysis. Compounding this issue is the fact that generalizations regarding the breadth of John Lewis's work are made throughout Floyd's monograph *The Power of Black Music* (1995), excluding Lewis from African American expressive culture in nearly all instances. After detailing the MJQ's "Now's the Time" performance in the previous quote, Floyd goes on to extrapolate that the entirety of the MJQ output evinces "spiritual vacuity" by way of a "paucity of ring tropes" and that the intent of this process was to make the music "respectable in 'proper' (that is white) social circles" (1995, 167).

A different perspective is put forth in this chapter. Faced with a lack of performance and recording opportunities at the beginning of the 1950s, many jazz artists sought to break new ground, broadening the jazz market through the expansion of performance venues and audience demographics. A syncretic approach to composition in which familiar jazz devices and Western art music devices were fused helped appeal to the modernist model of jazz development espoused in academic circles. Yet many of these works went even further, creating Western art music sonorities through the innovative deployment of jazz vernacular devices, clearly demonstrating applications of the Signifyin(g) act as interpreted by Henry Louis Gates (1988). While the degree to which these acts were overt varied from project to project, their presence can be discerned across the compositional spectrum. In the case of the MJQ, however, a perception of vernacular denial related to this compositional approach would lead to a broader stripping of African American identity in discussions surrounding the group members' behavior. Such claims evince a reverse of the racial stereotyping outlined by Porter (2002), calling special attention to the "manners" and "gentility" of the group as if these concepts were foreign to African American culture. This reading of the MJQ, interrogated in chapter 2, demonstrates the ultimate cost of interpreting African American syncretic music apart from its particular historical context.

2 • "Bearded Undertakers"

Rhythm and Reputation

The 1957 Nat Hentoff interview with John Lewis that I discuss in the opening of this book is undoubtedly a rich text. Lewis's frustration with the press's critique of his music is palpable throughout—potentially fueled by a sense of betrayal grown out of Hentoff's prior endorsements of Lewis's modernist approach. Yet at the same time, Lewis downplays his embrace of Western art music conventions, asking rhetorically at one point, "Have we played out our use of fugal structures? We only play three. . . . How can it be said that that aspect of what we do has been played out?" (Hentoff 1957b, 15)—a truly intriguing comment given Lewis's recent involvement with the Jazz and Classical Music Society. And in yet another tension-filled moment, Lewis seems pushed to the edge when confronted with praise for the "sensitive and responsible attitude of the [MJQ]," stating plainly, "We're grown men . . . and we conduct ourselves as grown men. There's nothing remarkable about that" (Hentoff 1957b, 16). While each of these issues raises a series of interesting questions, if there is one note that rings louder than others in this interview, it is a sense of lost control over how Lewis's music and legacy were being conveyed to the public through the trade press.

This is not to say that the trade press somehow treated Lewis unfairly. Indeed, over the course of the 1950s, Lewis's syncretic approach was given more than considerable attention in feature articles, editorials, and interviews that appeared in the North American magazines *Down Beat* and *Metronome* as well as in international publications such as the German journal *Melos*, the Parisian publication *Jazz Magazine*, and the British *Jazz Journal*. The vast majority of these assessments deployed familiar and outwardly fair journalistic methodologies, placing (or attempting to place) Lewis's work somewhere within the vast contemporary jazz milieu. In order to do so, journalists endorsed the model of musical evolution discussed in chapter 1, describing Lewis's work as a step forward—in either a right or a wrong direction—but always with an end point far from jazz's folk roots in mind. Lewis had, in tandem, seemed to encourage this sort of understanding through his early comments on the importance of "structure" in jazz (Hentoff 1953a, 8), his circulation of notes outlining the structural features of his music to journalists (Hentoff 1954b, 27), and his development of the Modern Jazz Society and the Jazz and Classical Music Society. Such actions make it easy to understand why certain ideas about Lewis's music gained traction in the popular press and at first glance make Lewis's attempt to add nuance to his legacy seem a bit out of step.

Yet the need for such nuancing becomes undeniably clear when one considers the effect descriptions of Lewis's music were beginning to have on depictions of Lewis's character. Lewis's penchant for dynamic control, instrumental balance, and complex structural devices had from the outset garnered critique caged in language that highlighted mental rather than physical engagement. Terms such as *interesting*, *intellectual*, and *cerebral* occurred more frequently in accounts of his music than commentary regarding physical response—a marker of authentic black music production deeply embedded within the public imagination (Gioia 1989; Radano 2003). By the mid-1950s this critical bent had begun to distance the behavior of Lewis and his colleagues from perceived African American cultural norms in the popular press, perpetuating the subtle but biting racial stereotype that professional behavior was, for all intents and purposes, a stand-in term for "white" behavior. In other words, stereotypical ideas about what jazz music should sound like and how jazz musicians should act appear to have collided in Lewis's reception in a manner that severely limited the possibility of what critics were prepared to accept as genuine acts of African American expression. Indeed, this seems to be the sort of issue Lewis is determined to confront in his claim that "there's nothing remarkable" about acting like "grown men."

In this chapter I aim to unravel the issues inherent in Lewis's trade press reception by first illuminating how loaded racialized language became (and still remains in many cases) a part of the jazz lexicon. Ronald Radano's (2003) work on the rhetoric of "hot" music serves as a useful platform for this discussion, as it highlights the fact that linguistic bridges between behavioral and musical realms can be seen to extend as far back as early European expedition reports of the African continent. With the help of Radano and others, I trace these linguistic and ideological clichés through early jazz writing and into the discourse surrounding Lewis's work. I then demonstrate how the use of such language crowded out discussion of Lewis's own comments affirming what he viewed to be an operational standpoint located within the boundaries of an African American artistic tradition. This argument allows Lewis's own comments regarding musical orientation to gain critical weight and begs for the investigation of ways in which we can understand Lewis as an artist with roots in a different sort of African American expressive culture than the one powerfully ingrained in the imagination of so many jazz enthusiasts.

Rhythm and Authenticity in Jazz Discourse

The idea that music of the African diaspora is, at its core, an especially "rhythmic" music has long guided the interpretation and analysis of musical genres linked in some way to the African continent. In the field of jazz studies, such overt rhythmicity was viewed as a key aesthetic ingredient during the first half of the twentieth century and was frequently used as a way of denoting a level of essential difference between jazz and Western art music. This understanding can be seen to permeate a spectrum of critical views—extending from Hugh Panassié's (1936, 4–5) "primitivist" perspective, in which the ability to "swing" resided in the biology of African descendants, to Barry Ulanov's (1952, 12) sociological viewpoint that conceptualized "rhythmic discipline" as a cultural practice brought by African slaves to the New World. Yet in both cases, the championing of overt rhythmicity as something uniquely African strikes a curious chord given the contemporaneous experimentation with rhythm occurring in the Western art music realm, notable, as Kofi Agawu points out, in the works of "[Elliot] Carter, [Steve] Reich . . . [and Igor] Stravinsky" (1995, 386). Why, we might ask, does the language of rhythm color so much of the discussion of African and African-derived music during this time period, despite the fact that a similar focus on rhythm was present in a wide variety of music from around the world?

Part of the answer to this question lies in the fact that most of what was known about African cultural practice in the 1950s was written with the intent of making it seem more different from other sorts of music than it might actually have been. Radano locates the origin of this sort of essentializing in early European travelogues about the African continent, in which perceptions of savagery and primitivism were linked, in a genetic sense, to African dance and musical performance as a way of highlighting the civility and order (if not the perceived supremacy) of parallel European cultural products (Radano 2003, 89–90). William Bosman's "New and Accurate Description of the Coast of Guinea" (1705/1814) provides one such example, demonstrating how the syncopation and volume of percussive parts in African music were sometimes exaggerated in order to "widen the gap [both culturally and genetically] between Europeans and Africans" (Radano 2003, 81). This is evident in Bosman's reduction of the intricacies of a group performance involving wind instruments and percussion to the level of an ad-hoc percussive improvisation both "horrid and barbarous . . . produc[ing] a sort of extravagant noise" (qtd. in Radano 2003, 81). According to Radano, such a comment "adopts what was by then a familiar racial association, comparing their [the Guineans'] performance to the regressive sounds and behavior of animals and children" (2003, 81). Following this description, Bosman warns against "'international' sexual relations" in an attempt to stem the flow of such musical practices into the European heredity pool (Radano 2003, 82). A belief in biological predisposition toward an overtly percussive musical style is thus clearly articulated in the structure of this argument.

Radano goes on to make the argument that such rhetorical practice followed depictions of African and African-derived music to the New World—a phenomenon clearly evident in early descriptions of jazz music. Indeed, Frank Salamone's work in this area highlights several examples in which jazz's "rhythmic vitality" was inextricably linked to comments about "Negro blood" (2005, 735). One of his key pieces of evidence—the defense of jazz offered by Frankfurt Conservatory director Bernhard Sekles put forth in a 1928 *New York Times* article—pulls few punches in this regard.

> The teaching of jazz is not only the right but the duty of every up-to-date musical institution. The majority of our musicians find themselves permanently or temporarily compelled to play in jazz ensembles. Aside from this practical consideration, a serious study of jazz will be of the greatest help to our young musicians. An infusion of Negro blood can do no harm. It will help to develop a wholesome sense of rhythm, which after all constitutes the life element of music. (qtd. in "Jazz Bitterly Opposed" 1928, 10)

Sekles's comment sets up "Negro" rhythm as biologically inherent, while describing the rhythmic abilities of working European performers, in contrast, as resulting from intellectual engagement. In this view, a sense of "Negro" rhythm could be developed in European students through study, while it existed in the genetic coding of African American performers.[1] Such understanding results in a paradox in which one route to authentic performance circumvents the need for biological transmission while the other continues to articulate a genetic imperative. In both cases, however, rhythm is essentialized as a key component of the jazz style, and the genus of jazz rhythmic sense is located within the biology of the African American race. This sort of thinking was in no way unusual among early jazz enthusiasts, and similar comments can be seen to permeate the work of Panassié (1936), Sargeant ([1938] 1975), Goffin (1944), and Blesh (1946), to name but a few.

Yet even in descriptions of jazz that did not outwardly mention African American racial difference, the idea that the genre contained some sort of magical rhythmic difference remained. Criticism along these lines typifies early coverage of the genre published in the American journal the *Musical Quarterly*. During the 1920s, several *Musical Quarterly* contributors were keen to stress a particular concern with the impact jazz might have on compositions of Western art music. Important to both sides of this debate was the influence that ethereal qualities ascribed to jazz rhythm might have on European cultural products. Expanding the genetic myth, these qualities were often depicted as a "musical infection" (Radano 2003, 235), spreading from Africa to the West and carrying with them the symptom of uncontrollable physical response. Paul Laubenstein's problematizing of jazz rhythm and the seemingly related symptom of physical reflex put forth in his 1929 article "Jazz—Debit and Credit" is emblematic of how this phenomenon was conceived in the pages of the journal. After mentioning the "physical hold" jazz induced on contemporary youth, Laubenstein explicitly dissects the components of the style's rhythmic conventions, writing,

> The mechanical domination is figured forth in the underlying "rhythm" of jazz, in its mass production, its rapid standardization and its speed. . . . What is new in jazz-rhythmics is the peculiar exaggeration and distortion of rhythm, the contrasts produced by freely moving figures gambolling in syncopation over an unvarying fundamental rhythm, both necessary for the proper jazz effect. (Laubenstein 1929, 609–10)

Laubenstein's depiction highlights the importance of both tempo and spontaneity in the creation of "jazz-rhythmics" as well as the fundamental role "rhythmics" plays in conjuring the "proper jazz effect." Similar importance is bestowed on rhythmic spontaneity in Randall Thompson's work for the *Musical Quarterly*, in which he documents jazz as a "rhythmical style":

> Rhythm, by definition, involves repetition. By establishing an unvarying beat, superimposing conflicting beats, and interrupting itself from time to time in rhythmic variations of the first magnitude, jazz achieves the very sum and substance of rhythmical style. (1932, 11)

The unpredictable nature of jazz rhythm in this description contributes to what Thompson refers to as the "spell of ragtime and jazz," a predilection toward which he felt both European and American composers were beginning to fall (1932, 15). Indeed, both Laubenstein and Thompson would appear in these passages to agree with the idea that jazz's essential aesthetic quality resided in its magical rhythmic power—a power that emerged via a mysterious confluence of speed, syncopation, and spontaneity—resulting in hypnosis at best and addiction at worst. Such an idea upheld the notion that jazz performance practice was uniquely different from Western musical practice even as it worked to bury theories of racial difference underneath broader mystical themes.

It is important to note that those who lashed out at the circulation of ideas about racial difference during the 1930s and 1940s were not immune to the legacy of such ideas—particularly the notion that a uniquely African rhythmic sensibility was required for successful jazz interpretation. Barry Ulanov, for instance, credits African lineage for the germ of rhythmic affect that would evolve into the "fundamental quality of rhythmic swing" (1952, 195), stating,

> One cannot and one should not, in the heat of forensic rage, dismiss the real contribution of African Negroes to jazz. Without looking to the mysterious reaches of the unconscious, one can find a considerable administration of rhythmic discipline imposed by Southern Negroes, whether of the first or third or fifth American generation, upon the music they found around them. (1952, 12)

Similarly, although Sidney Finkelstein (1948) is strongly critical of Rudy Blesh's (1946) claims of a genetically encoded musical aptitude among African Americans, he makes assertions about jazz's rhythmic foundation in terms that strongly echo the language of essential racial difference surveyed thus far. Take, for example, an early sentence from Finkelstein's *Jazz: A People's Music* that attempts to define the aesthetic feel of the jazz genre: "Jazz is often a music of great basic simplicity, and gripping rhythmic force" (1948, 24). Here use of the term *gripping rhythmic force* as a defining element of the jazz style perpetuates both the central role of rhythm in the genre as well as its ability to induce a physical hold. Later comments on the collective rhythm section go even further:

> The most splendid and new percussive achievement of jazz was its collective rhythm section, powerful in its beat yet constantly varying in timbre. . . . Through it jazz has restored rhythm as a powerful, independent musical voice. (Finkelstein 1948, 44)

Implicit in both of these comments is the idea that jazz rhythm is not a subtle rhythmic effect; it is both pervasive and "powerful," always changing, and a key component of the jazz sound. While Finkelstein denies a link to the African continent, he maintains that rhythm plays a symbolic role in articulating African American musical difference, where African American music is viewed as an arena open to contributions from people of all races.

As the works of early jazz discourse surveyed here show, the legacy of theorizing rhythmic difference in African American musical production was well entrenched across the spectrum of jazz politics by the 1950s. The impact of such an understanding on subsequent jazz journalism appears then to have been twofold. On a base level, critics of all camps continued to write about rhythmic spontaneity and prominence as a ubiquitous part of the jazz sound. On a secondary level, an emotive response seen as linked to overt rhythmic effects became entrenched as a key criterion in the decoding of jazz authenticity. As Ted Gioia reflects about criticism from the following decades,

> Performances which fail to attain the frenetic and energetic ideal postulated by the stereotype are labeled "cerebral"—one of the most damning adjectives in the critical vocabulary of jazz writers. In contrast, the most excessive demonstrations of musical chaos are often lavishly praised so long as they are done "with feeling." (1989, 138)

Therefore, artists composing music that either neglected rhythmic spontaneity, masked rhythmic spontaneity, or elicited a response of "cerebrality" *despite* rhythmic spontaneity risked having their works interpreted as having been conceived outside the African American expressive realm. All three routes to inauthentic performance are problematic in that they emerge from a body of criticism more concerned with sonic representations of race than the processes involved in the composition of African American musical works themselves. Certainly the works of Finkelstein (1948) and Ulanov (1952) endeavor to free themselves from this history of racialized discourse, but even in these progressive studies the weight bestowed on rhythm appears indebted to older ideas about the nature of musical performance in the African diaspora. Reading about the reception of Lewis's syncretic works during the 1950s with the critical trends of the previous thirty years in mind allows us to see how the language of intellect and subtlety could indeed impact perceptions of overall cultural alignment.

The Effect of Rhythmic Essentialism on Lewis's Portrayal in the Popular Press

Certainly the circumstance of Lewis's initial popular press coverage marked his work as rhythmically different from that of other jazz musicians from the outset. As stated earlier, this attention began in connection with Lewis's arrangements for Dizzy Gillespie in 1946. Importantly, in discussions of Gillespie's 1946–47 ensemble this collaboration often plays a quieter role to that of Gillespie and his Cuban percussionist Chano Pozo. Jairo Moreno points to the latter relationship as an attempt by Gillespie to engage with the "North American modernist vanguard," realized in this case through the pairing of jazz and Latin rhythms (2004, 98). This brand of syncretism can be seen to align with the 1940s outreach strategies of Thornhill and Davis discussed in chapter 1, given the increasing number of Caribbean immigrants and the growing popularity of Latin American music in New York during the 1940s (discussed at length in Korrol 1983). In addition, paralleling the critical trends outlined in the first part of this chapter, documentation of this burgeoning music scene tended to essentialize the rhythmic elements of rhumba and related Latin American musical styles, as these genres, like jazz, were seen to extend from musical practices on the African continent. This is apparent in Bill Gottlieb's decoding of rhumba in 1947 as a product of the "same African roots" as jazz, evident in its rhythmic presentation: "Their music, for rhythmic fire, lush coloring and jazz feel, can hold its own with the products of the best hot orchestras" (1947a, 10). In turn, some practitioners described the link with Africa as being even more authentic than the one shared by jazz. Cuban bandleader Machito posited that "rhumba rhythms are both more primitive and more rhythmically complex than jazz" as a result of Caribbean music's resistance to dilution: "We play this way in Cuba for over a hundred years" (qtd. in Gottlieb 1947a, 10).[2] Regardless of the veracity of such a statement, depictions of Latin rhythm as closely tied to African music during the late 1940s may have cast Lewis's compositions for the Gillespie ensemble on which Pozo did not play as somewhat removed from the African American expressive realm.

At the very least Lewis's interest in Western art music allowed Gillespie to position the two styles of composition against each other. In the lead-up to his 1947 Carnegie Hall concert, the Latin and classical sounds of Gillespie's program feature prominently in *Down Beat*'s coverage, suggesting their inclusion in a press release. After a brief overview of the event, the magazine foreshadows the premiere of two major works, one an "Afro Cuban Suite" utilizing both a "conga and bongo drummer" and the other an unnamed "concerto" by John Lewis ("Bebop to Carnegie Hall" 1947, 5). Follow-up reviews comment on the same pieces, setting one firmly in the jazz realm via a discussion of rhythmic elements and the other in the classical realm through a discussion of form. Michael Levin's assessment of the "Afro Cuban Suite," conventionally referred to by the name of its two movements, "Cubano Be, Cubano Bop" (1947),[3] takes place under the text subtitle "powerful, but rough" and links audience approval to its rhythmic character:

> The crowd unquestionably liked the *Cubano Bop* number with its added bongo and congo [*sic*] drum soloists the best. Illustrating a point the *Beat* has often made that there is much jazz can pick up on from the South American and Afro-Cuban rhythm styles. (1947, 1)

In contrast, Levin discusses Lewis's work "Toccata for Trumpet" (1947) mostly in terms of its intellectual allure: "Formalistically, the *Toccata* appealed to me: Lewis displayed an economy of means and an interesting series of ideas that make him a man to be watched in the writing field" (1947, 1).

Levin's comments regarding the formal elements of the "Toccata" are by no means erroneous. Lewis had begun courses for a master's degree in music at the Manhattan School of Music in early 1946, and his composition appears to reflect this influence, breaking with the formal conventions of the blues and AABA bebop contrafacts (the work is through-composed and stands in contrast to the riff-driven "Cubano Be, Cubano Bop" on which Pozo performs). However, Gillespie's twenty-two-bar improvisation over an ascending saxophone riff and fast-swinging rhythm section echoes the overtly rhythmic performance aesthetic viewed by many as central to the authentic jazz sound. While it is understandable that this element of the composition received little focus in Levin's discussion, as it appears to have been intentionally masked by the composed parts of the work, it is significant to note that the language of form and structure that formed Levin's assessment would soon overshadow discussion of rhythm in Lewis's works even when the composer purposely directed listeners to his rhythmic sensibilities.

Lewis's 1953 interview with Nat Hentoff is emblematic of such tensions. Following the 1953 midyear release of the MJQ's first album, *The Modern Jazz Quartet*, Hentoff ran two Counterpoint articles in which he cast Lewis as a "particularly perceptive experimenter" in "extended form" (Hentoff 1953a, 8). The recording inspiring such contextualization included Lewis's first fugal work, "Vendome" (1952), and an arrangement of Jerome Kern's "All the Things You Are" (1939) in which the piano and vibraphone introduce the work's theme over a composed interplay of bass and cymbal rolls. As stated previously, Lewis was quick to point out in the first of these columns that these structural devices were employed in an effort to "widen" the jazz audience. But in a less frequently discussed part of the interview, Lewis can be seen to steer the conversation toward rhythmic concepts he views as underpinning the group's success:

> Take rhythm. Any kind of improvisation—unless you're playing by yourself—is going to be more or less contrapuntal. But in jazz, except for the best Dixieland people and a few others, there's often been a rhythmic dullness. The bass, drums, and piano should do more than simply supply chords and a basic pulsation. Now Kenny has never been caught in this rut. He doesn't get stuck with any one rhythmic pattern. In our work we also stimulate counterpoint rhythmically this way: when someone is playing a solo, the other instruments will play ideas in the background, ideas subordinate to those of the soloist. They don't slip back and just keep time. (Hentoff 1953a, 8)

Here Lewis echoes the essentialist rhetoric of jazz critics from both the modernist and traditionalist camps by demonstrating the continued importance of spontaneous, improvisational, and interactive rhythmic effects. In other comments, such as "all the instruments in our group supply rhythmic propulsion. . . . Anybody who plays on whatever instrument *must* supply rhythmic propulsion" (Hentoff 1953a, 8; emphasis in original), Lewis articulates the physical hold component of the essentialist argument, albeit in more subtle and musical terms than those surveyed in the first part of this chapter. Such comments can be seen to temper Hentoff's questioning around form, framing Lewis's work for the *Down Beat* audience as authentic jazz in the established language of authenticity. Yet while Hentoff clearly sees value in Lewis's descriptions (they are, after all, the published excerpts of a longer interview), his follow-up piece engages even less with the rhythmic components of Lewis's syncretic projects.

Interpreting Hentoff's second Counterpoint column, published a month later, in January 1954, is a complex process because much of his discussion is guided by notes Lewis provided yet the text itself is devoid of quotation marks. Such reporting results in ambiguous expression, making it nearly impossible to separate the critic's thoughts from Lewis's own ideas. Hentoff's discussion of "The Queen's Fancy" (1953) provides a pertinent example of this problem:

> *The Queen's Fancy* shows another simple, effective combination of form and improvised spontaneity. This begins with a written five measure theme, sort of a fanfare. After it comes a new contrasting idea in a kind of three-part song form that's treated in a contrapuntal fashion. (1954b, 27)

The first sentence of this quote can almost definitively be attributed to Hentoff, as it is more or less an expression of opinion, but the third sentence, discussing a "kind of three-part song form . . . in a contrapuntal fashion," seems to use language from outside Hentoff's specialty area. Complicating this reading is the fact that the language embedded in the third sentence suggests interpretation (Hentoff's qualification "in a kind of" speaks to this point). It does seem likely that Lewis's notes included a good deal of information regarding European structural devices, as Hentoff's earlier discussion of "Vendome" begins with a description of the composed "subject," "answer," and "countersubject" before surveying the work's sectional divisions using terminology such as "episodes" and "expositions" (1954b, 27). But Hentoff's discussion of the function or purpose of these devices cannot be read as a direct reflection of Lewis's intent, given the article's imbedded subjectivity.

Indeed, Lewis's views expressed verbatim in the 1953 Counterpoint column and Hentoff's interpretation of Lewis's notes in the 1954 Counterpoint column stand slightly askew. In the 1953 column, Lewis appears to have seen European structure as a way of expanding the reach of the vernacular, in as much as the vernacular voice manifested in the rhythmic propulsion and spontaneity he championed. In the 1954 column, Hentoff conceptualizes the structural elements of Lewis's work as bringing coherence to vernacular elements themselves. This latter point is evident in Hentoff's discussion of Lewis's work "Django" (1954):

> Milt Jackson will improvise on a chord progression that suggests the first theme but is not exactly like it. On this chord progression Milt will improvise in two keys, and he will be able to play almost anything he feels like therein, because the progression, itself, will be sufficiently reminiscent of the first theme to hold the performance together. This, then, is another way in which the musician can retain his jazz freedom while making it easier for the listener to assimilate the work as a whole, rather than as a disjointed series of solos (1954b, 27).

Here Hentoff focuses on the ease of engagement that repeated chord progressions will provide, and although this type of organization does not seem to differ greatly from established jazz conventions, its integration into a discussion that begins with a fugal analysis has the effect of making the structure of "Django" appear different from jazz norms. Furthermore, it is this formal difference that Hentoff depicts as aiding the listener's understanding of Jackson's improvised solo. Such discussion crowds out comment on the improvisation itself in terms of melodic and rhythmic content and leads to an overall critical assessment in which the value of the work is tied almost exclusively to its structural components.

Again, there is certainly good reason for Hentoff to have interpreted the work in this way. In addition to the notes provided by Lewis, the composer's 1953 comment cited in chapter 1 ("If there is more of a reason for what's going on, there'll be more overall sense, and, therefore, more interest for the listener" [Hentoff 1953a, 8]) appears to beg a structural focus. Yet this comment was followed in the 1953 Counterpoint column by Lewis's discussion of the importance of the work's underlying rhythmic sense. Taken together with Lewis's marketing approach, analyzed in chapter 1, the tension in these columns might be more appropriately read as the purposeful juxtapositioning of both European and jazz influences aimed at simultaneously expanding and stewarding Lewis's appeal. Hentoff's focus on what would have been perceived as the novel element of this syncretism, European formal devices, aids one side of this strategy. Yet at the same time it foreshadows a style of assessment in which discussion of structure and control in Lewis's compositions would gradually limit alternate readings.

Part of the responsibility for this trend lies with Lewis himself. Despite the dissonance between the 1953 and 1954 columns, Lewis did not immediately counter the claim that value in his work was to be found primarily in the structural realm. If anything, Lewis exploited this reading as he pushed for venue expansion along the lines discussed in chapter 1. As a result, critics were undeterred in essentializing the structural components of his compositions, invoking an inversion of the racialized rhythm motifs tied to authentic jazz performance. In other words, Lewis's apparent focus on structure fit so neatly into the "cerebral" side of Gioia's (1989) "cerebral" versus "with feeling" paradigm that a notion of Lewis's works as intellectual artifacts more aligned with European culture than with AfroAmerican culture emerged in the popular press almost unquestioned. Hentoff's assessment of the 1955 Modern Jazz Society concert at Town Hall is made in these terms, once again praising Lewis's ability to build improvisations into a work "so that the listener was left not with fragments but with an integrated experience" while linking such design to a larger perception of cerebrality:

> No one combines his quality of touch (even better than Wilson's and equal to Halberg's if not Tatum's), his classical (in the denotative sense) taste, and his ability to swing deeply while appearing so quietly fastidious. (1955a, 8)

The urbane qualities of control ("quietly fastidious") and European alignment ("classical taste") highlighted in this assessment are echoed in Ralph Gleason's review of a MJQ performance in San Francisco:

> The music of the MJQ is fragile, to be sure; it is delicate, too, but it is never dull. . . . To those who will listen, there are moments when

> the sound these four men make has the same shattering effect as a line by Donne or a sketch by Picasso. (1956, 18)

Here Gleason aligns Lewis's work broadly with European artifacts through mention of its subtlety—a connection he then makes specific through the inclusion of Donne and Picasso as parallel artistic figures. John Wilson's coverage of the MJQ's 1958 tour in the *New York Times* demonstrates similar European alignment; only this time specific artistic figures are replaced with the broader term "European intellectuals":

> The restrained, rather intellectual jazz played by the Quartet (piano, vibraharp, bass, drums) was felt by some observers to have proved more accessible than other types of jazz might be to the older European intellectuals (1958a, X9).

Importantly, these comments are followed by Wilson's discussion of Lewis's use of "old forms" such as the "canon" and "fugue" (1958a, X9). This descriptive milieu, in which adjectives regarding intellect merge with subjects of European culture in the evaluation of compositions praised for their formal elements demonstrates how drawing attention away from rhythm, the use of blues sonorities, and improvisation allowed Lewis's music to avert primitivist portrayals and garner ascriptions of intelligence and discipline. While discussion of vernacular components was not totally lost—Gleason (1956, 18), for instance, writes that "the blues they have are the bluest," and Hentoff (1955a, 8) refers to Milt Jackson's ability to "swing" as a positive performative element—it is considerably downplayed in the summative statements regarding the group's ethos above. Such a portrayal surely worked in support of Lewis's outreach strategy but carried with it the unfortunate effect of resurrecting attitudes regarding perceived behavioral differences between African American cultural participants and Western artists.

Perceptions of Behavioral Difference in the MJQ's Reception

A conception of the MJQ's behavior as different from jazz norms is evident when quotes citing the "stature," "sensitivity," and "dignified appearance" of the group are compared with popular press depictions of bebop musicians from the late 1940s—portrayals derived in part from what Lopes (2002, 210) refers to as perceptions of the "hipster cult." The "hipster," in Lopes's view, refers to a social identity in which artistic disposition lies paramount and often manifests as eccentricity in dress and behavior. The construct emerged in tandem with the bebop genre, and many practitioners embraced the label as a way of affirming their desire to pioneer something new without abandoning an underlying sense of unity. As Dizzy Gillespie writes,

> A "square" and a "lame" were synonymous, and they accepted the complete life-style, including the music dictated by the establishment. They rejected the concept of creative alternatives, and they were just the opposite of "hip," which meant "in the know," "wise," or one with "knowledge" of life and how to live. . . . They were apathetic to, or actively opposed to, almost everything we stood for, like intelligence, sensitivity, creativity, change, wisdom, joy, courage, peace, togetherness, and integrity. (1979, 297)

Admirable as Gillespie's reflections are, the popular press frequently conflated the antiestablishment music related to this mentality with behavioral eccentricities in a way that mirrored the type of racialized discourse surveyed by Radano (2003). As Ingrid Monson notes,

> When transposed downtown and scrutinized by mixed audiences and the press, the stylistic aspects of the musical scene—the clothes, the hats, the talk, the goatees, the drugs—would breathe life into the very primitivist presumptions that the new modern musical movement, with its commitment to art, sophistication and social protest most deeply opposed. (1995, 411–12)

Overlap between discussion of the hipster culture and behavioral depictions in which artists were cast as slaves to their inner workings are woven throughout popular press writing of the time. Echoing the language discussed at the beginning of this chapter, *Time* magazine drew on racially loaded language in its description of bebop as a world full of "feverish practitioners" dressed in "berets, goatees and green-tinted horn-rimmed glasses" ("How Deaf Can You Get" 1948, 74). A *Down Beat* article focusing on pianist Thelonious Monk in turn begins with a description of his hipster dress, "goatee, beret and heavy shell glasses" before transitioning to a discussion of artistic temperament that implicitly questioned his professionalism:

> He's so absorbed in his task he's almost mysterious. Maybe he's on his way to meet you. An idea comes to him. He begins to work on it. Mop! Two days go by and he's still at it. He's forgotten all about you and everything else but that idea. (Gottlieb 1947b, 2)

Notwithstanding Lopes's (2002) and Monson's (1995) claims, this overt return to the motif of innate drive seems to have arisen out of a plurality of causes. As shown here, antiestablishment dress and behavior played a part, but as several further quotes in the popular press indicate, spontaneity and dissonance in the music itself may have proved just as important in driving critics back to the behavioral clichés associated with "Hot" jazz criticism. In 1946 *Time* ran an article referring to bebop as "hot jazz overheated," an essentially rhythmic reference, before continuing with a description that aligned the style with "bawdiness" ("Be-Bop, Be-Bopped" 1946, 52). Similarly, the speed and dissonance of melodic solo lines in the genre drove Carter Hartman of the *New York Times* to label the music "semi controlled frenzy" (1948, X13). The complexity of sorting out exactly how primitivist portrayals continued to infiltrate readings of bebop does not, however, negate the fact that such depictions affirmed a rift between the behavior of Lewis and the MJQ and that of the larger bebop community.

Curiously, the MJQ's use of suits served as a particularly frequent opening device in discussions of this perceived difference. A 1957 *Esquire* article, for instance, opens with a passage comparing the group's appearance to that of "a splinter group . . . [of] Baptist ministers" before transitioning to a behavioral description of the quartet's "dedicated and serious" attitude ("Slipped Disk" 1957, 12). In *Down Beat*, Ed Sachs described Lewis's arrival in a "mortician's uniform" to a 1959 interview before commenting on his "calm, poised, and agreeable" demeanor (1959, 18). Further evidence of the trope can be found in the *New York Times*, where John Wilson related how many in the jazz community felt the formal dress of the MJQ had given them the appearance of "bearded undertakers" before juxtaposing Lewis with the "casual rough-and-tumble of . . . old-time jazz musicians" (1960, 47).

This focus on dress is intriguing, particularly because it was not especially odd for jazz musicians to wear suits in both everyday life and in performance. Even the MJQ's occasional use of tuxedos—to which, it must be noted, these journalists are not referring—had some precedent. As Harvey Cohen points out, Duke Ellington and his orchestra frequently dressed in tuxedos—a practice that extended back to their work at the Cotton Club in the late 1920s (2004, 296, 310). Louis Armstrong, in turn, wore a tuxedo so frequently when he was starting out that he gave it a nickname: "my old Roast Beef" (Giddins & Armstrong 1986, 236). The suits that the members of the MJQ wore when they were not in tuxedos—their "mortician's uniform," as Sachs put it—were, in fact, fairly reflective of jazz stylistic norms. Certainly berets and horn-rimmed glasses were absent, but in relation to other elements of style, the group does not seemed to have dressed exceedingly better than those performing regularly at Birdland, the Five Spot, or the Village Vanguard. One need only turn to the photojournalism of W. Eugene Smith (Stephensen 2009) or the photography of Herman Leonard (Leonard 2010) to appreciate the ubiquity of suit jackets, slacks, and ties in both jazz rehearsals and performances that took place over the course of the decade. However, the act of making the MJQ style of dress seem different, even though it was not, did play into the narrative that the group was moving away from African American cultural norms.

Often the distance traveled in these assessments required reviewers to conceptualize Lewis in terms oppositional to African American culture at large. Sachs, for instance, relays the following quote from an anonymous source:

> John is quite free of the anti white feeling that in smaller or larger parts is fairly prevalent among many Negro musicians. One reason may be that he ran into practically no race friction in New Mexico while he was growing up. Another is that by now, he is so internationalized, that he has experienced and enjoyed people and social contexts in many areas where race doesn't count. (1959, 19)

While the anonymity of Sachs's source makes it difficult to fully contextualize the comment, the clear division between the behavior of the larger body of "Negro musicians" and Lewis's behavior does speak to an attempt to solidify Lewis's difference in sociological terms. In addition, the location of the comment within the article, immediately preceding a description of Lewis's travels to Europe and his "constantly favorable" critical reception on the Continent (Sachs 1959, 19), seems to connect European success with cultural realignment. It is Lewis's "internationalization," it would seem through this pairing, that allows him to effectively deliver his music to a European audience without being caught up in the behavioral trappings of African American culture. John Wilson's report for the *New York Times* in which the MJQ members are described as "bearded undertakers," discussed earlier, in turn highlights how some in the jazz community were beginning to view Lewis as a biologically inferior jazz musician:

> They accused the group's musical director and pianist John Lewis, of stifling Mr. [Milt] Jackson (who was a major figure of the bop period in the Nineteen Forties) and of being devoid of any jazz instinct himself." (1960, 47)

The return to the idea of "jazz instinct" in this quote via a discussion of nonaligned hipster dress and a reference to musical control (the "stifling" of Jackson) demonstrates how the web of associations discussed throughout this chapter just as easily combine to strip an artist of perceived biological coding as they do to affirm perceived biological predisposition. In this argument Lewis is implicitly connected to the instinct-less "whites" of Sekles's genetic paradigm ("Jazz Bitterly Opposed" 1928, 10) by way of musical style. Later positioning of Lewis and vibraphonist Milt Jackson as opposing forces in the quartet would further revive criticism based on such "primitivist" assumptions.

This is particularly evident in the way Jackson and Lewis are compared in a 1961 concert summary written by Don De Micheal. De Micheal begins by discussing the strict attention to detail involved in the concert preparations (the cleaning of the piano keys by Lewis; the tuxedos worn by the group members) before going on to claim that these elements add up to the elimination of "visual distraction" during MJQ performances. Referring to Milt Jackson, however, De Micheal views resistance to this agenda:

> At the Ann Arbor concert, he appeared to be following the rules, but as the evening progressed, the rules seemed to go out the window. The tail of his tuxedo jacket, which had been unbuttoned from the first, flapped as his movements became more animated. His feet spread farther apart. His wrists, undulating as if on ball-bearings, were graceful blurs as he guided the mallets over his vibraharp. His head bent farther down. When he played a phrase that seemed to delight him, he looked out over his glasses to see if what he had played had struck anyone else as it had him. When it was necessary to move to the upper octave of his instrument, he made a discreet leap as he moved.
>
> His solo over, he retired to the background, but, where before he had stood solemnly, his stance was now relaxed. Smiling, he nodded his head slightly in tempo, his fingers snapping occasionally when the other three played in an especially strong manner. (1961, 18)

While De Micheal's comments are not as overt as the "primitivist" commentary surveyed by Radano (2003), they are striking in their intense focus on Jackson's physical behavior. Not only do they set Jackson apart from the rest of the group, they do so from the perspective that Jackson was incapable of adapting to the social norms adopted by the MJQ. This separation creates the context for viewing Jackson's playing as more authentically grounded in the jazz tradition, as it evinces the type of behavior associated with magical rhythmic performance. Lewis's behavior is in turn depicted as culturally distinct, evident in De Micheal's comments regarding Lewis's response to an enthusiastic fan requesting one of Jackson's blues compositions in the middle of the concert:

> The concert's finale was given over to a several-part composition written by Lewis, who announced and explained each part. Before the third section, as he was explaining his attractive, but complex, piece of work, a man in the first row shouted, "*Bags' Groove!*" Lewis

> recoiled as if a bucket of ice water had been thrown in his face. He replied with dignity, "We'll play *that* later." (1961, 18)

Lewis's control and "dignity," as described by De Micheal, contrast with the unpredictability and emotion of Jackson's on-stage behavior. In a telling decoding of this difference, De Micheal eventually enters into a comparison of musical styles, writing,

> There is much of contrast between Lewis and Jackson. It can be seen in the music they write. Jackson's is usually more simple and takes the form of blues or the 32-bar song much more often than does Lewis'. While Lewis appears to like formality, Jackson does not. "I don't feel comfortable in formal clothes or formal settings," he said. "I dig being completely relaxed—although music has always been a serious thing with me." (1961, 20)

In De Micheal's article, what begins as a discussion of behavioral difference ends up being a discussion of compositional form, thus confirming the fact that perspectives on musical aesthetics were occasionally linked to behavioral depictions even in musical styles far removed from early jazz. Jackson's apparent aversion to the strictures of form is shown to align with the qualities of spontaneity identified in his behavior, just as Lewis's penchant for musical structure is seen to be congruent with his austere on-stage attitude. Critical trends essentializing African rhythmic characteristics are likely responsible for the persistence of such categorization. Just as jazz musicians who utilized overt rhythmic effects in early jazz were cast in the primitive realm, those who chose alternate routes to performance in later years ran the risk of being viewed as operatives from outside the African American cultural arena. Although Lewis had spoken about his reliance on rhythmic ideas early on, his failure to continually articulate this aspect of his work to the popular press allowed perspectives on the novel elements of his compositions, their formal components, to dominate discussion. Such broad strokes conflated Lewis's dimensions as a composer with an easily articulated archetype, a stigma that persisted until the time of his death in 2001.

The summative statements of his obituaries speak to this point. In his remembrance for *Down Beat*, Fred Bouchard draws on a European allusion rather than jazz comparisons in his comment that "like his lifelong inspiration J.S. Bach, Lewis consistently exhibited meticulous craftsmanship" (2001, 22). Echoing Bouchard's allusion to Bach, Lewis's *New York Times* obituary claims that the "MJQ's music was largely a reflection of Mr. Lewis's classical training. . . . Lewis drew as much inspiration from Bach as he did from Gillespie," a comment that seems to indicate that the composer was at least equally split between European and vernacular realms (Keepnews 2001, B9). A year later Bouchard would push the allusion to Bach even further, not only claiming that Bach was Lewis's "lifelong inspiration" but that, like Bach, "Lewis drew on a wellspring of sublime melodic invention, and set it in meticulously crafted orchestrations, often as fresh as Bach inventions" (2002, 28). Finally, in *Billboard*, Lewis was described as having "a penchant for longer, classical forms such as the fugue" and running a group that, in implied contrast to other jazz ensembles of the 1950s, contained "no horns, which meant no spit, no sweat and no screaming" (Goldberg 2002, 26). The location of value in these assessments falls squarely on the way in which the formal elements of Lewis's works aligned with a European compositional ethos. With the limitations of critical trends in the popular press now identified, such evaluations must be read with some skepticism.

Indeed, they seem to tell a different story than the one Lewis would endeavor to promote toward the end of his life. In an interview for *Down Beat* in 2000, Lewis opened up to Eugene Holley about the significance of the "formal" aspects of his compositions, painting a more complicated picture of their intent:

> The primary thing for us was the interplay, which took a long time to achieve. The whole point of a composition is to make a piece that incorporates improvisation into it as seamlessly as possible, so you won't know what's improvised and what's not. It took a long time for that to happen, but that was the goal we worked towards achieving. (Qtd. in Holley 2000, 39)

Developing this idea further, Lewis spoke about trying to "incorporate the blues in everything I play, to find some way to make the blues speak, and to do it in a polyphonic way" (qtd. in Holley 2000, 43). Such comments echo those Lewis had made decades earlier in his first *Down Beat* interview with Hentoff: "We have to keep going back into the gold mine . . . the blues, and things that are related to it" (Hentoff 1957b, 15). It is a testament to the resiliency of primitivist commentary in the popular press that so little attention has been given to reconciling such claims with the dominant themes of Lewis's historical reception.

One of the things we learn from such an inquiry, as shown in this chapter, is that essentializing form and rhythm places artificial limits on cultural identity. It is therefore no surprise that constant critique along these lines irked Lewis into his "incredulous" standoff with Hentoff in the anecdote that begins this book. While certainly well meaning, Hentoff and his peers were operating within a field that utilized a style of language that limited not only what might be viewed as genuine jazz but what might be viewed as "normal" African American behavior. In the following chapter I set out a way for us to contextualize Lewis's frustration through a discussion of the values and musical practices of the African American middle and upper class. Adding this lens into the historical mix and exploring Lewis's reception in this world helps erode the established narrative around Lewis's works while simultaneously enabling an expansion of thought around what might be conceived of as authentic African American musical expression, both within jazz and beyond.

3 • "Finesse, Precision and Logic"

Musical Traditions and the African American Elite

On the night of February 22, 1946, Maestro Dean Dixon took the stage at Carnegie Hall to conduct the American Youth Orchestra, an interracial ensemble composed of exceptional young musicians from across the New York area (Du Bois 1946, 15). Dixon had founded the group in 1944 after receiving a prestigious Rosenwald Fund fellowship ("46 Get Rosenwald" 1945, 2), and their debut was lauded in the African American press for presenting a pathway that "well-qualified" African American musicians might follow into "the classical field" ("Another Race Barrier Falls" 1944, 12). Throughout 1946 Dixon would lead the orchestra through some of the more challenging works of the Western art music canon ("Dean Dixon Back" 1946, 10), and the February 22 concert was to be no exception. Over the course of the evening the ensemble would perform works by Khrennikov, Rachmaninoff, and Sam Morgenstern, showing off to an interracial audience both their technical proficiency and their expressive prowess (Du Bois 1946, 15).

One audience member, the noted intellectual and critic W. E. B. Du Bois, was particularly impressed with what he saw. Writing in the *Chicago Defender* the very next day under the headline "Winds of Time," Du Bois made the following observations:

> This concert was not merely a plea for race tolerance. It was a great deal more than this. It was the American Youth Orchestra composed of musicians without reference to race and color. A black girl with a violin sat in front far to the left. Dark men played brass and wind

> instruments but above all guiding this whole orchestra of hundreds of instruments was a young, handsome black man, Dean Dixon, who seemed to hold their thoughts and hearts in absolute control. . . .
>
> It has often been said that art is the clear, straight path to democracy and while I have continually doubted this I have wanted this to be true. Certainly as I look back upon our path in this land I can see nothing that has guided us more consistently toward freedom and accomplishment than our literature and music, our sculpture and painting, our drama. Our political efforts despite our triumphs have failed us; our economic emancipation has hardly more than begun; our physical revolt died a-borning. But our art forms have not only made America, they are an integral part of the 20th Century. (1946, 15).

Du Bois's comments in the *Defender* are particularly intriguing in that they speak to a complicated notion of ownership over the music performed by the American Youth Orchestra. In Du Bois's view, the American Youth Orchestra was not a white ensemble in which African Americans participated. It was an ensemble that at the very least evinced a shared sort of ownership, but at most, as Du Bois mentions at the end of the quote, made public and promoted long-standing African American facility and familiarity with and love of Western orchestral music. In other words, Du Bois appears to argue in this passage for the music performed by the ensemble to be heard as an iteration of the African American musical voice—as an acceptable expression of African American cultural accomplishment intrinsically linked to a unique historical path.

In this chapter I endeavor to illuminate how this conception of African American musical identity developed over the course of more than a hundred years and to trace its effect on the coverage John Lewis received in the African American press—a style of coverage uniquely different in tone from that surveyed in chapter 2. Beginning with a discussion of cultural changes promoted by African American church leaders during the 1800s, I demonstrate how nondemonstrative behavior and an appreciation for European musical styles were gradually adopted into the social life of middle- and upper-class African American Christian denominations across the

United States as part of what Evelyn Higginbotham (1993) has referred to as "the politics of respectability." These politics advanced an agenda of cultural transformation that challenged racist assumptions about who African Americans were and how African Americans should act. Yet more importantly, the inward focus of such a movement—its goal of empowering segregated African American communities—allowed for "respectable" behavior and taste to become a celebrated part of a newly emergent form of African American identity. Although such behavior paralleled the social codes of the hegemony, this fact did not detract from the value bestowed upon it by community leaders in terms of its ability to advance African American economic, intellectual, and spiritual development. Indeed, as I discuss in my survey of African American middle-class musical life during the 1940s and 1950s, a persistent focus on the performance of Western art music along with the showcasing of Westernized spirituals seems to have reified belief in a malleable sort of African American culture indebted to a particular historical legacy while concurrently open to outside influence.

In the final section of this chapter I return to the story of Lewis's music, only this time I study how it was received in a critical realm that endorsed such malleable ideas about African American culture. In particular, I examine how the acceptance of Westernized spirituals and syncretic concert works composed by African Americans set in place a language for discussing and evaluating other sorts of modern African American musical developments, such as Lewis's work with the MJQ. While the language of this reception—its focus on intellect and refinement—remained quite similar to that used in the jazz press's evaluation of Lewis, I demonstrate that its function in the African American press differed dramatically. Far from positing that musical marks of "refinement" denoted a move toward European assimilation, the African American press largely accepted such stylistic choices as "par for the course" in terms of what they viewed as an expansive and diverse field of African American musical expression.

The Black Church Prior to 1950 and the "Politics of Respectability"

Attempts to negotiate a version of African American identity that was both uniquely African American and embracing of dominant American cultural norms can be seen to underpin much of the history of African American Christian worship in the United States. In his monograph *The Rise of Gospel Blues* (1992), Michael Harris sets out a brief overview of change throughout the evolution of the African Methodist Episcopal Church (AME)—"the first black denomination in the United States"—in which he illuminates nearly 150 years of tension between congregation and ministry regarding the compatibility of folk practices and religious decorum. Initially, these debates revolved around the continued use of the Ring Shout—a form of worship involving singing, dancing, and hand clapping that was performed in a style considered overly demonstrative by the AME leadership (Harris 1992, 3). Inspired by outward-looking looking ideologies of racial uplift, AME clergy like Bishop Daniel Alexander Payne worked tirelessly during the antebellum era to exorcise black musical practices like the Ring Shout from the church, encouraging instead the performance of "European classical instrumental music" and the establishment of choirs (Harris 1992, 8). Seeing out such a project was, however, no easy feat. Payne would later decry in his autobiography the resistance he had often felt for "not let[ting] them [congregants] sing their 'spiritual songs'" ([1891] 2001, 93). Yet Payne's goal in enacting such changes does not seem to have been the wholehearted assimilation of African Americans into white culture. Indeed, the AME Church itself was established in response to dissatisfaction with the white Methodist Episcopal Church and "the second-class membership" afforded black participants (Harris 1992, 5). In Payne's view, founding the AME had enabled an "independence of character" to emerge in its African American membership, a development he hoped would lead AME congregants to "feel and recognize our individuality and our heaven-created manhood" ([1891] 2001, 12). In other words, despite looking toward established white churches for cues on how religious life should be celebrated, Payne remained convinced that the AME's physical and conceptual independence from its white counterpart would ultimately strengthen the self-awareness and self-investment of its members.

In her discussion of "the politics of respectability," Evelyn Brooks Higginbotham explores the paradox of how African American denominations could assert claims of bolstering individuality while simultaneously conforming to dominant social norms. Focusing on the black Baptist Church of the early twentieth century, Higginbotham charts out the manner in which female activists promoted "manners and morals" in their communities as a way of challenging stereotypical expectations of African American behavior. This agenda was seen by some as unshackling the church community from the legacy of having value imposed upon it from the outside; or more to the point, it was seen as a way of asserting an ideology of self-determination against a backdrop of "crude stereotypes" and "'scientific' racism." Yet those who promoted this agenda were not satisfied with mere behavioral parity between African American and white Americans and implored church members to enact the values of "temperance, cleanliness of person and property, thrift, polite manners and sexual purity" even more rigidly than the white Christian populace did. Such a pursuit allowed Baptist communities to assert equality and individuality simultaneously—to be, in Higginbotham's language, "both black and American" as they *perfected* the respectable behavior with which others continued to struggle (Higginbotham 1993, 188, 193).

Similar attempts to erode racist assumptions and promote "respectability" as a core African American value can be seen to have driven the ideology and social initiatives of Christian denominations more strongly associated with upper- and middle-class African Americans during the same time period. Indeed, Davarian Baldwin's *Chicago's New Negros* (2007) explores the central role such politics played in asserting a societal boundary between Chicago's "old settler" families and the waves of African American migrants coming to Chicago from the American South during the 1920s. In Baldwin's view, demonstrations of conservative behavior in African American Chicago neighborhoods helped "establish a hierarchy of distinction that provided distance from but also dominion over the newly arriving migrant masses" (2007, 59). Such social stratification then worked to define the rough shape of African American urban centers through the first half of the twentieth century.

The central role religious institutions played in seeing out this cultural project was made apparent in early surveys of African American religious life produced during the first half of the century. In his sociological study of Episcopal, Presbyterian, and Congregational churches in Chicago during the late years of the Depression, for instance, Vattel Daniel detailed a middle- and upper-class preoccupation with "conservatism, conformity, thrift,

[and] industry" that effectively echoed Higginbotham's behavioral "politics." Such values, in Daniel's view, informed the mind-set of those involved in "civic affairs" in Chicago, especially affairs in which "race" was deemed to be a factor (1944, 23). This orientation is particularly evident in the commentary of Robert S. Abbott—founder of the *Chicago Defender* and a member of first an Episcopal and later a Presbyterian church—who implored the religious leaders of Chicago in 1935 to fund a finishing school for African American girls. His rationale, put forth in the pages of the *Defender*, claimed,

> Unless our attention is directed more seriously toward the solution of our social problems we shall be forever troubled with prejudice. . . . Our behavior, our decorum, our speech and laughter in public or private places, at teas, receptions and recitals indicate to casual observers that there is need for more culture and cultural inclination. I trust that some day our girls may be so transfigured culturally as to take their places with grace, dignity and poise beside those charming aristocratic ladies who are presented to the Buckingham palace each year. (Abbott 1935, 11)

Abbott's suggestion that African American churches foot the bill for such a school speaks to his belief that a central part of the mission of these institutions was the promulgation of respectability. Furthermore, the tone of Abbott's comments reflects a conviction that African American culture at large could in fact benefit from such an initiative—that "decorum" and "grace" (words that appear to be code for nondemonstrative or conservative behavior in this passage) should be incorporated into the story of who African American people were and become markers of African American identity.

Undoubtedly, some have viewed this agenda as the unpardonable promotion of assimilation into white culture. In his monograph *The Negro Church in America*, E. Franklin Frazier denounces the "transfiguration" Abbott writes about as evidence of an African American middle class seeking "identification with and acceptance by the white middle class" through its rejection of "Negro heritage, including . . . religious heritage" (1964, 85). Frazier's student Nathan Hare in turn called out "Negro ministers" for being "pathological imitators of . . . white clergymen" and for endorsing a politics of "mimicry" in their congregations (1965, 35, 46). Yet the persistent fact of segregation between African American and white communities rendered Frazier's and Hare's appraisals, in some ways, moot. Writing in 1944 on the subject of "The Negro Church: Its Weakness, Trends, and Outlook," Gunnar Myrdal noted that Episcopalian and Presbyterian preferences for conservative behavior seemed to have little impact on assimilation, arguing instead that "the Negro church fundamentally is an expression of the Negro community itself" ([1944] 1971, 874–75). That is to say, for Myrdal, the behavior of the congregation *was* noteworthy in that it denoted commitment to the political goal of "moving the American Negroes onward in their struggle against caste," but it did not mark a capitulation of independence ([1944] 1971, 874). African American behavior may have been changing, and notions of white middle-class behavior may have driven that change, but continued segregation ensured that any cultural shifts that did occur functioned primarily in terms of local community development.

The articulation of this sort of malleable African American culture in the comments of Myrdal, Abbott, and Payne underscores the central theme of the New Negro movement in America. Promoted by African American intellectuals such as Alain Locke and Charles S. Johnson during the 1920s and 1930s, New Negro ideology viewed African American culture as a dynamic force capable of maintaining and celebrating certain aspects of African American history while simultaneously incorporating new ways of thinking and living into the fold. Locke in particular was an advocate of breaking down the notion that "Negro culture" began and ended with folk traditions. In his essay "The Negro's Contribution to American Culture," Locke charts with great detail the way in which "Negro Art" incorporated the aesthetic trends of "realism, regionalism, [and] proletarianism" while maintaining a unique perspective honed from the African American experience (1939, 527–28). The manner in which hegemonic notions of respectability were incorporated into the ethos of African American religious practice appears to have worked in the same way. Early proponents of a separate African American church recognized the potential of the organization to strengthen the African American position in America. For better or worse, many decided that the best path forward was the adoption of behavioral trappings espoused by white middle-class patrons of parallel churches. Yet over the course of more than a hundred years, such attitudes became a part of the ideal vision of what African American identity should look like—at least when leaders of the African American church put forth such visions. This conception of being African American continued to center on race (Abbott was, after all, concerned with "our behavior" and "our girls") but remained dynamic enough to accommodate a spectrum of expression and cultural practices borrowed from across American society.

Music in the Black Church, 1870–1950

In the musical realm, such hybridity is perhaps most evident in the reintroduction of African American spirituals into religious contexts towards the end of the nineteenth century. Sterling Stuckey's work on early African American music traces the roots of spirituals to songs sung as part of the Ring Shout ceremonies of African slaves (1987, 30). As Christianity was adopted by slave populations, the lyrical content of these ceremonies changed, but the melodic content retained colloquialisms that continued to set it apart from Western art music. As the ethnomusicologist John Wesley Work III wrote in 1940:

> There is a certain elusive quality heard in the native singing of the melodies that defies musical notation. For lack of suitable symbols, it is impossible to record on paper many of these songs as they are sung in their native environment. Extravagant postamenta [*sic*], slurs, and free use of extra notes serve to mystify the collector of these songs who strives for accuracy. ([1940] 1998, 25–26)

Mirroring the language of essential difference surveyed in chapter 2, commentators on African American spirituals in what Work refers to as their "native" form often resorted to allusions that highlighted the spirituals' perceived backwardness and immaturity. As Fredrika Bremer pointed out after the performance of several spirituals at a Cincinnati-based African Methodist church in 1850, "The hymns and psalms which the negroes have themselves composed have a peculiar *naïve* character, childlike, full of imagery and life" (qtd. in Epstein 1977, 223). Arthur Buckminster

Fuller, a chaplain of the Unitarian Church, in turn wrote of attending an African American religious meeting at Fort Monroe in 1862 in which he ventured the opinion that the singing of spirituals was "a little more demonstrative than I am accustomed to or suits my taste. . . . O, they [the singers] were so mournful, so despairing (who wonders at that?) in their view of this life; but they changed to wild paeans when they spoke of an immortal state" ([1863] 2007, 199). Such a reading of the performativity of spirituals worked against the goals of African American church leaders bent on breaking free from primitivist stereotypes and led to their somewhat anachronistic presence in urban African American churches by the 1870s (Harris 1992, 113).

Indeed, at least in the realm of Episcopal, Presbyterian, and Congregational Churches—those denominations most concerned with charting a new behavioral course—spirituals might have disappeared entirely if not for the innovative experimentation of a select group of performers during the final decades of the century. These developments might best be described as a Westernized approach to the performance of spirituals and owe a debt to the pioneering efforts of the Fisk Jubilee Singers. Formed under the tutelage of Fisk University treasurer George L. White, the group's first incarnation in 1867 focused on the preparation of works associated with the "white 'art' repertoire." The aim of such an initiative was to both raise money for the struggling institution and to showcase to the wider public how much "former slaves had benefitted from higher education." Yet their performances of Western art music attracted far less attention than their occasional performances of spirituals—a facet of their programming that began to grow in earnest during the group's 1871 tour (Brooks 2004, 193). White's fixation on the transformative effect of higher education seems to have in turn informed his direction of those spirituals, leading to a break with the demonstrative and unpredictable nature of African American spiritual singing described earlier and instead pursuing what Work referred to as:

> A style of singing the spiritual which eliminated every element that detracted from the pure emotion of the song. Harmony was diatonic and limited very largely to the primary triads and the dominant seventh. Dialect was not stressed but was used only where it was vital to

> the spirit of the song. Finish, precision, and sincerity were demanded by this leader. . . . Mr. White strove for an art presentation, not a caricature of atmosphere. ([1940] 1998, 15)

White's musical decisions left in place many key sonic components of the spiritual—the frequent use of pentatonic scales, for instance, and the rhythmic syncopations that played such a crucial role in establishing the genre's character. Yet he had stripped the genre of its more salient marks of "otherness," those musical features that had often caused people to remark on its overly emotional nature. This new style of performing spirituals was received enthusiastically by both white audiences and African American audiences that endorsed the "politics of respectability," leading to several successful tours undertaken by the Fisk Jubilee Singers between 1871 and 1878 as well as the establishment of similar choral organizations at the African American colleges Hampton and Howard (Brooks 2004, 194).

In turn, the Fisk Singers' more reverent style of performing spirituals was widely welcomed by leaders of African American churches, who had long attempted to subdue congregants wishing for more acknowledgment of the African American experience in their places of worship. As Michael Harris neatly summarizes,

> Whereas old-line directors had considered the spiritual in its classic form to be crude and its first descendent musically trite, they found the anthem/octavo spiritual a worthy medium through which to restore some aspect of their racial heritage from which it had been so effectively expunged. (1992, 114)

Yet incorporating the use of these works into the liturgical practice of African American churches at the turn of the century remained beyond the pale of how far many church leaders seemed willing to go.[1] Instead, arranged spirituals began appearing in concert programs performed outside of worship hours. Functioning as social and cultural hubs, many urban African American churches had long set in place concert series aimed at celebrating and promoting community expertise in Western art music. A biography of the African American singer and composer Harry Burleigh's early life assembled by Jean Snyder (2004) provides ample evidence of both the breadth and scope of such performance opportunities extending across the urban centers of Cleveland, Buffalo, and New York. Burleigh had made a name for himself in these cities as a classically trained baritone proficient in art songs, but on the back of the Fisk Jubilee Singers' success, he began introducing solo arrangements of African American spirituals into his church concerts around 1900 (Brooks 2004, 479). Burleigh was followed in this regard by Robert Nathaniel Dett, who led the Hampton Institute Choir in the performance of arranged spirituals and art songs at churches and recital halls across the country during the 1920s and across Europe in 1930 (Brooks 2004, 491).

Those observing these concerts in the African American press were impressed with the way in which this new take on the spiritual appeared to reify New Negro ideology in sonic terms, demonstrating to the world the sophistication and technical proficiency African American musicians could attain in the performance of works with folk roots. In particular, commentary on the "training" required to perform in the new spiritual style and the "control" with which the music was delivered pervades African American press coverage of the genre. Typical of this type of reporting are the comments made by Gamewell Valentine of the *Atlanta Daily World* about a concert given by the Fisk Singers at the First Congregational Church in Atlanta on March 22, 1935. Valentine writes, "As to be expected, Fisk maintains her supremacy in the dignified interpretation of spirituals and their singing had fine tone production, rhythm, authority and that finesse which only Fisk possesses" (1935, 1, 3). Laced through this description are acknowledgments of the Fisk Singers' nondemonstrative approach and the idea that such a result stemmed from the training these musicians received at Fisk rather than their own genetic predispositions. A similar understanding of the value of the Westernized spiritual can be seen in Frankye Dixon's comments about the Hal Johnson Negro Choir made several years earlier in the *New York Amsterdam News*: "Any prepossessions you may have had against Madrigals and Spirituals as being unvocal or harsh or crabbed will melt like mist before the summer sun. . . . Hal Johnson is to be greatly commended for his untiring efforts in the training and the banding together of such a representative group." Dixon would in turn highlight Johnson's "excellent choral arrangements" and the "intelligence in interpretation" evinced by members of Johnson's choir as assurances "that a universal welcome will soon be the reward for these living representatives of the only true native school of American music" (1928, 9). The point here is that the language of musical "subtlety" and "intellect" woven through these reviews can be seen to demonstrate the impact respectability politics had on assessments of modern African American musical developments in elite circles.

Of course the spiritual was not the sole musical vehicle of modernist thought explored by African American composers during this period. An important parallel aesthetic project can be seen to have occurred in the concert works composed by Burleigh and Dett, as well as their contemporaries William Grant Still, Florence Price, and William Dawson. Dett, for instance, would compose the concert oratorio *The Ordering of Moses* between 1931 and 1932 in order to fulfill the assessment requirements for his master's degree from the Eastman School of Music. The work had a foundation in the African American spiritual tradition in that it used the melody of "Go Down, Moses" as a unifying device, but at the same time, the work's extended form placed it outside the arranged spiritual model (Ryder 1997, 370). In 1935 Burleigh would in turn move beyond the realm of spirituals and publish the art song "Lovely Dark and Lonely One," based on a text by Langston Hughes. In this work Burleigh pairs a series of motivic gestures rooted in Western art music compositional practice with a "harmonic and melodic structure . . . [based] on a succession of seventh and ninth chords" suggestive of the blues (Snyder 1997, 191). Still, Price and Dawson ventured even further afield, writing symphonies in which vernacular tropes and Western compositional language were fused. Still's *Afro-American Symphony* (1930) integrated the twelve-bar blues form and the pentatonic blues scale into a "modified sonata form" in its first movement (Floyd 1995, 109), while Dawson's *Negro Folk Symphony* (1932) employed a pentatonic motive as a structural link between the themes of various movements derived from the melodies of African American spirituals (Strong 1997, 358). In line with Still and Dawson, Price would embrace a pentatonic theme and folk-inspired syncopated rhythms in her Symphony in E Minor (1932), which would in turn draw heavily on orchestration effects explored in Dvorák's Symphony no. 9, *From the New World* (Brown 1997, 942).

As with the spirituals sung by the Fisk Jubilee Singers and related groups, the African American press endorsed the works of Still and Dawson as excellent visions of what modern African American music might sound like. Inherent in this commentary was language that pointed to the "cerebral" nature of these works as evidence of their cultural value. Still's *Afro-American Symphony*, for example, was praised in the *Defender* for demonstrating both "subtlety and skill," factors that allowed Still to demonstrate "his own genius" ("Race Symphony" 1935, 5). A similar critique of the work was offered by the *Pittsburgh Courier*, which applauded the way "'blues' themes and banjo parts" were "intricately woven to make up the colorful fabric of the whole" ("Still's Symphony" 1936, 8). Dawson's *Negro Folk Symphony* in turn was celebrated in the *New York Amsterdam News* for harnessing the emotionalism of African American vernacular forms, evident in the critique that "one feels the religious fervor, the suffering and the humor of the Negro, all skillfully woven into three movements" (Overton 1934, 4). Such comments echo the enthusiasm with which syncretic spirituals were received and unequivocally endorse the compositional idea of fusing folk material with Western art music conventions.

Yet curiously, the performance of syncretic spirituals and other concert works did not come to eclipse the performance of canonical works of Western art music in African American social settings during this period. As church concerts continued throughout the 1930s and 1940s, equal attention appears to have been given to the performance of works by Western art music composers such as Handel, Mozart, Beethoven, and Chopin (among others) and to the performance of compositions by African American artists. Consider, for instance, the program performed by the junior choir of the Mt. Carmel Baptist Church in Washington, D.C., on April 20, 1942, in which the music of Dett was paired with that of Grieg, Brahms, Mozart, and Elgar ("Junior Choir" 1942, 17), or the program performed by contralto Jewell Yancey Humphrey at the St. Paul AME Church in St. Louis on November 25, 1946, in which "excerpts from operas by the old masters in French, German and Italian" were paired with "ever-beloved Negro spirituals arranged by Jonson, R. Nathaniel Dett and Brown" ("Contralto Here" 1946, 19C). Examples of similar programs emerge in connection with a range of African American Christian denominations across the decade, providing further evidence of what appears to have been a fairly common programming format (see "Ohio" 1946, 11; "Tarrytown" 1947, 17; Campbell 1948, 18).

Two factors seem to have contributed to such continued focus on Western art music works. The first was that a bona-fide aesthetic appreciation for Western art music held by middle- and upper-class African American concert patrons seems to have solidified during this period. Such an appreciation is perhaps most evident in the negative—that is, in reviews of concerts that did not quite live up to expectations. Cultural critic Grace Tompkins, for instance, expressed less than total satisfaction with singer Frankie Fambro's performance at a 1941 concert in which her delivery of "Mozart's Alleluia lacked the delicate finesse and smooth legato singing necessary for an excellent performance . . . show[ing] a tendency toward breathiness and an inability to sustain the longer phrases" (Tompkins 1941, 18). Venturing into even more technical terms, in a critique of Eva Vorhies's piano recital at St. Martins Episcopal Church in New York, a reviewer for the *Defender* first applauded the difficulty of the program, on which both Beethoven's "Waldsetein" sonata and Liszt's "Mephisto" waltz were performed, before going on to complain that "overindulgence in the use of the damper pedal is her [Vorhies's] greatest fault" ("Eva Vorhies" 1942, 1). Such expressions of preference denote more than a superficial or passing engagement with Western art music and paint a picture of an informed and engaged public eager for opportunities not only to hear classical music performed but to hear it performed well.

A second factor that may have fed into continued engagement with Western art music was the way Western art music proficiency was aligned with success in the tertiary education sector. Indeed, performer biographies that preceded discussion of concert programs in the African American press were frequently laden with lists of universities and courses attended as well as the names of musical mentors who had helped the performers along the way. Represented in these lists were both historically African American institutions such as Wilberforce University ("Singer Thrills" 1944, 17A) and Howard University ("Junior Choir" 1942, 17) as well as integrated institutions such as the University of Pennsylvania ("Eva Vorhies" 1942, 21) and the University of Minnesota ("Applaud Duo" 1954, 14). As the following discussion of a performance given by twin brothers Rudolph and Adolph Thornton at St. Marks AME Zion Church in Indianapolis demonstrates, such a discursive frame allowed communities to endorse a model of successful adulthood that incorporated both tertiary training and respectable music taste.

> A packed house greeted the two maestros who are graduates of Crispus Attucks high school and have made great strides in the field of music. They are former students at Lucille S. Collins Conservatory of Music and also studied under Norman L. Merrifield, concert pianist of the Indianapolis Philharmonic [*sic*] Symphony Orchestra.
>
> Thunderous applause greeted the brothers as they played a duet, "The Star Spangled Banner," a special arrangement by John Stafford Smith. It was expertly rendered, without a flaw.
>
> Following this rendition, Adolph played the works of Beethoven and other composers, while Rudolph devoted his part of the program to compositions by the great artist Chopin and others.
>
> After the program, the talented twins were given a reception in the parlors of the church, where they received the plaudits of their friends and associates. ("Twin Brothers" 1950, 24)

The Thornton brothers' reception reveals the degree to which Western art music proficiency and tertiary education were woven together in the minds of some African American communities as marks of ideal social advancement. This mode of thinking is reflective of W. E. B. Du Bois's endorsement of a humanities-rich education as a pathway to racial uplift in his 1903 essay "The Talented Tenth." Similar to the goals of respectability politics, Du Bois's vision of a strong African American community revolved around disproving assumptions about African American talent and aptitude through the successful deployment of tertiary education programs on par with those offered to whites. Specifically, Du Bois rejected the notion that the best hope for racial uplift lay in industrial training, as promoted by Booker T. Washington, arguing in contrast that "education must not simply teach work—it must teach Life" and that "the sending out of teachers whose training has not been simply for bread winning, but also for human culture, has been of inestimable value" ([1903] 2007, 198, 205). Showcasing students who had successfully studied the arts at tertiary institutions provided one way for communities to publicly celebrate the advancements they had made in securing the reins of self-determination as well as make the case that the community itself was capable of producing members of Du Bois's envisioned leadership class. In this way, the performance of classical music helped shore up boundaries between those who continued to pursue a folk, or what Guthrie Ramsey (2003, 40) has referred to as a "provincial outlook," and those who pursued more "cosmopolitan" identities.

Further evidence of this willful stratification can be seen in the way members of the "cosmopolitan" set rejected musical styles derived from folk practices they perceived to be overly demonstrative. Just as the early form of the spiritual had been rejected in African American church communities, popular music in the form of jazz served as a particular lightning rod for those looking to break free—or maintain their distance—from folk-based identities. Writing a year before he promoted his idea for a "finishing" school in the pages of the *Defender*, Robert S. Abbott set about critiquing jazz in the same essentialist language used by the the *Musical Quarterly* authors surveyed in chapter 2. Under the heading "Jazz Is Scandalizing," Abbott wrote of young African American women "tearing down every conceivable hope of redemption . . . [and] abandon[ing] themselves into such frenzied epileptic contortions as 'snake-hip,' 'black-bottom' and the vulgar dance de ventre [*sic*] known as the 'rhumba'"(1934, 11). Lawrence Levine's documentation of jazz reception across African American periodicals in the 1920s and 1930s uncovered similar views about the music's value. Levine cites *New York Age* critic Lucien H. White, who wrote in 1921 that jazz appealed "only to the lover of sensuous and debasing emotions," as well as Maude Cuney-Hare of the *Crisis*, who in 1936 denounced jazz in language that set it far outside the nondemonstrative realm: "Music should sound, not screech; Music should cry, not howl; Music should weep, not bawl; Music should implore, not whine" (qtd. in Levine 1989, 12).

From a contemporary viewpoint, such perspectives are certainly difficult to stomach. While they provide evidence of an intellectual project aimed at rescuing the power of African American definition from the hands of those who would stereotype, they simultaneously embrace a racialized and essentialist reading of jazz music that harks back to some of the uglier moments of "primitivist" critique. In turn, it has not been uncommon for scholars committed to promoting the value of the folk aspect of African American music to read such views within a framework of manipulation—to look at comments about the evils of jazz as evidence of a sort of brainwashing of middle-class African Americans regarding the value of folk products. Writing in 1963, LeRoi Jones (who would later change his name to Amiri Baraka) chastised the likes of Abbott, Lucien White, and Cuney-Hare in his claim that middle-class African Americans had engaged in "willful dilutions" of African American music in order to answer "persistent calls to oblivion made by the mainstream of the society" (Jones 1963a, 131). More recent discussion of the phenomenon has been increasingly nuanced but continues to highlight the power dynamic of a dominant culture imposing its will on a minority culture. In Guthrie Ramsey's view, for instance, "'the politics of respectability' championed by the black professional and upper-class citizens" evinced an agenda of "disciplin[ing] black bodies into bourgeois submission" (2003, 51). No doubt Ramsey is referring to the bourgeois behavior of the African American upper class in this statement, but use of the term *submission* in connection with a form of behavior modeled on white culture denotes a conceptual imbalance of power. Taking the broad view, I do not argue with this sentiment. Given all of the evidence I have relayed thus far, I feel it is safe to say that a bourgeois mindset driven by white notions of respectability worked to shape middle- and upper-class African American identities—both social and musical—throughout the first half of the twentieth century. As both Jones/Baraka and Ramsey argue, and I would concur, it is important to acknowledge the flow of power in the way these identities were shaped and the forms of expression such shaping clearly put at risk.

Yet at the same time, it is difficult to deny the fact that African Americans like Abbott, Lucien White, and Cuney-Hare experienced and contributed to a way of being African American that felt genuine to them. The musical world in which they lived clearly celebrated Western art music, Westernized spirituals, and syncretic orchestral works. Social church events in middle- and upper-class communities revolved around the performance of canonical Western art music works, and expertise in classical music performance achieved through tertiary study was given a good deal of column space in African American newspapers of the time. These facets of musical life may have had limited success in altering hegemonic notions of African American musical culture—those persistent ideas that I chart out in chapter 2—but such a fact does not detract from the certainty that they held both aesthetic and political value for the communities in which they were realized.

Moving Classical Music beyond the Church during the 1940s and 1950s

As Ramsey has noted, this world would undergo significant change during the middle decades of the century. Preliminary evidence of such a shift can be seen in the increased coverage "entertainment-dance music" received in the pages of the *Defender* during the late 1940s and the decrease in coverage afforded "blacks in classical music, who had at one time dominated the society pages" (Ramsey 2003, 51). Yet caution needs to be exercised when interpreting this evidence, as performances of classical music undertaken by African American musicians do not seem to have waned in the postwar years. To the contrary, throughout the late 1940s and the 1950s African American artists who had trained in tertiary institutions (and some who had not) became increasingly interested in moving classical music outside of church settings and into the wider community arena. The urban centers of New York and Los Angeles in particular witnessed developments in the promotion of classical music among African Americans through the establishment of community orchestras and the organization of non-church-based recital programs. The support given these initiatives by the African American press continued to highlight their perceived value in terms of local community enrichment and speaks to the variety of artistic styles informing African American cultural spheres at the time John Lewis would begin to forge his musical voice.

A central factor in the expansion of community-based classical music initiatives during this period appears to have been the influx of classically trained African American musicians into a society that continued to endorse the idea of segregated symphony orchestras. In her survey of African American classical music organizations since the 1800s, D. Antoinette Handy writes of how, by the 1950s, "impatience" had set in for "black 'classically' trained instrumentalists" in relation to "the snail-paced progress being made in [the] integration of American symphony orchestras." As a result, African American musicians increasingly started to pursue the development of "'integration concerned' orchestras" as a way of "afford[ing] opportunity to highly gifted musicians regardless of age, sex, or national origin" (Handy 1981, 9–10). To be fair, an African American orchestral presence was not without precedent in the United States. Handy points to "the Ida Club and Lyre Club symphony orchestras in New Orleans" as well as N. Clark Smith's "Little Symphony Orchestra in Chicago" during the late 1800s, along with a host of others, to forward the notion that the idea for such initiatives was already in the air (1981, 7). Yet the need for more similarly minded institutions was plain enough even to the classical music critics of the *New York Times*, who admitted in the mid-1950s that major symphony orchestras continued to "act largely as if Negro string, wind, brass and Percussion players did not exist" (Taubman 1956, X9).

Maestros Dean Dixon, Everett Lee, and Leroy Hurte were early pioneers in the fight against the status quo through their development of interracial orchestral societies in New York during the 1940s and 1950s. Dixon's American Youth Orchestra, organized in 1944, was understood early on to be a vehicle purpose-built for the "break[ing] down" of "barriers of prejudice and discrimination" that continued to stymie African American orchestral employment (Holt 1944, 6). The ensemble accomplished this not only by offering professional training—which many participants had already received as part of their upbringing—but by contributing to what might be considered "facts on the ground" in terms of African American orchestral presence. In direct reference to Dixon's American Youth Orchestra and Everett Lee's Cosmopolitan Symphony Orchestra, founded four years later in 1948, Lester Granger of the *New York Amsterdam News* summed up the phenomenon in the following terms:

> For many years it has been the dream of serious Negro musicians to find outlet for their talents in the larger, widely recognized symphony orchestras. But these world-famous groups have held their ranks tightly, contemptuous of the efforts of qualified Negro musicians to join their numbers. But in recent years something has been done about this situation by persons who love music deeply and democracy even more. (1948, 11)

Indeed, both Dixon's and Lee's orchestras appear to have served as turning points in the battle for orchestral employment. Lee's interracial Cosmopolitan Symphony Orchestra would in fact go even further than Dixon's American Youth Orchestra in this regard by nature of the fact that it was in and of itself a professional ensemble with a payroll. The success of such an enterprise in meeting its financial obligations impressed critics in the African American press, particularly those aware of the fact that such success occurred "in a town where even long-established music groups were dipping into red ink" (Scott 1949, 13). In connection with Granger's observations, such coverage belies the fact that financial security for classically trained African American musicians resided front and center in the minds of those assessing the cultural value of these new interracial orchestras.

Yet providing economic reward was not viewed as their sole societal benefit. The emergence of integrated orchestras once again provided the African American press the opportunity to celebrate the achievements of middle-class community members. The coverage of Lee's debut, for instance, enabled a simultaneous public recapitulation of his success both as a professional CBS Radio staff member and as an educator at the Berkshire Festival and Columbia University (Northern 1948, 13). Coverage of the launch of the amateur New York Orchestral Society in Harlem in 1953, conducted by Leroy Hurte, in turn presented an opportunity for talking up community achievements in both education and occupation. While the *New York Age* was quick to outwardly promote the idea that the orchestra established a platform for people of "all walks of life" to come together under the umbrella of a "respected symphonic orchestra," its discussion of the society's membership revealed a decidedly less diverse reality ("New York Orchestral Society" 1953, 7). Only middle-class occupations are highlighted in the article (Andrew Johnson is described as a "minister-musician" and Alvin Moore is described as a "cop-by-day and violinist-by-night"), while members' affiliations with Columbia University and the Greenwich House music school are featured prominently. Furthermore, the *New York Age*'s description of an audition process in which "scores of persons were heard and screened" but only eleven made the initial cut speaks to the sort of privileged training one would have needed to acquire in order to participate.

The location of the concerts held by groups like the American Youth Orchestra, the Cosmopolitan Symphony Orchestra, and the New York Orchestral Society in turn demonstrates a shifting geography for African American classical music performance during the late 1940s and early 1950s. Certainly there was a precedent for African American classical music performance outside church settings in the decades prior. Harry Burleigh performed at colleges and YMCA halls as early as the 1890s (Snyder 2004, 225), while Town Hall in New York served as a particularly useful venue for African American performers with high profiles, such as Roland Hayes ("Roland Hayes" 1937, 20), Marian Anderson (I. Smith 1938, 19), and Jules Bledsoe during the 1930s (Berlack-Boozer 1938, 10). Yet the nature of having a large African American or interracial ensemble without a particular "home" church required the pursuit of non-church-based performance spaces from the very start of these projects. The American Youth Orchestra's Carnegie Hall debut was, for example, followed in short order by a series of performances at Hunter College ("Covering Concerts" 1945, 6), while the Cosmopolitan Symphony Orchestra's debut in the Great Hall of City College ("Everett Lee to Present" 1947, 6) was followed by performances at Town Hall ("Everett Lee to Conduct" 1948, 16). The New York Orchestral Society in turn can be seen to have utilized the Harlem YMCA auditorium during its short life before Hurte moved to Los Angeles, where he would conduct the interracial Angel City Symphony Orchestra in performances at East Los Angeles Junior College and the Wilshire Ebell Theatre ("Angel City Symphony" 1958, A12).

Apart from developing new spaces for performance, the increased profile for African American conductors built through these concerts seems to have set in motion the wheels of integration for several historically white ensembles. Hurte's early work with the New York Orchestral Society, for instance, was followed by requests that he guest conduct the Peter Meremblum Orchestra in 1956 and a Western Symphony Association concert in 1957 ("Leroy Hurte Directs" 1960, C2). Everett Lee was in turn recruited in 1951 to conduct the Louisville Philharmonic orchestra (the first southern orchestra to be led by an African American) and the New York City Opera Company in 1955 ("Negro Maestro Makes Bow" 1955, 1). Dixon's developing profile would, on the other hand, lead to leadership positions abroad, first with the Stockholm Symphony Orchestra ("Dean Dixon to Conduct" 1953, 4) and then with the Gothenburg Symphony Orchestra ("'Life' Points out Northern Bias" 1957, 2). The dedication with which the erosion of racial boundaries evident in the developing careers of these conductors was followed by the African American press speaks to the importance such developments held for press stakeholders.

The combination of this sort of coverage, the expansion of African

American and interracial Western art music ensembles, and the continued promotion of Western art music works both inside and outside of African American church settings during the 1940s and 1950s paints a slightly different picture of the cultural milieu within which John Lewis operated than is normally acknowledged in discussions of his music. Certainly those views distancing Lewis from African American culture discussed in chapter 2 hold water if the limits of African American cultural expression are locked into the realms of folk practices and demonstrative performativity. Yet such an understanding of Lewis seems less tenable when one considers the plurality of thinking around what might have constituted bona-fide cultural expression in the minds of middle- and upper-class African Americans during the postwar years. Indeed, Lewis's interest in Western art music conventions and Western art music ensembles like string quartets and symphony orchestras (interests discussed in depth in chapter 4) place him quite evenly in step with the likes of Hurte, Dixon, and Lee. From this perspective, Lewis's music appears to evince a weaving together of versions of African American identity at play during the 1950s rather than an assimilationist move toward a European cultural aesthetic.

Lewis's Reception in the African American Press

Lewis's coverage in the African American press can be seen to endorse this very idea. Yet before such coverage can be unpacked, it is important to note some intellectual shifts in relation to how jazz was valued in middle- and upper-class African American circles during the 1940s and 1950s. This shift can most simply be described as a "warming" to jazz and seems to have arisen out of two linked societal changes. The first was that musical developments in jazz during the 1930s and 1940s appeared to debunk many aspects of the popular "primitivist" myth, affirming instead an inherent modernism in jazz more suitable to the ideological outlook of New Negro adherents.[2] The development of bebop in particular served as a striking example of how jazz music might transform in complexity, and while many felt the bebop genre was no less demonstrative than the sort of "Hot" jazz Abbott decried in the pages of the *Defender* during the 1930s, the very fact of its transformation stood as reason enough in the

African American press for it to be celebrated as a milestone in African American cultural development.[3]

The second issue that seemingly played a part in shifting the opinion of the African American middle and upper class was the increasingly overt role jazz musicians and ensembles played in the broader struggle for equal rights. Indeed, increased coverage of jazz music in African American periodicals seemed to go hand in hand with reports on the difficulties African Americans faced in terms of negotiating segregated seating policies, access to performance venues, and access to accommodation. Often, both musical and political commentary were rolled together in these accounts. The *New York Age*'s reporting on Louis Armstrong and Bennie Goodman's April 17, 1953, Carnegie Hall concert, for instance, provides lengthy descriptions of the musical innovations attributed to each performer before transitioning to a description of Goodman's role in leading the charge for integrated jazz orchestras ("Goodman-Armstrong Team" 1953, 12). Coverage of the Jazz at the Philharmonic tour in the same year is similarly structured, speaking to the diverse lineup of musicians before embarking on a discussion of how the tour represented a "triumph over the forces of bigotry throughout the country, and the world" ("Granz' 'JATP' Swings" 1953, 19).

In some cases, the sort of cultural work toward integration achieved by jazz ensembles was cast as being even more effective than the political action undertaken by African American civil rights leaders. In a critique of the "top down" model of leadership that characterized the civil rights struggle of the early 1950s, Mary Bethune of the *Defender* ventured the opinion that perhaps better role models could be found in the jazz realm, singling out Lionel Hampton in particular as someone "alive to progress, and alert to the needs of the people of which he is a part. He has his finger on the pulse of the plain people—and most of us are plain people" (1950, 6). A similar notion forms the cornerstone of a 1954 "Simple Says" column written by Langston Hughes for the *Defender* in which Hughes humorously skewers the high-minded intellectual discourse of an imaginary "Race Relations Seminar" by suggesting that the seminar might have worked better if it had incorporated a jazz band into the program:

> With a jazz band, they could work out integration in ten minutes. Everybody would have been dancing together like they do at the

> Savoy—colored and white—or down on the East Side at them Casinos on a Friday night where jam holds forth—and you would have been integrated. (1954, 9)

Such coverage clearly denotes a change in position toward jazz music. Yet it must be acknowledged that such a change did not appear to signal a dramatic shift in respectability ideals. Rather, the growing endorsement of jazz in the African American press seems to have stemmed from a renewed understanding about the meaning of jazz music itself. Evolution in musical style and jazz's demonstrated success in facilitating integration erased (or at least minimized) notions of jazz's backwardness or "primitive" nature in these outlets, allowing the musical genre to be newly interpreted as a valuable and sophisticated cultural product.

Lewis's music in particular played well into this new understanding as its sonic brand audibly linked to the Westernized spiritual approach and the syncretic concert work approach endorsed by the African American press during the 1920s and 1930s. Indeed, coverage of African American spiritual groups based on the Fisk Jubilee model and the orchestral works of Still and Dawson seems to have set in place a way of talking about modern African American music ripe for describing Lewis's works. In particular, the manner in which reviews of these earlier innovations walked a tightrope between acknowledging folk roots and celebrating new sonic components linked to notions of "cerebrality" and refinement appeared, to many, directly applicable. The *Atlanta Daily World*, for instance, highlighted both the MJQ's popularity among "jazz lovers" and its "unique combination of compositional skill, instrumental technique and musical direction"—three qualities easily grouped under the idea of musical control—in its coverage of an upcoming MJQ concert at Morehouse College ("Modern Jazz Quartet Here Saturday" 1959, 3). In the lead-up to a performance at Orchestra Hall in Chicago, Bob Hunter of the *Defender* would in turn speak to the group's improvisatory foundations before applauding it for being able to "control . . . all its [jazz's] wildness" (1962, 10). Likewise, in its coverage of the opening night of the 1964 UCLA jazz series, the *Los Angeles Times* wrote of the group's "improvisatory freedom" and "earthiness" as part of a paradoxical style that also included "finesse, precision and logic" (Clar 1964, C15), terms nearly identical to those Work used in his description of the Fisk Jubilee Singers' "finish, precision and sincerity" ([1940] 1998, 15). On the surface, such a reception does not appear markedly different from comments made about the group in the jazz press and mainstream newspapers. Ascriptions of intelligence and control abound in both sets of publications and there is no shortage in either of comments supportive of the group's more "provincial" improvisatory elements.

Yet there does exist a notable difference between these sets of publications in terms of how the significance of Lewis's innovations was interpreted. As I discuss in chapter 2, Lewis's use of Western art music compositional devices and his pursuit of a nondemonstrative performance aesthetic led many reviewers to conceptualize his music as a departure from the realm of African American expression. The newness of such an approach would lead many to venture the notion that a novel style of music was being forged between European and African American cultural realms and that while this style of music was indebted to both cultural arenas, it belonged fully to neither. Such debates are largely absent from the coverage Lewis's music received in the African American press. That is to say, while Lewis's syncretic projects were closely followed in these publications, they were not showcased as breaks with tradition as they were in the jazz press. The *Defender's* coverage of Lewis's Parisian ballet project *The Comedy* in 1960, for instance, details the work's basis on the improvisational practices of the commedia dell'arte without ever suggesting that such a basis might be considered problematic ("Modern Jazz Quartet Wins Acclaim" 1960, A17). *Down Beat's* coverage of the same project, in contrast, uses as its focal point the debate about how some had viewed "the ballet-like dance" as having "little to do with jazz" ("Precious Asset" 1960, 9). The *New York Amsterdam News*'s coverage of the MJQ's participation in a music series at Town Hall titled "The Symbolic Sound of Impressionism" in turn would laud Lewis's score for the film *Sait-on jamais* (1957) for bearing a "striking similarity in both tone-coloring and tone picturing" to the "impressionist music of 19th Century France." These comments were placed alongside coverage of the MJQ's receipt of a National Association for the Advancement of Colored People award for "cultural contributions in the field of music" ("Music for Moderns" 1957, 13). *New York Times* coverage of the same work, in contrast, focused on the music's "borderline" stylistic status and took place underneath the headline "Serious or Jazz?" (Wilson 1958b, X12).

It is of course understandable that the jazz press and jazz reporters for the *New York Times* would be primarily concerned with matters related to musical developments within the *jazz* genre. Yet the conclusions of these critics—their idea that if Lewis's work wasn't jazz, it was either a part of the European musical tradition or part of a brand-new American musical tradition taking shape under the Third Stream banner—seems to have missed an opportunity to read the music as part of African American music-making traditions that had long embraced Western art music aesthetics. In other words, the apparent novelty of Third Stream music, a novelty evident in jazz critics' descriptions of it as a "developing" music (Wilson 1958b, X12) or as a "brand of music . . . whose name we know not, whose form we are just making" (O'Connor 1957, 18) seems to overstate the case when one considers the legacy of syncretic spiritual traditions and syncretic orchestral works composed by African Americans in preceding years. There are, of course, plenty of asides to syncretic precedents in the jazz realm in discussions of Third Stream music. The extended works of Duke Ellington, for instance, are mentioned by Wilson (1961, X16) as direct precursors to the works presented on Lewis's recording *The Modern Jazz Quartet and Orchestra* (1961), and both Ellington and James P. Johnson are credited as forebears to what Charles Smith (1959, 39) referred to in *Down Beat* as a "burgeoning of composition in jazz" taking place in 1959. Yet even in these discussions the framing of Ellington and Johnson as "pioneers" belies a hesitancy to read facility or interest in Western art music conventions as something commonplace within the African American middle-class experience.[4]

Given the African American press's extensive documentation of African American stewardship and engagement with Western art music in the preceding years, it is unsurprising to note that these publications viewed Lewis's work through a different lens. In particular, the rhetoric of novelty is stripped out of assessments of Lewis's career published during the 1950s and early 1960s. Consider, for example, the reporting on the diversity of recording projects Lewis both supervised and took part in as an A&R man for Atlantic Records, published in the *New York Amsterdam News* in 1962:

> Lewis has already begun recording a new series of albums in various parts of the world. The series will include all kinds of music. On a trip to Europe Lewis supervised recording dates in several countries.

> In Stockholm, Sweden, he produced an album in which he also appears as a performer with the Swedish violinist Svend Asmussen. The album, which will be released in the fall, is entitled "European Encounter."
>
> In Milan Italy, Lewis recorded a modern classical chamber work, the "Five Movements for String Quartet, Opus 5," by Anton Webern, with the well-known Italian string quartet, Quartetto Di Milano.
>
> Lewis also recorded extensively in Germany. In Baden-Baden, he supervised an album with Albert Mangelsdorf, the most famous, and reputed to be, the best jazz trombonist in Europe. Lewis played piano in this album. ("Atlantic Records" 1962, 22)

Missing in this account is the editorializing that so persistently followed Lewis in the jazz press—the constant interrogation of what Lewis was doing and how well he was doing it. In its place we find instead a matter-of-fact description of Lewis's achievements in his new role. His suitability to oversee the range of projects described is not explicitly set out, and this, in fact, is the point of difference between the trade press and the African American press. African American involvement with Western art music like Webern's String Quartet was not a remarkable event for those contributing to the *New York Amsterdam News*. Therefore, Lewis's involvement with the work did not require special explanation.

A similar ideology surrounds Harold Keith's review of the MJQ's *Sait-on jamais* recording, published in the *Pittsburgh Courier* in 1958. In contrast to Wilson's (1958b) assessment of the music underneath the heading "Serious or Jazz?," Keith's review of the work avoids any attempt to make sense of the score's apparent Western art music bent, choosing instead to simply document what he views as its sonic success. Keith begins his report without proviso, writing,

> [The] MJQ's latest release for Atlantic can be labeled as an unqualified triumph. The LP disc, based upon the original writings of pianist John Lewis, presents a magnificence of composition which has, in its swath, captured all of the lace and fluidic beauty of Venice, one of the most beautiful cities in the world. (1958, 16)

Keith goes on to mention the "grace and tragic pageantry" of the work "Cortege" and the "beautiful pictorialization of [the character] Sophie" in the work "One Never Knows," drawing on the language of musical "respectability." Yet Keith avoids mention of the work's significance in terms of a larger musical movement or, in fact, of its similarities to any parallel European aesthetic paradigms. Indeed, beyond the mention of Venice, no other references are made to either Europe in general or to compositional conventions normally associated with Western art music. A similar critical approach is used in a retrospective article on the MJQ run in the *Defender* in 1963 in which the language of musical "control" abounds but no direct links to Western art music or the Third Stream movement are made ("Modern Jazz Quartet Top Unit" 1963, 29). In fact, across the publications the *Chicago Defender*, the *New York Amsterdam News*, the *Pittsburgh Courier*, the *Los Angeles Times*, and the *Atlanta Daily World*, no mention of the term *Third Stream* in connection with Lewis or the MJQ appears to have been made at all between the term's emergence in 1957 and the group's ten-year anniversary celebrated by the *Pittsburgh Courier* in 1965.

It therefore seems safe to assume that in the eyes of the African American press, Lewis's engagement with Western art music did not evince a groundbreaking move toward a new musical ideology. And when one examines the history of music making in middle- and upper-class African American communities during the first half of the twentieth century, it becomes clear why. For at least seventy years before the formation of the MJQ, a tradition of weaving folk and classical musical styles together had existed within the realm of the African American spiritual and the concert works authored by Burleigh, Dett, Still, Dawson, and Price. Such an approach found its rationale in what Higginbotham (1993) refers to as the "politics of respectability" and what Baldwin (2007, 30) refers to as "old settler ideology"—aligned political mind-sets in which the capacity for self-determination was felt best demonstrated through the mastery of hegemonic cultural practices. The musical side of these politics, embodied in syncretic works, would find additional purchase in the continued support for a musical social world organized around the performance of canonical works of Western art music. Lewis's music was an exceptionally good aesthetic fit within this paradigm, as it capitalized on growing interest in modern jazz music emerging in middle- and upper-class African American circles while simultaneously adhering to the rules of sonic decorum well entrenched in the ideology of respectability.

What then might an awareness of this orientation mean for the way in which we interpret the mechanics of Lewis's music? It seems to me that the views of middle- and upper-class African Americans toward Western art music during the 1950s hold a good degree of relevance in terms of how we might read the intent of Western art music conventions such as fugal processes, suite formats, composed contrapuntal passages, and the like in Lewis's work. In chapter 1 I suggested that when we view these compositional elements in connection with Lewis's attempts to reach or build new jazz audiences, they might be conceptualized as part of a double-voiced compositional strategy in which those unfamiliar with the jazz genre were introduced to it through the use of more familiar sonorities. This same mode of thinking in part helps explain the way Lewis's works may have functioned in relation to the experiences and musical tastes of middle- and upper-class African Americans. The development of modern jazz styles in which "provincial" elements were embedded within "intellectual" frames led to a renewed (or brand-new) appreciation for jazz within this demographic, and Lewis's works can undoubtedly be read as part of this trend.

Yet we might also think of Lewis's use of Western art music conventions as emerging from the experience of being part of the African American middle class. Raised in Albuquerque by a grandfather who was a small business owner (Balliett 1971, 176), Lewis' childhood contained all of the hallmarks of middle-class life set out in the African American press. He was trained in the performance of classical piano from a young age, studying privately until the age of twenty-two, when he left home to join the army (Lyons 1983, 77). His family were members of the Methodist Church—an affiliation he would later paint in contrast to the more demonstrative Pentecostal Church in Albuquerque (Holley 2000, 40)—and his educational pursuits mirrored those applauded by the African American elite. Turning away from the pressure to study dentistry imposed by a family friend, Lewis enrolled in arts and science classes at the University of New Mexico in 1940 before being drafted into World War II in 1942 (Lalo 1991, 15; Lyons 1983, 77). Upon his return in 1944, he confirmed his commitment to a liberal arts education by enrolling with an anthropology and music double major (Balliett 1971, 176). Years later Lewis would confirm the effects of this middle-class journey on his appreciation for classical music, claiming,

> Classical music is something you do because you're a middle class person. At least, that was the case where I lived and grew up with my family. Which I loved dearly; it was great to be exposed to as much as possible. ("MJQ Views" 1987, 28)

This spectrum of experiences seems to beg for a reading of Lewis's music that takes into account the larger story of African American middle-class music making.

In the following chapter I therefore seek to tell multiple stories about how the compositional design of Lewis's works might be understood within the context of various African American music-making traditions. On one level I explore the compositional implications of a double-voiced recruitment agenda evident in works produced across Lewis's first decade of ensemble leadership. I support this position by asking the reader to consider the context of these works' performance, the sorts of audiences in attendance and the works' paratextual frames. Yet at the same time I endeavor to show that many of Lewis's musical decisions seemed to be driven by a fascination with Western art music born out of his Western art music training in the United States and his relationship with jazz modernists both at home and abroad. In other words, even when a double-voiced intent might be identified in Lewis's work, one can easily point to other forces surrounding him that may have had an equal impact on his aesthetic decisions. As I discuss in this chapter, being guided by such forces is not a uniquely "white" phenomenon. A proud legacy of African American stewardship and engagement with Western art music apart from double-voiced syncretic works exists, and Lewis's music can just as easily be understood as an extension of this tradition. It is not my intent in making this claim to argue that such a tradition functioned entirely separately from the musical traditions of the white hegemony. Indeed, as the movement toward integrated orchestras shows, considerable overlap and line blurring can undoubtedly be seen to occur between the two. My intent in pointing to African American stewardship and feelings of ownership around Western art music is simply to take some steps toward eroding notions of aesthetic ownership based on race alone while at the same time finding a way to honor notions of tradition as they may have been experienced within a particular historical moment. Ideas about tradition are powerful and valuable but they are not universally felt, and it is the acknowledgment of this diversity that positions us the best for understanding the ways in which Lewis's works functioned within the complex landscape of ideas about culture that defined 1950s America.

4 • Composition in Context

Lewis and the MJQ, 1952–62

The central compositional vehicle for Lewis's musical vision during the 1950s was a quartet composed of vibraphone, bass, drums, and piano. Breaking with industry norms, the group set out not under Lewis's name, but under a title that pointed directly to the innovative style of music the four members were committed to exploring—it was to be a Modern Jazz Quartet in both name and mission.

Although the group officially formed in 1952, its origins can be seen to extend back to Lewis's first major gig on the East Coast. After spending three years in the army—two of which he spent playing with drummer Kenny Clarke—Lewis moved to New York in 1945 and began classes at the Manhattan School of Music while waiting out receipt of his union card. Apart from a few one-nighters in groups run by Allen Eager, Eddie Davis, and Hot Lips Page, it wasn't until Clarke's return to New York in 1946 that Lewis began participating in the jazz scene in any sort of sustained manner. The most significant development along these lines was his introduction to Dizzy Gillespie via Clarke in 1946. Gillespie hired Lewis first on a temporary basis and then, satisfied with the result of the three-month trial, asked Lewis to join up for a series of ninety one-night shows on the road beginning in September 1946 (Balliett 1971, 164). As Lewis continued to extend his tenure in the band, a small subgroup of the ensemble began to take shape, made up of Lewis on piano, Clarke on drums, Ray Brown on bass, and Milt Jackson on the vibraphone. This precursor to the MJQ would play between Gillespie's big band sets and served as a side ensemble for the musicians when the band would go on vacation (Lyons 1983, 79). Ray

Brown left the group in 1952—a result of his apparent expense, according to Lewis—and Percy Heath was brought in as the new bass player (Balliett 1971, 162). The core of the MJQ was then set, and apart from the replacement of Clarke with drummer Connie Kay in 1955, the group would remain a consistent unit for the next twenty-two years.[1]

There must have been a sense early on that the music these four (and later Kay) would play together was going to be different. As Lewis reflected years later, "There were things wrong in the music around us that we all agreed on, and some of them were long, long solos and that formula on a tune of everybody playing the melody in the first chorus, followed by a string of solos, and then the melody again" (Balliett 1971, 162). Even before the quartet was established, Lewis had begun exploring solutions to this problem through his arrangement efforts. His works for Gillespie seemed more structured than others in the ensemble book and he had played a central role in crafting the *Birth of the Cool* recordings.

In this chapter I turn my focus directly to what it was that made Lewis's compositional approach unique. While part of such a project requires the documentation of specific aspects of Lewis's compositional style, I also endeavor in the following pages to interpret the design of these works in relation to the messy and paradox-ridden historical context from which they emerged. One focal point of my analysis is therefore the manner in which many of Lewis's compositions from the 1950s and early 1960s responded to the economic pressures detailed in chapter 1 by leading new audiences into an appreciation of jazz. Indeed, throughout this historic period Lewis can be seen to have reinvented hegemonic conventions through the clever deployment of vernacular devices—a compositional approach ripe for double-voiced analysis. This musical play often began with the evocation of Western art music, usually through a combination of the use of straight rhythmic time, melodies devoid of blues sonorities, fanfares, composed counterpoint, and composition titles referring to European forms (or simply to European locales). These expectations were then teased in a myriad of ways, including the introduction of blues sonorities into composed counterpoint, the use of improvised counterpoint, the use of improvisation to meet relevant Western art music criteria in the exposition and episode sections of "fugues," and the reinterpretation of formal strictures implied by multimovement formats on the basis of folk conventions. This mimicry of Western art music through the innovative implementation of what many considered to be vernacular devices effectively packaged "new" material in the shell of the familiar as Lewis strove to locate and recruit audience members from the Western art music world.

Yet at the same time, many of Lewis's compositional innovations appear to have arisen out of a modernist mind-set that transcended the paradigm of subversion. Or more to the point, Lewis's modernist sensibilities seemed to simultaneously advance notions of African American musical identity not solely focused on the preservation of the folk. So while on one hand we can view Lewis's compositions as leading Western art music patrons into an appreciation of jazz, on the other we can view them as operating within a more standardized model of musical modernism. In other words, Lewis's syncretic compositions can also be understood as expressing a unique vision of a desired future musical landscape, and the fact that such a vision overlapped in many ways with the syncretic ideas of African American composers such as R. Nathaniel Dett and William Grant Still allows us to continue to interpret them within notions of African-American musical tradition.

Considering both versions of compositional intent together is not, as it might first seem, an impossible task. In his exploration of the same musical period, Guthrie Ramsey introduces the term *Afro-modernism* as a way of focusing on two key questions: "What was modernity to African Americans at the historical moment under consideration? How were their attitudes to it worked out artistically and critically?" (2003, 97). In relation to Lewis, there are no easy answers to these questions. Given Lewis's background as a member of the African American middle class steeped in classical music training as well as a pianist fascinated by and active in the New York jazz scene, it seems likely that multiple conceptions of musical progress may have been at play in the compositional design of his works. Discussing these different conceptions simultaneously allows us to unpack in an honest way possible pluralities of mind, and only through this acknowledgement of paradox can we begin to chip away at the relationship between Lewis's works and the complex historical moment from which they emerged.

Furthermore, my discussion of Western art music conventions in Lewis's oeuvre also focuses on how Lewis engages with and explores Western art conventions in a celebratory manner. Of particular interest in this regard is Lewis's exploration of commedia dell'arte characters—extending from his 1956 work *Fontessa* to his 1960 album *The Comedy*—and his pursuit of increasingly diverse instrumental ensembles during the latter part of the 1950s. These musical pursuits cannot be separated out in every case from what I have deemed to be a recruitment agenda or a development of New Negro compositional ideology, but at the same time they should not be read entirely within these contexts. As I explain in the second half of this chapter, Lewis's musical training and relationship with European modernists exhibited influence on his compositional process in a manner not always easily tied to subversive or assimilationist uplift strategy. Indeed, given the different cultural landscape of jazz scenes in postwar France and Germany, it is possible to read many of Lewis's works performed in these contexts as responding to existing notions of modern jazz espoused by European critics and musicians rather than engaging with American racial politics. I do not mean to suggest that these narratives are not tightly woven together. I simply aim to point out that reading this material as celebratory rather than subversive helps in understanding the global dimension of Lewis's compositional voice.

An investigation into such phenomena is of course not without its limitations, and it should be expressed at the outset that the analyses in this book are concerned with works produced by Lewis in connection with the MJQ, as well as other ensembles, during the first decade of his ensemble leadership only (1952–62). The limitation of my analysis to this decade arises as a condition of what DeVeaux might refer to as the moment's historical particularities. The economic and social pressures that shaped various conceptions of jazz during the 1950s and that I survey in the first three chapters of this book were undoubtedly unique. And while several shifts in the aesthetics of jazz music did occur within the first ten years of Lewis's ensemble leadership, a major conceptual change in the jazz world as a whole would not be seen until the emergence of the Black Arts movement of the early 1960s. It is this latter fact that makes it impossible to incorporate Lewis's later 1960s works into the same conceptual paradigm used to examine his 1950s oeuvre.

As Paul Lopes (2002) explains, a broad embrace of "Black Nationalism" intrinsically linked to the energy of the civil rights movement during the early 1960s added a further layer of tension surrounding what might constitute "real" black music. In musical terms, many in the jazz art world lived out this political ideology by overtly embracing African American folk tropes, a move that effectively positioned "Cool" and "Third Stream" artists firmly against the wall (Lopes 2002, 251). In part, this "blues-heavy" approach can be linked to what Omi and Winant have described as the "rearticulation of black collective subjectivity," an ideological shift in the civil rights movement that encouraged the idea of African American collective identity, thus contrasting with the dominant civil rights paradigm of the 1950s in which "race-thinking" was viewed as working against equality (1994, 96–100). While one decade of output may seem a somewhat arbitrary limitation to place on the study of such an important phenomenon, the increasing militancy of the Black Power movement in the years immediately preceding the passage of the Civil Rights Act by the U.S. Congress in 1964 (Haines 1984, 38) and its residual impact on the jazz art world (Hersch 1996, 117) make it difficult to discuss the meaning(s) of Lewis's syncretic works produced throughout the 1960s without including a lengthy exploration of the radically new social and political landscape. Such investigation would, however, form a natural extension of the arguments put forth in this book.

Ambiguity and Difference in Lewis's Early Works, 1952–56

As discussed in chapter 1, Lewis and the MJQ made their first commercial recording in 1952 for the record label Prestige. The session tracks included two jazz standards, "All the Things You Are" (1939) by Jerome Kern and "Rose of the Rio Grande" (1922) by Harry Warren, as well as two of Lewis's own compositions, "La Ronde" (1952) and "Vendome" (1952). The subsequent marketing of these tracks involved two initial 78-rpm releases. The first was issued with "All the Things You Are" on the A-side and "La Ronde" on the B-side and the second with "Vendome" on the A-side and "Rose of the Rio Grande" on the B-side. All four tracks cut on the December 22, 1952, recording date were then rereleased on Prestige LP 7059 under the title *Modern Jazz Quartet with Milt Jackson* in 1953.

Lewis's syncretic approach in relation to the jazz standards recorded in December 1952 is most obvious in his treatment of the "heads," defined here as the amalgamated unit of the work's main themes and underlying harmonic form. The convention of beginning a work by playing through the head and then transitioning to an open improvisatory section before returning to a statement of the main theme defined much of the bebop-era approach to performance (DeVeaux 1997, 203). Lewis's use of an asymmetrical seven-bar introduction to "All the Things You Are," which paired cymbal rolls and bass ostinato with a fragmented melody, as well as the composed contrapuntal line played by the bass and piano underneath the vibraphone's initial thematic statement on "Rose of the Rio Grande," set these works apart from the bebop norm from the outset—although not so far apart as to make their relationship unrecognizable.[2]

Lewis's original compositions, however, would go further. The 1952 recording of "Vendome" in particular is notable in this regard, as it employs fugal gestures, a facet of the work Lewis would highlight in notes provided to Hentoff in 1954 in advance of Hentoff's Counterpoint columns discussed in chapter 2 (Hentoff 1954b). Thomas Owens's analysis of the work describes its adherence to fugal conventions in terms of its bona-fide fugal exposition "based on a neo-Baroque subject . . . answered in the dominant" (1976, 26). This exposition is followed by what both Hentoff and Owens refer to as improvised "episodes," and the alternation of composed thematic statements based on the exposition with these subsequent episodes form the structure of the work. This structure, in turn, directly reflects common Western art music expectations regarding what fugal process entails.[3]

Yet "Vendome" embraces adherence to Western fugal processes in a subtler way as well through its employment of modulatory passages within episodes. Paul Walker has pointed to modulation within episodes as a conventional aspect of Western art music fugal writing (Walker 2010, ¶1), and table C in appendix A chart out these harmonic shifts within the episodes of the work. Each exposition is prepared by a modulatory passage embedded within an improvisatory episode and all expositions following the initial opening demonstrate a change in tonality from the immediately preceding exposition. Taken together with the use of fugal subjects and answers in Lewis's expositions, extensive preplanning seems to permeate "Vendome."

Still, without an extant score, it is frustratingly difficult to determine the extent of written or preplanned melodic parts composed for individual members of the quartet—and this ambiguity seems largely the point of the work. Obviously the thematic content of the piece was composed, and other moments of preplanning might be discerned in relation to unison melodies, repeated contrapuntal lines, and melodic interplay in transitional or bridging passages. Yet the preplanning of many other melodic moments remains unclear. Consider, for example, the independent contrapuntal line Lewis plays behind Jackson's improvised solo in the third episode of "Vendome." Its straight-time feel and the fact that it facilitates a modulation from E minor to G major draws it out of the ensemble texture, reminding the listener of the contrapuntal effects that determine the character of the expositions. At the same time, it grows naturally out of Lewis's chordal comping during the first part of Jackson's solo, leading the listener to hear it as part of an improvisatory accompaniment. When one considers the expansion goals I discuss in chapter 1, this tension might be seen as driving a double-voiced design. By performing improvised parts in a manner that sounds composed or by doing the opposite, performing composed parts in a manner that sounds improvised, Lewis is able to infuse his work with perpetual questions about where improvisation and preplanning/composition begin and end. These questions lead members of both jazz and Western art music audiences into a discussion about unfamiliar conventions, and in this way, the work achieves a didactic goal.[4]

Such didactic ambiguity can in turn be discerned across much of Lewis's output from the early 1950s. For instance, on June 25, 1953, six months after their first recording session, the MJQ recorded another four tracks for Prestige. Again the session included two jazz standards, "Autumn in New York" (1934) by Vernon Duke and "But Not for Me" (1930) by George Gershwin, as well as two of Lewis's own compositions, "Delaunay's Dilemma" (1953) and "The Queen's Fancy" (1953). As with the group's approach in 1952, the tracks were released as double-sided 78-rpm singles before being incorporated into the multitrack LP *Modern Jazz Quartet with Milt Jackson*.[5] Composed and improvised counterpoint feature prominently on these sides, and the ability of these features to conjure Western art music associations is evident in the album's critical reception. As Hentoff wrote for *Down Beat*,

> Lewis' writing is of a charm, meaningful direction, and spare unpretentiousness. There is also a quiet humor as in *Vendome* and *The Queen's Fancy* which bring to mind an 18th century cat, time-machined to now, and wailing on a sunny morning in May. (Hentoff 1953b, 16)

The pairing of "The Queen's Fancy" and "But Not for Me" on one of the initial double-sided singles from this date echoes the blurring of composed and improvised contrapuntal lines discussed in relation to "Vendome" above. Located on the A-side of the record, "The Queen's Fancy" introduces a Western art music expectation from the start by beginning with a straight-time fanfare (example 4.1) before transitioning to a contrapuntal passage in which thematic statements are offset against each other (example 4.2).

Example 4.1. "The Queen's Fancy" (1953). Prestige LP 7057. Fanfare, mm. 1–5. Transcription.

Straight-time and preplanned contrapuntal passages are then compartmentalized, bracketing improvisatory passages and signaling a division between what might be seen as the work's Western and non-Western sides (see appendix A, table D). Yet the B-side of the recording, Lewis's arrangement of "But Not for Me," complicates the symbolic role of juxtaposed melodies in "The Queen's Fancy" by utilizing contrapuntal lines colored by blues sonorities as backings to improvised passages (example 4.3). The most obvious example of this can be seen in the third measure of Milt Jackson's solo, transcribed in example 4.3, where the piano employs both pendular thirds and a flat seventh over the E♭ harmony.

Example 4.2. "The Queen's Fancy" (1953). Prestige LP 7057. Offset thematic statements, mm. 14–19. Transcription.

Example 4.3. "But Not for Me" (1930) [1953]. Prestige LP 7057. Improvised counterpoint, mm. 91–97. Transcription.

In connection with the scored counterpoint of "The Queen's Fancy," the likely improvisatory genesis of Lewis's contrapuntal lines and their "bluesy" content in "But Not for Me" reveal much about the function of counterpoint in Lewis's oeuvre. For instance, it is easy to hear both sides of the release as "contrapuntal" and even as "contrapuntal" in a fairly similar way—as utilizing clear melodic lines structured into phrases and then juxtaposed against each other. From this perspective, the sonic effects of composed and improvised counterpoint blur across the sides of the 78-rpm single. Yet at the same time these effects are made distinct through the unique application of rhythmic effects (straight time vs. swing time) and their melodic design (strictly diatonic vs. blues inflected). Such celebration of difference allows for counterpoint to form a bridge between stylistic realms while not obliterating all that has been deemed to be unique about these realms. Therefore, the simultaneous blurring and reifying of boundaries in these works enables listeners to hear in general terms both Western and non-Western musical worlds even though the limits of where, exactly, one begins and one ends remain unclear.[6]

Such plurality of musical difference undoubtedly underpinned the acclaim and professional momentum the group would experience following the 1953 recording session. Indeed, the MJQ's access to jazz venues rose upon the release of these recordings, with 1953 and 1954 seeing a good deal of performances by the group on both the East and West Coasts of the United States. The MJQ's first major booking at Birdland in New York during October 1953 gave way to engagements in Boston, San Francisco, Los Angeles, and Philadelphia (Giddins 1998, 384). Yet despite an obvious desire by venue owners to book the group, jazz club audiences were slow to respond positively to the MJQ's music. Heath's recollections of the group's 1954 Birdland residency discussed in chapter 1, in which audience chatter more than once forced the group to simply get up and walk off the stage, indicates the difficulty Lewis and the MJQ faced in connecting with jazz fans—at least within the context of jazz clubs. Yet Lewis remained undeterred and would continue to introduce syncretic works into the group's repertoire over the coming year.

Indeed, such an approach appears to have undergone considerable development in advance of the MJQ's next recording for Prestige, made on December 23, 1954, and January 9, 1955. In particular, the manner in which conventional jazz practices and references to Western art music are integrated in the "La Ronde Suite" and "Django" (two works from the resulting LP, *Modern Jazz Quartet Volume 2*) demonstrate new sorts of experimentation with musical form. Specifically, there seems to be an increased interest in these works in how formal structures normally associated with jazz might be caged within references to Western art music. The 1955 recording of the "La Ronde Suite" accomplishes this goal by utilizing the multimovement expectation induced by the term *suite* to present a series of variations on the 1952 "La Ronde" form (see appendix A, table E). Each movement in the "La Ronde Suite" is therefore roughly similar in structural design to the 1952 model, utilizing alternations in tempo and featured soloists as a means of creating diversity (see appendix A, tables F.1–F.4). Embedded within these movements are extended improvisatory passages that occur over a twelve-bar blues. While the blues form itself is not modified to invoke Western art music alignment, its use across the movements, grouped by the term *suite*, creates a dialogue with Western art music at the macro level. In other words, there is undoubtedly a degree of semantic play going on here. Despite its name, the "La Ronde Suite" can essentially be understood in analytical terms as a series of twelve-bar-blues showcases, evincing an overt attempt to use a formal convention from the jazz realm to articulate a Western art music concept.

Lewis's "Django" focuses on a different formal aspect of jazz practice—the use of vamps—and sets this convention side by side with a chromatically shifting chord progression emulating facets of European guitarist Django Reinhardt's style. Givan identifies the latter as consisting, in part, of harmonic modulations "partially driven by the use of strict motivic transposition" (2010, 146), and an examination of the opening bars of Lewis's "Django" reveals a similar process at play, with a motive repeated four times over the course of nine measures and the tonicization of both chords iv and III by way of secondary dominants.

The chromaticism of this opening is then echoed in the chord changes upon which Lewis and Jackson solo, and the improvisatory passages that outline these modulations may be understood as an initial level of syncretism in the work. Yet a stronger moment of dialogue between musical genres can be found in an embedded four measure repeated vamp on the chords G♭7 and D♭7 during which Heath performs the following bass line (example 4.4).

Example 4.4. "Django" (1954). Prestige LP 7057. Bass line over four-measure vamp, mm. 45–48. Transcription.

The prominence of the flat seventh in the riff and what could be construed as a IV–I chord choice given the modulatory nature of the work echoes gospel and R&B organizational practices. Indeed, such "plagal" gestures form a central part of Kernfeld's (2002, 635) understanding of the connection between the two styles. Positioning this section against the bulk of the "Django" aesthetic can therefore be seen as framing the sort of repetition viewed in chapter 2 as an essential part of African American music within the chromaticism of an individual style of jazz invented off the American continent.

On the one hand, Lewis's study of Reinhardt certainly constitutes homage, as the use of strict motivic transposition presented underneath Reinhardt's name undoubtedly aims to celebrate the guitarist's unique musical approach. Yet in connection with the semantic play of the "La Ronde Suite," the embedded use of the plagal vamp seems to indicate a simultaneous desire to create a work that adds up to more than the sum of its parts. Indeed, in some ways the vamp has the effect of "Americanizing" the "Django" aesthetic, or at least of bringing into relief the difference between the style of Django Reinhardt and those essentialized elements of jazz discussed in chapter 2. While discerning which intent sat more prominently in Lewis's mind is indeed a difficult task, there is little doubt that the work foreshadowed a clear pivot to more prominent engagement with European cultural references on the group's next album for Prestige, *Concorde* (1955).

The session tracks for *Concorde* were recorded on July 2, 1955, and again included a mix of jazz standards and originals, including a blues with a canon-like head ("Ralph's New Blues" [1955]) written by Milt Jackson and Lewis's second fugal work, from which the album takes its name. *Concorde* refers to the Place de la Concorde public square in Paris, a fact evident in the locale's sketched representation on the album cover. As a point of contrast, other jazz artists for Prestige tended to highlight individuality over place in the titles and album cover content of their 1954 and 1955 releases. Bob Weinstock's action photography of Miles Davis, Sonny Rollins, Bennie Green, and Bob Brookmeyer often captured the musicians with instruments poised at their lips, positioned in front of microphones. These images then served as backdrops for album covers with self-referential titles such as *Miles Davis All Start Sextet* (1954), *Sonny Rollins and Thelonious Monk* (1954), *Bennie Green Blows His Horn* (1955), and *The Dual Role of Bob Brookmeyer* (1955). The absence of the MJQ from the *Concorde* album cover, the depiction of the Place de la Concorde, and the decision to go with a non-self-referential title positioned the album against the bulk of Prestige releases, setting the group apart from other jazz artists in a way that echoed Lewis's move toward "modern music" venues during the same year.[7]

The recording was also unique in that it marked a change in the group's personnel. Kenny Clarke, whose connection to Lewis extended back to their time in Dizzy Gillespie's big band, decided to leave the group in February 1955 (Giddins 1998, 385). Clarke's ability to improvise had been highlighted extensively in the works Lewis composed—most notably on "La Ronde" and the "La Ronde Suite"—yet his replacement, Connie Kay, was admittedly averse to the practice. As Kay explained to Whitney Balliett in 1971, "I don't like to take drum solos at all. Drums are a flat instrument. . . . I know how I feel when other drummers solo. It seems like you've heard them all before" (qtd. in Balliett 1971, 167). In addition to this alternate view on improvisation, Kay produced a very different sound on the instrument. While Clarke's performance practice had derived from the effusive rhythmic accompaniment of the bebop era, Kay showed an interest in the clarity of individual sounds, eventually emerging as "an adept colorist . . . seated behind an array of drums, chimes, triangles, and cymbals" (Giddins 1998, 386).

In musical terms, the ambiguous contrapuntal effects established in Lewis's earlier works once again rise prominently to the fore on this album. In addition to Lewis's polyphonic "Concorde"—the double-voiced nature of which I discuss in chapter 1—the standard "Softly as in a Morning Sunrise" (1928) by Romberg and Hammerstein is arranged with a four-bar double-time introduction in which displaced entrances of an introductory theme lead into independent contrapuntal lines before transitioning to the AABA form of the work and improvised solos backed by improvised melodic licks. The balance of independent polyphony in the opening of Jackson's "Ralph's New Blues" and the polyphonic comping behind the blues form that composes the body of the work in turn fits neatly into the blurred-lines aesthetic approach I describe in relation to the group's earlier recordings.

Yet this particular collection of works also demonstrates a break with precedent in terms of which audience Lewis would seek to engage through the deployment of these effects. As I discussed earlier, despite critical praise and successful jazz club bookings during 1954, Lewis's musical initiatives struggled to find a foothold with nightclub patrons. His foundation of the Modern Jazz Society in 1955 indicated a promotional shift aimed at addressing this problem, its declared purview enabling Lewis to highlight his music's "modernism" rather than its jazz credentials. The selection of "Concorde," "Softly as in a Morning Sunrise," and "Ralph's New Blues" as works to be performed as part of the inaugural concert program in turn indicates which works in the quartet book Lewis felt to be most emblematic of his particular modernist brand.

Selecting Town Hall as a venue for the project was, furthermore, a particularly clever move in terms of facilitating audience recruitment from beyond the jazz realm. In specific terms, the venue's historic role in bringing together both African American and white patrons of classical music would have opened the floodgates to potential recruits. As I describe in chapter 3, Town Hall held a special significance for African Americans who chose to steward and develop Western art music. The venue had been one of the few large-scale rooms open to performers such as Roland Hayes, Jules Bledsoe, and Marian Anderson in New York during the 1930s, and it had served as an important platform for interracial orchestras such as Everett Lee's Cosmopolitan Symphony Orchestra and Dean Dixon's American Youth Orchestra during the 1940s. In the months preceding the Modern Jazz Society concert, the venue had hosted the interracial New York Concert Choir (Diton 1955, 5) and the African American classical pianist Una Hadley ("Praise Goes to Town Hall Pianist" 1955, 8). Performing within this context would therefore not only have allowed Lewis's music to connect with a variety of Western art music aficionados, it would have placed it conceptually on par with other strains of modern African American music celebrated by middle-class African Americans, ranging from the arranged spirituals of R. Nathaniel Dett to the symphonic works of William Grant Still.

This purposeful framing of the MJQ as a vehicle for "modern" music in turn seems to have driven Atlantic Records to recruit the group in the same year. Giddins (1998, 386), after all, credits producer Nesuhi Ertegun for approaching the group as part of his vision to encourage "modern sounds" on the label. Their first recording for Atlantic, *Fontessa* (1956), again included a mixture of originals and jazz standards, including the works "Woody'n You" (1942) by Dizzy Gillespie, "Willow Weep for Me" (1932) by Ann Ronnell, "Angel Eyes" (1946) by Matt Dennis and Earl Brent, and "Over the Rainbow" (1939) by Harold Arlen and E. Y. Harburg. Curiously, Lewis's interpretation of the standards on this album seemed to incorporate fewer Western art music conventions than his previous arrangements while highlighting the use of blues sonorities early on, a development facilitated in part by the works' heads. Indeed, the straight-ahead arrangements of these melodies signaled a departure from many of Lewis's early arrangements of jazz standards, in which Western art music engagement was embedded into opening passages through the deployment of composed contrapuntal lines underneath themes and the use of straight rhythmic time and ostinatos.

Yet Lewis's original compositions continued to explore the contrapuntal ambiguity that was quickly becoming a signature aspect of his compositional style. Like "Concorde" and "Vendome," Lewis's "Versailles" (1956) is based on the thematic interplay of fugal processes—although in this case, appears to utilize at least some improvisation in its expositions. As Thomas Owens related in 1976, "John Lewis told me recently that the quartet worked from the written subject only; nothing else about this piece—neither its overall structure, key areas, chord progressions, nor accompanying ostinatos—was ever written down" (1976, 30). Such absence of written music, however, must not be confused with a lack of planning. For as Heath would later reflect, the contract with Atlantic brought with it a new attitude regarding preparation: "It wasn't like other record dates where you go in and the guy scratches out some chords and hands it to you at the date, like a lot of the Miles recordings. Everything was not only rehearsed, it was *refined* before we got to the studio" (qtd. in Giddins 1998, 387; emphasis in original). The fact that reconciling these two accounts (i.e., the amount of preplanned material versus the amount of improvisation in the exposition) is so challenging from the position of a blind listening makes "Versailles" one of the most successful examples of contrapuntal ambiguity in Lewis's oeuvre.[8]

Furthermore, contrapuntal ambiguity extends into the improvised episodes of the work, infusing the whole of the composition with questions about what is improvised and what is preplanned. Take, for example, the use of subject motifs played by Jackson during Lewis's solo. Like both "Vendome" and "Concorde," the work aligns the sound of independent counterpoint with Western art music practices through a fugal exposition (example 4.5) before employing it as an accompaniment feature of improvised episodes (example 4.6). Example 4.5 demonstrates how Lewis is able to infuse the fugal subject and answer with blues sonorities (pendular thirds in the first full measure of the C-major subject and F-major answer) as well as the chromatic inflection of the flat ninth, a prominent part of the jazz lexicon during the bebop era (second full measure of the C-major subject and F-major answer). Jackson's riff-like backings during Lewis's solo draw on the blues-derived flat fifth before sounding repeated subject motifs, an approach that both maintains and expands the presence of blues tropes established in the exposition. Yet because the nature of preplanning in the exposition is already unclear, the listener is left hearing such moments of repetition without a clear sense of which musical world they emerge from. In other words, if the quotation of subject motifs in "episodes" or "choruses" is just as normal in Western fugal process as it is in jazz practice (as Walker [2010], in his definition of fugal process, assures us it is), then it becomes exceedingly difficult to tell which tradition is being realized during Jackson's employment of subject quotations during Lewis's solo.

The title work, "Fontessa" (1956), in turn pursues a similar strategy, evident in how extemporizations of various themes morph into improvised solos and vice versa (see appendix A, table G). While such a practice is not at all outside the realm of standardized jazz practice, the straight-time setting of the initial "Fontessa" theme successfully alludes to Western art music. Lewis would in turn heighten this connection by explaining in the liner notes how the work's various themes were meant to conjure various figures from the "Renaissance Commedia dell'Arte" theatrical tradition. In explanation of the work's design, he writes,

> FONTESSA is a little suite inspired by the Renaissance Commedia dell'Arte. I had particularly in mind their plays which consisted of a very sketchy plot and in which the details, the lines, etc. were improvised.

Example 4.5. "Versailles" (1956). Atlantic LP 1231. Exposition, mm. 1–8. Transcription.

> This suite consists first of a short Prelude to raise the curtain and provide the theme. The first piece after the Prelude has the character of older jazz and improvised parts are by the vibraphone. This piece could perhaps be the character of Harlequin. The second piece has the character of less older jazz and the improvised parts are played by the piano. The character here could perhaps be Pierrot.
>
> The third piece is of a still later jazz character and develops the main motif. The improvised parts are by the drums. This character could perhaps be Pantaloon. The opening Prelude closes the suite.
>
> Fontessa is the three-note main motif of the suite and is perhaps a substitute for the character of Colombine. (J. Lewis 1956, 1)

These stock characters—the miserly Pantaloon (Pantalone), the astute Colombine, the mischievous Harlequin, and the naïve Pierrot—are all depicted on the cover of the *Fontessa* album. Again, determining exactly what is composed and what is improvised in relation to iterations of the themes based on these characters remains beyond the aural realm, and this gray

Example 4.6. "Versailles" (1956). Atlantic LP 1231. Thematic motif behind piano solo, mm. 25–40. Transcription.

area seems to have been pursued largely on purpose. By highlighting to an audience the idea that art from Western culture may also contain improvisatory components, Lewis effectively deepens in "Fontessa" the ambiguity between what might be seen as being linked to jazz practices in the work and what might have been seen as its "Western" components. In other words, the aural question shifts from discerning between what is improvised and what is composed to the impossible task of figuring out which aspects of improvisation draw inspiration from jazz and which aspects draw inspiration from the commedia dell'arte tradition.

The illumination of this and similar compositional strategies in the early works of Lewis's oeuvre helps flesh out in specific terms the musical mechanics driving Lewis's reception in both the jazz and the African American press. Indeed, after just this brief survey, it becomes abundantly clear why members of both camps utilized European allusions in their discussions of Lewis's music. The works themselves wear their engagement with European culture on their sleeves. Not only do they utilize French names, deploy Parisian imagery, and shout out to the commedia dell'arte as part of their paratextual frames, they span the allusory gamut of European musical styles, moving from fugues to suites to an homage to Django Reinhardt. Yet underneath these surface elements lies a more profound compositional agenda in which composed and improvised elements are woven together in such a way as to make their culture of origin unclear.

In the arena of the Modern Jazz Society concert, the sonic result of such an approach may have been interpreted in a variety of ways. To those who grew up as part of the New Negro movement, it may have signaled the subversive preservation of the folk, or an act of vernacular music uplift, as did the arranged spirituals of the previous decades. Younger African American patrons may have simply heard it as the natural sonic representation of Lewis's experience as an African American middle-class musician fusing the plurality of his musical experiences into a coherent style. And still another cohort may have heard it as an attempt to modernize the genre of classical music by infusing jazz-based improvisational practices and blues sonorities into Western forms. The ambiguity of Lewis's music—particularly that of its contrapuntal facets—lies at the heart of why it was able to speak in so many different ways, and while this may have made it difficult for music critics to pin it down in terms of intent, such flexibility would ultimately contribute to the expansion of Lewis's musical reach both at home and abroad.

An Expansion of Confidence: The MJQ's 1956 European Tour

Indeed, Lewis's early recordings with the MJQ made considerable waves in European jazz circles even before the group's first European tour took place in the fall of 1956. Lewis's "Vendome" in particular intrigued the German jazz critic Joachim Ernst Berendt, who had spent the majority of the postwar years trying to rehabilitate the image of jazz in German society. As I mention in the introduction to this book, throughout the early 1950s Berendt embraced a strategy of articulating jazz's worth by comparing its features to "serious" music. His 1955 assessment of "Vendome" in the pages of the music journal *Melos* is unambiguously made in these terms through a careful piecing together of how the work's expositions and episodes unfold. Yet Berendt seemed simultaneously aware in this assessment of the composition's didactic power—its ability to fool the listener into hearing improvisation as composition—writing, "Much of what seems obviously 'European' in the music of the Modern Jazz Quartet, was subconsciously improvised by the musicians, who—except for John Lewis himself—are dedicated to the jazz tradition alone and who do not for a single moment suspect that anything they play could be 'European'" (1955, 349).[9] Such ambivalence gave the MJQ a unique status in Berendt's mind in terms of the cultural work they could be deployed to perform within the German jazz scene, and over the next several years he would take on an active role in promoting the group through his position as jazz editor of the southwestern German radio station Südwestfunk (SWF).

Within the French context, it was Lewis's work "Milano" (recorded in 1954 for the *Concorde* album) that would strike a chord in advance of the group's arrival. André Hodeir, the famous French jazz critic and composer, would arrange and record the work with his ensemble Le Jazz Groupe de Paris in the summer of 1956. Hodeir's relationship with members of the MJQ extended back to the liberation of Paris and his befriending of the deployed Kenny Clarke during the waning months of World War II (Haggerty & Clarke 1985, 203). For nearly a decade after the war, Hodeir's interest in modern jazz (and bebop in particular) would be pursued alongside a fascination with serialism and avant-garde music, resulting in projects as diverse as his bebop collaboration with Clarke titled "Laurenzology" (1948) and his composition "Jazz et Jazz" (1952) for piano and magnetic tape, written in connection with the Groupe de Recherche de Musique Concrète (Pautrot 2006, 4–5). His establishment of Le Jazz Groupe de Paris in 1954 served to further develop his compositional palette through its purposeful emulation of the Miles Davis Nonet's aesthetic (Pautrot 2006, 6). Hodeir's arrangement of "Milano," released on the group's second album, is emblematic of this particular period, effectively draping the timbral effects conjured by Davis's ensemble over the bones of Lewis's polyphonic chart.

In contrast to Berendt's idea that the value of the MJQ's music lay (at least for Berendt's political reasons) in the echo of the Baroque, Hodeir seemed more impressed with the way in which the music played by the group signaled a progressive move into new musical territory. Although he avoided mention of the MJQ in the original publication of his *Hommes et problèmes du jazz* (1954), his revised edition, translated into English and published two years later in the United States under the title *Jazz: Its Evolution and Essence* contains a lengthy discussion of the significance of the MJQ's music. Hodeir begins this passage with a critique of Lewis's "allusions to classical and pre-classical European forms," calling out "Vendome" in particular as being "close to . . . pastiche," but then changes course, writing the passage I cite in the introduction to this book:

> Lewis' most remarkable conceptions bring into play the necessary relationship between the infrastructure and the superstructure, as well as a renewal of the spirit of collective creation that this idea implies. . . . He deserves unreserved praise for having faced up to the problem of the relationship between theme, arrangement, and solo, which is the most critical and the most formidable problem the modern jazz-man has to solve. In fact, it may be the problem on which the whole future of jazz depends. (1956a, 278)

In December 1956 Hodeir (1956b) would contribute a French version of this passage to the magazine *Jazz Hot*, building a case in France for Lewis's importance in the development of jazz as well as for the style of jazz Hodeir himself seemed interested in writing. His relationship with Lewis would in turn develop over the coming years through a series of compositional collaborations and performances aimed at transforming these ideas into sonic facts.

In October 1956 the MJQ would arrive in Europe for the first time and record a series of tracks for South German Radio (SDR) in Stuttgart. Their trip to the Continent was made possible by Norman Granz's decision to include the group as part of the Birdland All-Stars (BAS) tour (with headliners Miles Davis, Bud Powell, and Lester Young) scheduled to kick off the following month at the Salle Pleyel concert hall in Paris. Their first concert of the tour on November 2, 1956, was followed by twenty-three shows within a one-month period, taking them across France and Germany (as well as Belgium, the Netherlands, Sweden, Switzerland, Denmark, and Italy). Following the tour, the MJQ would take on their own two-week residency at the club Saint-Germaine in Paris (Lalo 1991, 69).

The recent release of five tracks recorded for SDR on October 26, 1956, reveals a great deal about Lewis's compatibility with German tastes in jazz during this period. They include two standards ("Willow Weep for Me" and "I'll Remember April"), Jackson's "Ralph's New Blues," a new arrangement of the traditional "God Rest Ye Merry Gentlemen," and Lewis's original large ensemble work "Midsömmer" (1955) (which had premiered at the Modern Jazz Society concert in 1955). Given Lewis's compositional trajectory in the U.S. context, the musical approach employed across these recording is unsurprising. The polyphonic head of "Ralph's New Blues" and the straight-time overlapping statements of the theme on "God Rest Ye Merry Gentlemen" position these works in a close conceptual relationship with "Vendome," maintaining and promoting what had become a signature element of Lewis's compositional style. Indeed, if just these two recordings are considered, it is difficult to discern any change in Lewis's approach and one might get the sense that any compatibility with Berendt's vision of what jazz art music might sound like was little more than coincidence.

Yet there is some evidence on these recordings that indicates a retooling of works toward Berendt's "serious music" ideal did take place. Consider, for instance, the striking difference between the MJQ's version of "Willow Weep for Me" made on January 22, 1956, for Atlantic and the version made on October 26, 1956, for SDR. As I stated earlier, the version of "Willow Weep for Me" recorded for the *Fontessa* album contains minimal allusion to Western art music. Blues sonorities are featured prominently from the start in Milt Jackson's interpretation of the head, and the rather straight-ahead approach to the rest of the tune sets it apart from Lewis's "augmented" standards like the 1952 version of "All the Things You Are" or the 1955 version of "Softly as in a Morning Sunrise." Lewis's backing of Jackson's interpretation of the head on the Atlantic recording is similarly straight ahead, repeating a falling major second figure (scale degrees 6-5), which is occasionally added to melodically in order to create an echo of the theme.

For the recording made for SDR, Lewis makes the small but crucial change of altering this backing figure to a falling minor second (scale degrees flat 6-5) before repeating it in various permutations against Jackson's version of the head. Lewis's insistence on this interval, the volume at which it is played, and the clashes that occur when Jackson plays scale degree 6 against Lewis's flat 6 all combine in a showcase of dissonance marking a clear departure from the aesthetic concept of Lewis's earlier arrangement.

Such showcasing of dissonance is pursued even further in Lewis's work "Midsömmer," recorded on the same date. Norman Granz commissioned "Midsömmer" in connection with "Sun Dance" (1955) for an envisioned LP of Lewis's extended compositions in advance of the 1955 Modern Jazz Society concert. It was originally scored for drums, bass, trombone, French horn, clarinet, tenor saxophone, bassoon, and harp (Hentoff 1955a, 8). The version recorded for SDR uses the Harald Banter Ensemble on the same chart while adding in Lewis and Jackson, who play short sections of improvised content in-between passages of impressionistic chordal passages voiced across the ensemble.[10] The frequent use of these nonfunctional coloristic chords makes clear allusion to French composers like Debussy and Ravel and points to an expansion of thinking around how dialogue between dissonance and consonance might be infused into Lewis's compositions. In this way, Lewis's rearrangement of "Willow Weep for Me" and his "Midsömmer" explore similar conceptual ground, using nonfunctional harmonic effects as a means of creating sonic tension and release.

Yet the significance of these recordings is in some ways less about the musical processes they document and more about what their existence tells us about German interest in these musical processes. In the U.S. context, Lewis's recordings had for the most part relied on a balance of musical components readily identifiable as jazz and compositional effects drawing on or conjuring Western art music. Even his move to Atlantic in 1956—a move supposedly aimed at ushering in a new era of modern sound on the label—continued this trajectory, pairing his extended work "Fontessa" and his fugal work "Versailles" with straight-ahead takes on jazz standards. The absence of such straight-ahead playing on the SDR recordings (only "I'll Remember April" comes close) indicates a different sort of valuation surrounding Lewis's music. In other words, out of the range of works in the quartet's book in 1956, only those clearly nodding toward Western art music were allocated tape in the group's first recording session on German soil.

Following the Birdland All-Stars tour, Lewis would go into the recording studio again, this time in Paris, to record the album *Afternoon in Paris* (1956) for the French label Versailles. The recording reunited original MJQ drummer Kenny Clarke with Lewis and bassist Percy Heath while adding into the mix French guitarist Sacha Distel and French tenor saxophonist Barney Wilen. While for the most part the tracks recorded were arranged in a way that allowed for as much blowing from Distal and Wilen as possible, elements of genre juxtaposition reminiscent of Lewis's early works can still be heard. Lewis's arrangements of the jazz standards "Willow Weep for Me" and "All the Things You Are," for instance, employ straight-time figures in their introductions. In turn, the theme of the Swedish folk song "Dear Old Stockholm" is broken up into an exchange between unaccompanied guitar, saxophone, and piano. While Distil and Wilen interpret their thematic figures in swung time, Lewis plays his section of the theme straight. Such juxtaposition allows for the simultaneous articulation of Western and non-Western rhythmic practices, indicating a degree of aesthetic similarity to the syncretic compositional practices Lewis deployed in his earlier recordings made in the United States.

Again, the musical processes documented on this album are not remarkably different from anything Lewis had done before. Yet the way such processes were received by French audiences does call for some comment. To be sure, Lewis's musical approach was not without its controversies in French jazz circles. *Jazz Magazine*'s coverage of the Birdland All-Stars tour included an article written in December 1956 that used the headline "We Pose the Question to 10 Jazzmen That Is on Everybody's Lips . . . Is the M.J.Q. Jazz?"[11] Such a controversial frame seemed at first to parallel the sentiments of the American jazz critics I survey in chapter 2. The article's follow-up questions were, however, far less contentious, indicating an apparent desire to protect the integrity of the group's artistic achievements regardless of whether the "10 jazzmen" interviewed labeled the MJQ a jazz group or not, such as: "Is it an interesting formula and valid in itself, but one which will have no impact on the evolution of jazz, like for example Django Reinhardt's string quintet?" ("Sous le signe du 'Birdland'" 1956, 21).[12] The logic of this follow-up question rested on the notion that the group's jazz credentials might to some extent be irrelevant to assessments of the group's value within the broader musical landscape. Such logic stood at odds with accusations leveled at Lewis for not being "funky enough," utilizing "too limited a range of expression," and relying "too much on fugal structures" (Hentoff 1957b, 15) in *Down Beat* three months later and led to some fascinating responses.

Most participants in the feature article—including former MJQ drummer Kenny Clarke—expressed unease with using the label *jazz* to describe the music of the MJQ.[13] Yet the majority of participants expressed general enthusiasm about the potential Lewis's approach might hold for the musical world in general—regardless of how it might eventually be labeled. Recent collaborator Sacha Distel referred to the "wonderful music" played by the group as a new musical "genre," and French pianist Henri Renaud claimed that Lewis was "making his own way" as "the only musician who [had] managed to integrate the contrapuntal language of classical music into jazz." Pianist Martial Solal, in turn, while voicing skepticism that younger jazz audiences would embrace the music of the MJQ, referred to the group as "a remarkable musical achievement." Trombonist Benny Vasseur would come out in even stronger support, describing their playing as "the music of the future" ("Sous le signe du 'Birdland'" 1956, 20–21). Certainly some members of the American jazz press would develop similar views over time, particularly in the wake of the group's follow-up European tour in the winter of 1957–58. The point here is simply to indicate that on the back of the frustrating Birdland residency of 1954—the residency that led to the formation of the Modern Jazz Society in 1955 and the Jazz and Classical Music Society in 1956—such a positive reception in Europe must have been a welcome change for the group.

If nothing else, the experience appears to have solidified for Lewis the idea that he was moving in the right direction. Knauer (1990, 48–49), for instance, writes of the impact Lewis's European reception had on the sorts of venues Lewis would seek out in the United States following his time on the Continent. Building on the venue expansion project Lewis had begun in 1955, the MJQ would recommit to seeking out the "atmosphere[s] [of] concentrated listening" (Knauer 1990, 49) they had experienced in Europe during the latter part of the decade by pursuing performances in art galleries (Wilson 1958c, 18), concert halls (Wilson 1959, 33), and contemporary arts festivals ("Arts and the MJQ" 1959, 10). Lewis would, in addition, pursue larger and larger musical projects during this period, in terms of both instrumentation and formal conception. While it is difficult to discern in these works any particular compositional devices Lewis may have "picked up" in Europe, their mere existence makes a different and, in my view, more intriguing point. It demonstrates increased confidence in the modernist project Lewis began when he formed the MJQ (regardless of whether one views Lewis's modernist bent as double-voiced or not)—a confidence derived from gaining acceptance in regions of the world where ideologies about the sort of music African American "jazzmen" might explore differed markedly from those entrenched in the United States.

Conceiving the "European" impact on Lewis in this way shifts the focus in discussions of Lewis's connection to the Continent. It allows us to break free from the tradition of parsing what Western art music conventions might be discerned in Lewis's works and instead turns our attention to how modern European culture may have affected Lewis's determination to pursue his compositional vision. The widespread endorsements of Lewis's music as something "valid in itself" in the French context, for instance, seem to have had the effect (at least temporarily) of lifting Lewis out of paradigms of comparison bound to classical music. In turn, the style of jazz art music endorsed by German jazz radio (evident in the recording session for SDR) would have reified for Lewis the idea that the jazz genre was itself malleable and that there was indeed an audience out there for the syncretic products Lewis was producing. These experiences pushed to the side questions of whether or not Lewis was a composer of "real" black music. In Europe at least, Lewis was a composer of "real" music, period, and his unique vision was welcomed.

Teaching Modernism at the Lenox School of Jazz

A parallel set of experiences seems to rest alongside Lewis's 1956 tour of the Continent in terms of building his confidence in his particular compositional approach: Lewis's involvement with the Lenox School of Jazz between 1957 and 1960. The Lenox School emerged out of the lecture series at Music Inn initiated by Marshall Stearns that I discuss in chapter 1. Lewis and the MJQ had participated in this series in the summer of 1956 and endorsed the overwhelming consensus of the attendees that the event be expanded into a summer school the following year (Wilson 1956, X9). Lewis was appointed director, and in August 1957 the Lenox School of Jazz launched its first season ("Jazz School's First Session" 1957, 13).

The ideology of the Lenox School curriculum revolved around two key ideas. The first was that formalizing jazz education was a useful thing to do. John Gennari points to coverage in the *Berkshire Eagle* advertising the school along these lines, depicting it as "the first effort to present jazz as a creative and vital art form which can be presented and taught as other art forms are taught, in a serious and vital relationship between the student and the creating artist" (qtd. in Gennari 2006, 219–20). The rough pedagogical design of the enterprise therefore mirrored that of a standard conservatorium program, employing both mentor-student pairings and sit-down classes in jazz history and composition. The content of these classes would, in turn, promote the second core idea on which the school was based—the notion that jazz was a modern and evolving music. Such an ideological bent is evident in the seminar titles alone from the school's first season. Over the course of the session, students were presented with a full evolutionary narrative of jazz, beginning with the seminar Music of Africa taught by Fela Sowande, followed by the seminar Primitive Beginnings of Jazz taught by Willis James, then Techniques in Jazz Composition, delivered by George Russell, and finally Jazz Frontiers, delivered by Bill Russo and Lennie Tristano ("School of Jazz" 1957, 23). Fundamental to the idea of such programming was that musical progress in jazz involved both the mastery of techniques from the past and the pursuit of musical works that pioneered new sonic "frontiers"—as Russo and Tristano would have it.

This ideology was in turn endorsed by both jazz and African American press coverage of the school, giving an additional measure of critical weight to the project. Such support in the jazz press is of course unsurprising given the "victory of jazz modernists over jazz traditionalists" in the "moldy fig" debate that had played out in editorials and letters in journals like *Down Beat* and *Metronome* during the 1940s (Lopes 2002, 218). Coverage of the Lenox School a decade later merely solidified the idea that jazz was an evolving music by highlighting the way music history at Lenox was taught. John Wilson's description of the 1956 Lenox seminars for the *New York*

Times is unambiguously made in these terms. Under the subtitle "Warring Camps," Wilson writes,

> One of the great stumbling blocks of the modern jazz musician has been his lack of knowledge or understanding of the background of the music he is attempting to play. This ignorance has been encouraged by the schism between the older forms of jazz and the newer ones, a split in which it has become fashionable for musicians on one side of the fence to offer little but scorn to those on the other side.
>
> But when moderator Willis Conover opened the discussion of "Rhythm" by asking Wilbur De Paris, whose music career began in 1907 with a carnival, and Sammy Price, who started playing piano professionally in 1914, to sketch in some of the early uses of rhythm in jazz, their remarks developed into a short lecture on the history of jazz rhythms simply because such modernist members of the discussion group as drummers Max Roach and Connie Kay, bassists Percy Heath and Ray Brown and pianist Dick Katz were so fascinated to learn where they had come from, musically, that it never occurred to them to interrupt. (1956, X9)

Coverage in the African American press tended to endorse the evolutionary narrative in a different manner by focusing on just how far jazz had come from its folk roots. The *Pittsburgh Courier*, for instance, would report on Bill Russo and George Russell's involvement in the 1958 Lenox season in terms laden with the language of modernist uplift surveyed in chapter 3. Russo is described in the article as a "composer who is currently composing a major work for the New York Philharmonic at the request of Leonard Bernstein and whose arrangements for Stan Kenton ushered in a new era for band arranging" ("Top Jazz Musicians" 1958, 15). George Russell is in turn referred to as a "composer, arranger and music theorist whose Lydian concept of tonal organization represents the most magnificent step in formalizing a jazz theory" ("Top Jazz Musicians" 1958, 15). Positioning the work of Russo and Russell against the hegemonic institutions of the New York Philharmonic and the arena of formalized musicology in no uncertain terms endorsed the idea of cultural syncretism—a key component of the "politics of respectability" governing the behavior of many middle- and upper-class African Americans. Such support aligned in broad terms with the support offered the school by the jazz press but simultaneously (and in its particulars) highlighted the legacy of a very different, class-oriented ideology of African American music making.

Most of the material performed by Lewis at the school during the 1957 season would not disappoint the spectrum of stakeholders committed at least in a general way to the idea of an evolutionary jazz narrative. Throughout 1957 Lewis worked to expand the musical ideas he had explored in connection with commedia dell'arte figures in his 1956 work "Fontessa." On August 24, 1957, Atlantic would record three new works by Lewis at Music Inn, titled "Harlequin," "Pierrot," and "Colombine," and release these the following year on the album *The John Lewis Piano* (1958).[14] In addition to Lewis on piano, "Harlequin" would incorporate drummer Connie Kay and "Pierrot" and "Colombine" would incorporate fellow Lenox faculty member Jim Hall on guitar.

Curiously, the thematic material Lewis associated with the characters Harlequin, Pierrot, and Colombine in his "Fontessa" suite is largely absent in these 1957 recordings. Yet degrees of aesthetic similarity between the works abound in other ways. In the liner notes to the *Fontessa* album Lewis writes that his section based on Harlequin employs "the character of older jazz," a character Lewis appears to understand in terms of blues tropes like call-response and the flattened fifth scale degree he infuses heavily into the passage (example 4.7). The 1957 version of "Harlequin" uses a different theme but continues to base this theme on blues components (example 4.8). For instance, the opening bars of the 1957 work are completely pentatonic, making as overt a link to the blues scale as the use of the flat fifth does in the earlier "Fontessa" setting. Furthermore, after a two-bar introduction in the 1957 version, Lewis can be seen to again deploy a call that is repeated with slight alteration and then answered over the second half of the melodic phrase.

The overtness of the blues aesthetic in both works opens the door for speculation about ways in which the blues may have been emblematic for Lewis of Harlequin's commedia dell'arte character traits. In particular, it is tempting here to point to Harlequin's status in the commedia dell'arte as a trickster figure appearing outwardly foolish but simultaneously "display-

Example 4.7. "Fontessa" (1956). Atlantic LP 1231. Harlequin theme, mm. 22–25. Transcription.

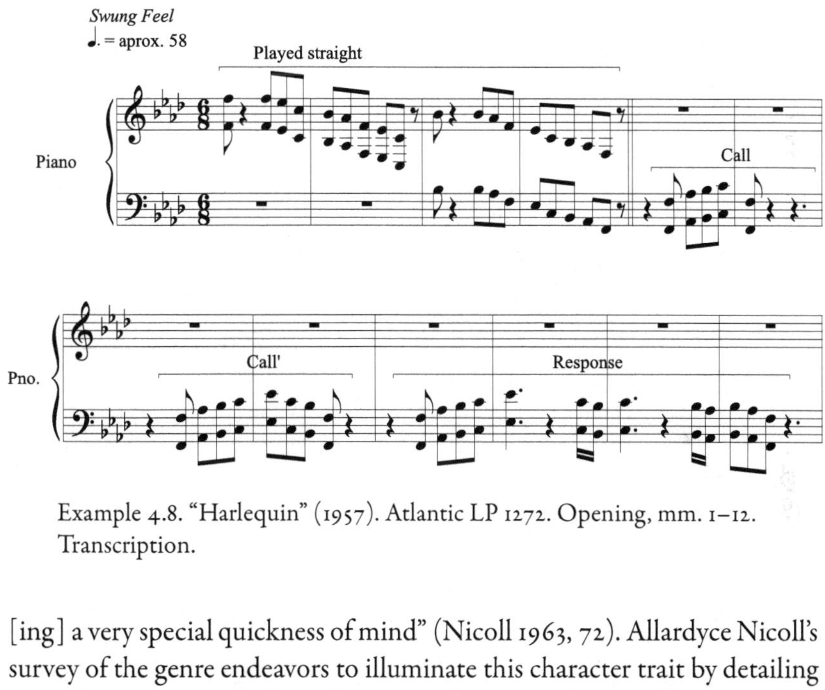

Example 4.8. "Harlequin" (1957). Atlantic LP 1272. Opening, mm. 1–12. Transcription.

[ing] a very special quickness of mind" (Nicoll 1963, 72). Allardyce Nicoll's survey of the genre endeavors to illuminate this character trait by detailing several scenarios in which Harlequin can be seen to do "two things at once," sometimes outwardly attempting to get out of a situation while subversively prolonging it for his own amusement or the reverse, outwardly committing to a particular action he does not want to do and then subversively sabotaging his chances at success (1963, 72). Harlequin's self-agency, despite his status as a servant and his appearance as a fool, neatly parallels in effect the double-voiced tropes of Houston Baker's "minstrel mask" and Henry

Louis Gates's Signifyin(g) theory. In other words, Harlequin's trickster faculties place him on the same level as those in African American profane discourse, able to say they are doing one thing while actually doing another.

Yet regardless of whether or not Lewis's Harlequin settings purposely allude to some sort of pan-tricksterism, they set in place a framework for future explorations of the Harlequin character based on blues sonorities. That is to say, unity between Lewis's 1956 Harlequin theme, his 1957 work "Harlequin," and the version of "Harlequin" he would record with the MJQ four years later as part of the group's 1962 album *The Comedy* is most apparent in the fact that all three of these works are the most blues-heavy works in the collections within which they appear. There is, of course, more thematic similarity between the 1962 version of "Harlequin" and the 1957 version of the work than there is between either of these versions and the Harlequin theme from "Fontessa." Yet an examination of the setting of other commedia-inspired themes from "Fontessa" in the 1957 Lenox recordings seems to confirm the idea that, at least initially, conjuring aesthetic rather than thematic similarity was at the forefront of Lewis's mind.

Consider, for example, the three-note "Fontessa" motif that Lewis associates with the character Colombine (example 4.9) and the four-note motif on which the "Colombine" theme of the 1957 recording is based (example 4.10).

Example 4.9. "Fontessa" (1956). Atlantic LP 1231. Colombine theme, mm. 1–3. Transcription.

The slow tempo at which both motifs are delivered and Lewis's choice to limit these motifs to just a few notes not only creates a unified Colombine aesthetic or musical character, it sets this character against the more elaborate and blues-inflected Harlequin themes. In turn, the constant modulations of both the section of "Fontessa" based on Pierrot and Lewis's "Pierrot" recorded in 1957 solidify Pierrot's musical character in terms distinctly different from both Harlequin and Colombine. Again, it is tempting to

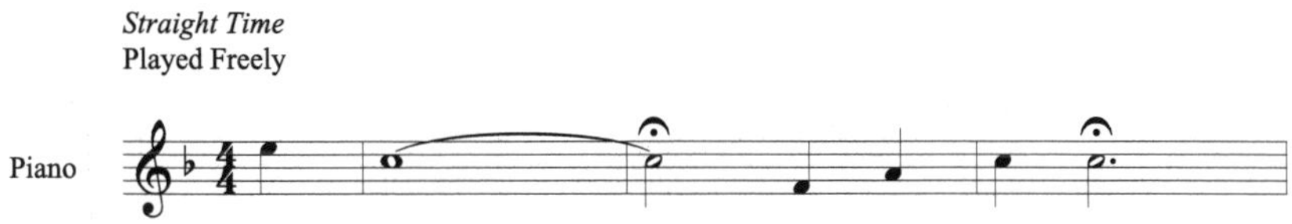

Example 4.10. "Colombine" (1957). Atlantic LP 1272. Opening, 0:18. Transcription.

read character traits such as "calculation" into the Colombine motif and "wistfulness" into the Pierrot themes, traits that largely defined the ways these characters were played. Yet whether such parallels are real or not is beside the point.

The real importance of these relationships is that they indicate an interest in the commedia dell'arte that extends beyond what might be considered a subversive "masking" of African American folk expression. Indeed, while the overt use of blues-heavy music paired with references to a commedia character like Harlequin might at first seem to be a double-voiced attempt to recruit into jazz curious patrons of Western art music, such a reading is complicated by the fact that the conceptual framework of Lewis's commedia dell'arte works does not seem exclusively tied to the jazz realm. In other words, it is knowledge of the commedia dell'arte tradition—and not necessarily jazz practices—that help us best understand the relationship between "Fontessa" and the 1957 works recorded at Lenox. These works do not tell the same story in a different way—a reference to jazz practice that would perhaps have been appropriate if Lewis had reset thematic material. They instead realize aesthetic characters—that is, ways of musical thinking—in different musical scenarios. Lewis's liner notes to the 1956 *Fontessa* album support this interpretation, referring to his Harlequin and Pierrot movements as "having the character of" certain jazz styles rather than exploring or developing particular themes (J. Lewis 1956, 1). It therefore seems reasonable to assert that by delivering to listeners the aesthetic characters defined in "Fontessa" in the context of the different melodic and harmonic stories he produced in 1957, Lewis was effectively engaged in the development of a musical version of the commedia dell'arte tradition. Such an idea would have been truly modern and progressive within the realm of improvised music in the mid-1950s and thus would have fit neatly into the ideologies driving the Lenox educational program.

Furthermore, throughout 1957 Lewis can be seen to have engaged in other projects that similarly highlighted a continued interest in exploring what were referred to at Lenox as "new frontiers." For instance, 1957 is also the year Lewis would write music for his first film, Roger Vadim's *Sait-on jamais*, the particularities of which I discuss at length in the following chapter. In turn, it was a year that would see him begin to score his multi-movement brass work *Excerpts from "The Comedy"* (recorded and released in 1960 on the Atlantic LP *The Golden Striker*). In addition to setting the characters of Polchinella (Pulcinella) and La Cantatrice in this work, Lewis would explore new ways of "masking" the blues by clashing major triads from different keys against the changes of a twelve-bar blues passage in C major (J. Lewis 1960, 3; 16). Such developments more than anything indicate a staying of the course for Lewis.

Yet the factors driving Lewis's motivation to stay on this path appear to have shifted. In chapter 1 I argue that Lewis's decision to "go modern" was at least in part mediated by financial concerns in the wake of the big band decline. My survey of the compositional design underpinning Lewis's early works in the first section of this chapter demonstrates how many of these pieces may have indeed enacted such an agenda by drawing listeners into jazz through the deployment of improvised counterpoint that sounded composed and vice versa. What makes studying Lewis's works from the 1957 Lenox season so interesting is that they break with the overtness of these early works. While "cerebral" elements linked to timbre, speed, and volume continue to sit readily on their surface, understanding their profound and actual connection to Western artistic traditions requires considerably more focused listening. In other words, audience appeal no longer appears to be the driving force behind Lewis's engagement with the West at Lenox. His appropriation of European cultural traditions instead seems to have become something much more personal—or at least something much less commercial. When we read such a shift in the context of the Lenox environment and Lewis's 1956 European experience it becomes clear that Lewis was supported in this transition by movements in jazz "thought." Indeed, despite the jazz press's suggestion that Lewis was moving away from the jazz genre through his exploration of different ways of thinking about compositional process, in the company of his compatriots at Lenox, Lewis's work was clearly ideologically on task.

Return to Europe and Lewis's "Third Stream" Works, 1957–62

Over the next four years, Lewis would continue to operate within this milieu of similarly minded artists and promoters. His return to Europe for a four-month tour with the MJQ beginning in October 1957 enabled further contact with European modernists such as Hodeir and the staff of SDR and SWF, the results of which can be heard on the album *European Windows* (1958) and on two albums released decades later: *Longing for the Continent* (1985) and *The Modern Jazz Quartet—Germany 1956–1958 Lost Tapes* (2013). In the aftermath of the tour, Lewis's interest in writing for increasingly diverse instrumental ensembles would in turn lead to his association with the emerging Third Stream movement and the recording of the now famous Atlantic LP *Third Stream Music* (1960), which included both Lewis's compositions and the works of Gunther Schuller and Jimmy Giuffre.

Although Lewis's compositional approach would not break markedly with the past during this period, this was the era of increased public discussion of the value of his works and the historical moment in which his apparent split from the jazz realm became solidified in the eye of the jazz press. Such tension between musical fact and public opinion appears to have been the result of a phenomenon in which Lewis's works for ensembles larger than the MJQ tended to be slapped with the Third Stream label while his writing for the MJQ remained conceptually linked to the jazz genre—a confusing distinction given the fact that similar compositional strategies informed both sets of works. Lewis's perceived distance from the jazz realm in the minds of jazz critics during this period therefore appears to have had more to do with his increased interest in using large ensembles than with the compositional devices he deployed within these contexts.

Lewis had, of course, explored large ensemble works prior to this period. The work "Three Little Feelings" that I discuss in chapter 1 and "Midsömmer," which I discuss in this chapter, utilized instrumentalists from beyond traditional big-band setups, such as French hornists, bassoonists, and harpists, in order to manifest unique timbral effects. What would make several of Lewis's post-1957 large ensemble works unique was that they marked the first time Lewis would write for established Western ensemble formats such as symphony orchestras and string quartets.

Lewis's loose association with these ensembles correlates with his return to Europe in October 1957 to perform with the MJQ at the Donaueschingen Music Days festival. The inclusion of jazz at Donaueschingen—an avant-garde music festival founded in 1922 and revived after World War II—began in 1954 with a work commissioned by Berendt and festival director Heinrich Strobel: Rolf Liebermann's *Concerto for Jazz-Band and Orchestra* (Hurley 2009, 25). In 1957 the festival organizers would make the decision to build on the success of the 1954 program by pursuing a wider jazz presence, inviting Hodeir's Jazz Groupe de Paris, Eddie Sauter's Big Band, and the Modern Jazz Quartet to perform. Innovative energy pervaded the resulting concerts, with Hodeir's and Sauter's works both drawing heavily on the atonal practices of the Second Viennese School and Lewis and the MJQ performing pieces that showcased a different sort of modernist approach: the reflexive use of composed and improvised counterpoint.

While Lewis's extensive touring in the aftermath of Donaueschingen would see the MJQ collaborate with a variety of ensembles—including Hodeir's Jazz Groupe de Paris, which would record Lewis's work "Sketch 3" and Hodeir's work "Ambiguité"—it was Lewis's earlier involvement with South German Radio during his 1956 tour that seems to have set in place his first encounter with a symphony orchestra. On February 20–21, 1958, Lewis was offered the opportunity to record with SDR's Süddeutscher Rundfunk Sinfonie-Orchester in Stuttgart. Choosing not to bring new works to the group, Lewis instead used the opportunity to reset works he had already recorded with smaller ensembles, including both "Midsömmer" and "God Rest Ye Merry Gentlemen"—tracks Lewis had recorded in 1956 for SDR—and the works "Three Windows" and "Cortege," which the MJQ had played at Donaueschingen and recorded as part of the soundtrack to the French film noir *Sait-on jamais*. The remaining pieces Lewis selected, "The Queen's Fancy" and "Two Degrees East—Three Degrees West" (1956), had their roots in smaller ensembles Lewis had recorded with (including the MJQ) in the United States during the previous years.

The result of these recording sessions would be the album *European*

Windows, released by RCA Victor in 1958. Importantly, when assessing the significance of this album it is crucial to note that the use of an orchestral ensemble appears to have had little effect on Lewis's compositional approach. Indeed, the paradox of contrapuntal practices functioning both as distinct cultural tropes and as a blurred aesthetic concept remains the most notable feature of the music, as is evident in Hentoff's reflections on Lewis's arrangements:

> Note the frequent use of counter-lines beneath soloists and between sections of the orchestra. Note too the clear, logical development of his themes; they are never swallowed or stifled by the orchestration. . . . And there is not a little influence from Lewis' jazz experiences here. The way, for example, the improvised flute and baritone solos flow naturally into and out of the surrounding texture so that they are always a continuing, organic part of the *whole* work. (1958, 1; emphasis in original)

While Hentoff's comments were made in reference to the entire album, they seem to speak particularly well to Lewis's reimagining of the work "Three Windows," from his score to *Sait-on jamais*. The overlapping thematic statements of the fugal exposition in this work are immediately followed on the *European Windows* recording by a forty-measure improvised flute solo performed by Gerry Weinkopf. The first thirty-two measures of this improvisation occur over an AABA form in C minor. Weinkopf then interjects subject motifs into his solo for eight measures while the bass plays the fugal countersubject. Gradual thematic layering continues to occur as Weinkopf moves from improvisatory material to a firmer statement of the fugal subject set against contrapuntal backings beginning in measure seventy (see appendix A, table H). The gradual increase of overlapping thematic backings during Weinkopf's solo and the eventual transition of Weinkopf's improvisation into a statement of the fugal subject itself affirms the interchangeability of contrapuntal techniques described by Hentoff. In other words, Weinkopf participates in the "fugal" nature of the work by providing both improvised independent counterpoint utilizing subject motifs against the statement of the fugal countersubject in the bass as well as by performing the subject itself amid the thematic layering beginning at bar 70. While such an approach does not differ dramatically from the use of improvisation in the MJQ fugal works "Vendome," "Concorde," and "Versailles," Lewis's choice to deploy this trope with the Süddeutscher Rundfunk Sinfonie-Orchester did mark a shift in the type of ensembles Lewis would seek out to realize such syncretic goals.

Confirmation of this shift would be made clear in September of the following year, when Lewis would team up once again with Gunther Schuller in the United States to produce a concert of jazz, Western art music, and fusion music at Town Hall, New York. Lewis and Schuller recruited the Beaux Arts String Quartet for this concert and designed a program split into three sections (similar to the format used by the Jazz and Classical Music Society), emphasizing different compositional approaches. The first section contained a performance of Haydn's Quartet, op. 74, no. 1, played by the Beaux Arts String Quartet; the second section was composed of the Modern Jazz Quartet playing selections from its repertoire of jazz standards, and the third section contained premieres of compositions by Lewis and Schuller written for a combined ensemble made up of the two quartets (Hoefer 1959, 46). These latter compositions, "Conversation" (1959) by Schuller and "Sketch" (1959) by Lewis, would be released the following year on the Atlantic LP *Third Stream Music*.

Far from a revolutionary break into a "Third Stream" paradigm, Lewis's "Sketch" can be unpacked almost entirely in reference to the concepts of contrapuntal ambiguity and the integration of "choruses" within composed contrapuntal passages—conventions Lewis had worked with as far back as "The Queen's Fancy" and "La Ronde." Drawing on this tried-and-true approach, Lewis uses the "Sketch" theme to link composed and improvised counterpoint in the opening measures of the work before pivoting to choruses of open blowing. In specific terms, he juxtaposes the "Sketch" theme against a composed bass line beginning at measure 21 (example 4.11) and then transitions to a section of improvisation (example 4.12) in which he reiterates an improvised version of the theme against an independent bass line (example 4.13) before embarking on the six improvised choruses that comprise the work's bulk.

The fact that Heath and Lewis both construct their improvised parts in relation to figures from the opening thematic passage outlined in example 4.11 before transitioning to the improvised choruses is, suffice to say, a

Example 4.11. "Sketch" (1959). Polyphonic thematic setting, mm. 21–25. Published score (set in Finale).

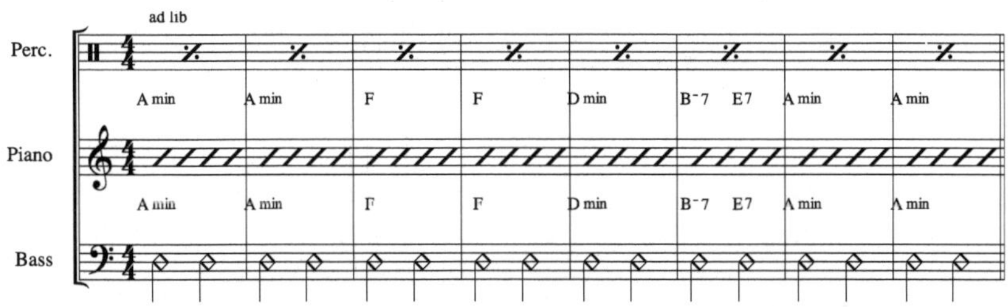

Example 4.12. "Sketch" (1959). First eight measures of open improvisation, mm. 35–42. Published score (reduced and set in Finale).

pretty unremarkable feat given Lewis's more ambitious engagement with contrapuntal effects in the past. True, an element of consistency emerges when "Sketch" is compared to Lewis's earlier works, and the use of a string quartet in "Sketch" might be understood as moving this compositional format into a new domain, yet the cognitive dissonance that made pieces like "Fontessa" and "Versailles" so interesting is largely eradicated by the straightforwardness with which composed and improvised counterpoint are deployed in "Sketch." Compounding this issue is the fact that the string quartet does not engage in contrapuntal interplay, offering only homophonic statements of the theme when called on to deliver thematic content.

Example 4.13. "Sketch" (1959). Atlantic LP 1345. Interpretation of first eight measures of open improvisation (piano and bass), mm. 35–42. Transcription.

Indeed, unlike Lewis's exploration of commedia dell'arte characters at Lenox, "Sketch" appears to evince a step backward toward a more superficial or "showy" approach to engagement with Western art music.

Yet inclusion of the work on the LP *Third Stream Music* would effectively make a different point. Seizing on discussion in the jazz press about an emerging "body of music . . . that is to some extent jazz and yet . . . just as much a part of serious music" (Wilson 1958b, X12), or in the words of Norman J. O'Connor, "a third brand of music, whose name we know not" (1957, 18), Atlantic's *Third Stream Music* LP essentially used Lewis's "Sketch" and Schuller's "Conversation" to define where the parameters of this new genre lay. In other words, by promoting works that in some way incorporated instrumental ensembles beyond big band setups as exemplars of the Third Stream movement, Atlantic's LP set in place a criteria for categorizing music that could essentially circumvent debates about compositional design.

The effects of this conceptual model are evident in the reception of Lewis's commedia dell'arte works realized in the late 1950s and early 1960s. As I stated earlier, Lewis's time at Lenox corresponded with both the development of a large ensemble brass work titled *Excerpts from "The Comedy"* and three smaller ensemble works titled "Harlequin," "Pierrot," and "Colombine," all of which draw on similar compositional language. The release of the brass work on Atlantic LP 1334 under the title *The Golden Striker* would overlap with the release of the album *Third Stream Music* and the two would be reviewed side by side in the pages of *Down Beat* in December 1960 in terms that would unequivocally unite them ("Spotlight Review" 1960, 36). Lewis's development of "Harlequin," "Pierrot," and "Colombine" for the MJQ along with the movements

"Polchinella" (recorded as "Pulcinella"), "Spanish Steps," and "Piazza Navona" from the brass work would be released on the Atlantic LP *The Comedy* in 1962. Despite the Western art music expectation induced by the commedia dell'arte associations of both projects and the neat compositional similarity in both the MJQ and brass settings of "Polchinella/Pulcinella," "Spanish Steps," and "Piazza Navona," only the brass ensemble work was framed initially as a Third Stream composition. As Gary Kramer writes in his liner notes to *The Golden Striker*,

> Considerable comment has been expended on John Lewis's independent use of both classical and traditional jazz devices in his work. Recently critic John S. Wilson hit upon the phrase "third stream music" to designate a new and growing body of music which, like John's, overlaps both fields to the point where it is hard to classify by older standards. (1960, 1)

Kramer's comments do not call out instrumental difference directly, yet such criteria seem to play at least a part in Third Stream attribution when this reading is compared with his discussion of the later MJQ version of the work. Using the improvisatory elements of *The Comedy* as opposed to its composed elements as evidence, Kramer endeavors to dispel confusion around the work's cultural origin in his liner notes to the 1962 album:

> It might . . . be a source of bewilderment to some that a *jazz* composer should be so obsessed by these quaint figures that come from a European tradition that antedates jazz by many centuries. John Lewis long ago perceived that there were many analogies between jazz and the Italian comedy, however. Its improvised character attracted him instantaneously; these plays were not written down, only a bare outline of a plot was posted in the wings, and the players had to take it from there. This was not an author's theatre; it was a *player's* theatre, just as jazz has been, in the main, an instrumentalist's medium rather than a composer's. (1962, 1; emphasis in original)

A comparison of Kramer's two essays seems to indicate a perception of there being different degrees of preplanning at play in the two variations of the work, yet there is little discussion of what the difference in composed elements might actually have been. Of course, when one considers the market mechanisms set in place by the Atlantic *Third Stream Music* LP, this sort of distinction makes a certain amount of sense. By providing a masthead for syncretic works that used large ensembles, the Atlantic LP effectively linked the Third Stream concept with works like "Three Little Feelings" and "Midsömmer"—pieces at the center of the new-venue-creation project discussed in chapter 1. Such use of the term might therefore be understood as having expanded the venue-creation project into the realm of commercial recordings. From this perspective it is then possible to see the "jazz" branding of Lewis's small-group version of *The Comedy* as a purposeful attempt to market the same sonic material (albeit this time in a state of undress, having shed its symphonic garb) to an audience not at all interested in the expanded ensemble aesthetic.

The point I am trying to make here is that despite the use of the Third Stream label to market Lewis's works "Sketch" and "Excerpts," a change in compositional approach large enough to designate an actual paradigm shift in these pieces is difficult to discern. Indeed, despite their different instrumentation, "Sketch" and "Excerpts" share a strong degree of aesthetic similarity with Lewis's earlier pieces "Fontessa" and "The Queen's Fancy," works that had helped Lewis establish a robust jazz profile—a profile strong enough to support multiple tours of European jazz venues and allow him to take on the directorship of the Lenox School of Jazz. By making this argument I am not suggesting that these works should necessarily be read as jazz works, only that the phenomenon of Third Stream attribution seems somewhat detached from the actual musical content of the syncretic works to which it is ascribed.

Of course there is no doubt that the *jazz* and *Third Stream* labels (along with the label *modern*) were all at one point or another used by Lewis as he developed and promoted his music both in the United States and in Europe during the 1950s. Throughout this chapter I have endeavored to demonstrate why such labels may have resonated more with certain demographics than with others and how Lewis benefited by framing his music in different ways. Yet at the same time I have tried to argue that Lewis's works are often more than what they appear to be in these settings. To the right set of ears, modern fugal works have the potential to be read as blues works in disguise and bluesy jams like "Harlequin" have the potential to be read as musical embodiments of the commedia dell'arte tradition. The capacity for these works to give rise to a spectrum of musical associations—despite whether one unpacks such a phenomenon in reference to the ideas of Baker and Gates—indicates a unique musical achievement often overshadowed by later assessments of the Third Stream genre (and Lewis's music, by association) as a cultural and aesthetic failure.

In this chapter I have tried to counter such assumptions by demonstrating that Lewis's works did indeed accomplish important cultural work. They advanced an aesthetic agenda of compositional ambiguity that catapulted Lewis to the front lines of the jazz modernism movement, allowing him to make advancements in jazz education, reestablish a jazz scene in German society, and move forward the work of New Negro composers that aimed to challenge ideas about the sort of music African American artists might create. Lewis may not have undertaken his modernist project with these specific goals in mind, yet thinking of Lewis's work in these terms, rather than in relation to which label best fits his music, allows for a more dynamic view of its ultimate value and historical significance.

5 • Lewis and Film Noir

There are two musical moments in the Robert Wise film *Odds against Tomorrow* (1959) that speak volumes as to how Lewis would carry his ability to frustrate aesthetic boundaries into the realm of film scoring. Both involve the main character, Johnny (played by Harry Belafonte), a jazz musician with a gambling problem struggling to reunite his estranged family. The first finds Johnny performing the song "My Baby's Not Around" (1959), backed up by the sound of the MJQ at a jazz club owned by the mob. Belafonte pantomimes improvisation along with Milt Jackson's vibraphone part while playing into stereotypes of the loose jazz musician (during the song the character's gambling debts are called in and immediately after the performance he begins sweet-talking an ex-girlfriend). After a meeting with the mob boss in which an ultimatum about repayment is issued, the tone of both the acting and improvisation changes. Gone is the easy confidence of the first scene as Johnny retakes the bandstand, now drunk and anxious, to perform the song "All Men Are Evil" (1959) with pop-jazz singer Mae Barnes.[1] After constantly interrupting Barnes with an unsolicited call-and-response, Johnny begins a frantic vibraphone improvisation that eventually causes the band to come to a halt. Here, Milt Jackson's sonic voice is united with Belafonte's emotional state, revealing the potential for improvisation in film to convey a complex array of emotions spanning distress, anger, and guilt. Such use of improvisation breaks free in this moment from the cartoonish jazz stereotypes of the first scene and points to the potential for more dynamic use of the convention within the film noir context.

I am, of course, not the first to point out that jazz was occasionally deployed in film noir toward diverse ends. Indeed, the supposedly ubiquitous role of jazz in film noir "as a trope for the darker side of the American urban experience" (Lopes 2005, 1468) is increasingly undergoing revision. Although there is little dispute that clichéd deviance triggers conjured from juxtaposed jazz bass lines and "world percussion" grooves permeate the form at large (Ford 2008, 120), many recent studies of the field have provided a broader understanding of how African American vernacular tropes function in the genre (Butler 2002, 2009; Cooke 2009). David Butler's (2002) monograph, for instance, demonstrates that while many 1950s noir films utilize deviance triggers along the lines Ford describes, moments of innovative jazz use that work against this cliché do at times emerge. Butler's most compelling case study focuses on the Robert Wise film *I Want to Live!* (1957) and charts the use of nondiegetic jazz scoring across a range of narrative strains connected to the internal soul searching of "falsely" convicted murderer Barbara Graham (2002, 116–27). Both Butler and film scholar Mervyn Cooke pursue this line of enquiry further in the edited collection *Thriving on a Riff: Jazz and Blues Influences in Literature and Film* (2009), highlighting moments in noir films from 1959 that continue to buck the deviance cliché, both in regard to preplanned jazz-inflected scoring and in the placement of improvised passages.

This particular approach to the use of jazz in film noir during the 1950s might be considered a natural extension of the genre's progressive use of music during the 1940s. Richard Ness, for instance, argues that film noir's rejection of narrative themes and tropes associated with prewar comedies and melodramas echoes in music tracks that break with "the tonal tradition of classical Hollywood film scoring" (2008, 53). Through an analysis of the films *Shadow of a Doubt* (1943), *Laura* (1944), and *Murder, My Sweet* (1944), Ness demonstrates how the use of "dissonance and atonality, . . . the breakdown of traditional diegetic/nondiegetic distinctions and the use of unusual instrumentation and experimental recording techniques" came to define "an overall *noir* musical style" by the dawn of the 1950s (2008, 52–53). Such "modernist leanings in soundtrack design"—as Mervyn Cooke (2009, 253) puts it—seem to have set in place a platform for musical experimentation in the form that would increasingly come to the fore during the second half of the decade.

As a particular example of this experimentation, Cooke points to Duke Ellington's score for the Otto Preminger film *Anatomy of a Murder* (1959). Engaging with claims made by Krin Gabbard that moments in the music track feel "randomly tacked on," Cooke argues that the progressive turn in film scoring in which the noir genre played an important part allowed for a more abstract relationship between "music and image" to develop. Such abstraction enabled composers to conceive of the music they would contribute to film as extensions of their own creative aesthetic projects and freed them from "narrative-dominated sensibilities" that had permeated earlier styles of Hollywood film production (Cooke 2009, 253). The result of such freedom may have resulted in a looser moment-to-moment relationship between image and music but would not, in Cooke's view, weaken the impact of a score on the overall aesthetic outcome of a film project. To the contrary, Cooke, quoting Royal Brown, argues that such approaches to film scoring enabled "a parallel aesthetic component to the film's visual and narrative structures" to emerge in which one might find unexpected "conjunctions of music and drama" that were both "oddly compelling and thought provoking" (Cooke 2009, 254–55).

Lewis's initial entry into the world of film music was no doubt facilitated by this increasingly expansive view regarding what might make up a film noir music track. Yet the scores Lewis would provide for his first two projects, Roger Vadim's *Sait-on jamais* (1957) and Robert Wise's *Odds against Tomorrow*, do not break totally with "narrative-dominated sensibilities" in the manner suggested by Cooke above. To the contrary, these scores seem to set in place Lewis's vision for a more expansive improvisatory voice in film delivered in aid of particular narrative strains. As Lewis claimed in a 1959 *Down Beat* interview, "Jazz hasn't been used yet to fill all of the needs of the motion picture. You haven't heard jazz used with love scenes or certain dramatic situations. The answer is improvisation that can be as tender or as dramatic as the scene demands" ("Jazz in Films" 1959, 16). His scores for *Sait-on jamais* and *Odds against Tomorrow* take action along these lines by frequently calling on various improvisatory styles to counterpoint and heighten the emotional content of particular narrative moments. At the same time, Lewis can be seen to conform to certain conventions of the noir genre established during the 1940s—particularly in relation to his use of deviance triggers that align with the musical model identified by

Ford above. The use of this familiar convention allowed Lewis to develop scores that fit a familiar auditory template while simultaneously expanding the use of improvisation across the length of the film. In other words, there is at least some potential to read these scores as double-voiced—as scores that actively package the unfamiliar within the boundaries of the familiar. Of course, such an approach need not necessarily be understood as a purposeful act of vernacular preservation in line with the Baker-Gates paradigm—especially given the dynamic nature of 1950s modernist thought explored in the preceding chapter. Nevertheless, such a methodology does demonstrate a level of compositional continuity between Lewis's concert works and film scores only tangentially mentioned in current surveys of Lewis's noir participation and is therefore ripe for exploration in this study of Lewis's music.

Deviance Triggers and Film Noir

Such an analysis, of course, must begin with a brief survey of how familiar musical tropes came to be, in fact, familiar within the noir context. Attempts at summarizing the noir construct span decades (Durgnat 1970; Schrader 1972; Silver & Ward 1992; Pfeil 1993; Vernet 1993), with perhaps the most inclusive interpretation put forth by Naremore in his overview of a "loose, evolving system of arguments and readings" that draws broadly on the negative in human relationships (1998, 11). Associations derived from this system inspire a related web of visual imagery ("low-key photography, wet city streets") and narrative traits ("pop Freudian characterizations . . . [a] romantic fascination with femme fatales") (Naremore 1998, 9). Butler (2002) is quick to identify jazz as a core component of Naremore's negative milieu, particularly in what are now considered to be the first wave of noir texts: *Phantom Lady* (1944), *D.O.A.* (1950), and *The Asphalt Jungle* (1950). All three of these works use either "live" performances by jazz musicians or diegetic props (a bar jukebox) to deliver vernacularly based musical accompaniment underneath morally ambiguous narrative moments. In *Phantom Lady* the protagonist, Kansas, slips into a sexually charged undercover persona in order to track down and seduce a witness at a jazz club; in *D.O.A.* businessman Frank Bigelow gets his drink spiked while being distracted by dancing at a jazz nightclub; and in *The Asphalt Jungle* the character Doc Riendenschneider plays jazz on a jukebox in order to get a young couple to dance, indulging his penchant for voyeurism. The "primitivist" connotations of jazz surveyed in chapter 2 help us make sense of why such choices were so frequently made and the difficulty involved in moving jazz's semiotic function beyond such moments.

Indeed, the pairing of jazz and deviance would come to form a resilient trope in the noir context as jazz transitioned from diegetic contexts to a clichéd reduction of itself in nondiegetic symphonic noir scoring of the 1950s.[2] Ford depicts this later scoring convention as an aggregate assembly of "musical codes" that are "exotic in a generic sense . . . without belonging to any specific place" (2008, 118). Its creation relied on the reduction of Latin and American popular music to core components and then the reassembly of these components into a stratified texture juxtaposed against a walking bass. As Ford explains,

> This music is less jazz than something written to sound like jazz. The polarity between walking basses and the figures superimposed against them becomes a metonymic reduction of the jazz sound, something composers rely on to conjure up an image of jazz and all that is associated with it: shades and beret, a smoky club after dark, etc. What this suggests is that composers seeking to *depict* jazz rather than simply write it will intensify that polarization between bass line and horn figure, or, more abstractly between figure and ground. (2008, 123)

Ford uses Henry Mancini's score to the Orson Welles film *Touch of Evil* (1958) to provide evidence of this effect, outlining the stratified music that begins the film as follows:

> After a unison fanfare that hammers out the tonic, a taunting percussion ostinato begins, at first slowly and then locking into a groove. At measure 16 the first ostinato line enters in the saxophones; at measure 30, a new line enters in the trombones, accompanied by a new bass ostinato. Then at measure 42, the texture splits into five layers: the percussion, the bass ostinato, a baritone sax ostinato, the trombone line (now doubled in the trumpets), and a new ostinato—a leering figure in alto and tenor saxophone. (2008, 120)[3]

A reading of this cliché as deviance trigger or trope can be seen in Ford's subsequent assessment that "here Henry Mancini does with a complex multilayered groove what the camera does in images, striking the film's tone of menace, its looming promise of interest to be paid on an accumulated debt of wicked deeds" (2008, 119–20). Further examples pairing the "world" percussion sound, bass ostinato, and layered horn lines of Ford's model with moments of transgression are illuminated in his discussion of the noir classics *The Wild One* (1953) with music by Leith Stevens, *The Sweet Smell of Success* (1957) with music by Elmer Bernstein, *I Want To Live!* (1958) with music by Johnny Mandel, and *Compulsion* (1959) with music by Lionel Newman. Indeed, the cliché would be used with such frequency in the 1950s that it would eventually develop its own moniker in anthologies of film noir music: "crime jazz."[4]

Such standardization of the reductive "crime jazz" trope appears to have, almost paradoxically, enabled a greater degree of vernacular engagement within other aspects of noir scoring. With the deviance trigger locked into such an easily replicated and recognizable convention, composers were free to experiment with the use of jazz harmonies, rhythms, and melodic features as accompaniments to other narrative strains. Butler (2002) identifies this concept as a driving force behind Johnny Mandel's "jazz based" symphonic score for *I Want to Live!* While Mandel continues to draw on the "crime jazz" cliché to induce anxiety, particularly notable in convicted murderer Barbara Graham's nightmare sequence (Ford 2008, 129), he simultaneously incorporates swing rhythmic time and a melody incorporating blues sonorities into a sequence in which Graham writes to her psychologist expressing a love of life and a desire to fight her execution sentence. While the latter scene cannot be construed as an entirely uplifting event, it is framed in the film as a moment of hope—there is the possibility, however fleeting, that Barbara's doctor will help save her life.

Yet at the same time that Mandel was eroding the jazz stereotype in his film score, director Robert Wise was upholding it in the placement of improvised music. Although Wise expressed a belief that West Coast or "Cool" jazz improvisation could carry with it more nuanced connotations than had typically been ascribed to jazz music in the past (Butler 2002, 119), the final release of the film evinces a continued tendency to connect improvised passages performed by an ensemble led by "Cool" jazz practitioners Shelly Manne and Gerry Mulligan with the themes of drug use, a seedy underworld, and internal conflict. Butler describes the establishment of this link in his overview of the film's opening jazz club sequence, in which Mulligan is featured:

> Wise . . . [shot] the majority of the club sequence through a variety of tilted camera angles that seem to be intended to create a sense of distorted perception, possibly due to the marijuana, in partnership with the jazz band. The sense of having entered a world of transgression is also suggested through the club's clientele. Mixed generation couples are visible, as well as black audience members, although they are always in the background. The 'two cool types' . . . are included and are coded for seediness, seen smoking in a corridor as the musicians play. (2009, 122)

While Butler suggests that the fleshing out of Graham's character enabled the sound of the Mulligan-Manne band to later symbolize a variety of "conflicting associations," it is never liberated entirely from the connotations of this opening scene, and Graham's most redeeming moment is cast in direct opposition to the ensemble.

This scene of transcendence occurs in Graham's cell and begins with Graham listening to a jazz radio program on which the Mulligan-Manne band performs. The music switches over to the news and her guard begins to search for a new station. Graham directs the guard to stop at the sound of classical piano with the line "There, leave that . . ." and then the revelation "There's lots of long-hair music I like." This exchange transitions to Graham's reflection on self-sacrifice. In an attempt to console the prison guard, who is struggling with a failed marriage, Graham describes the pain of giving up her own marriage for the sake of her husband's career. The scene is ultimately redemptive, with the condemned counseling the free through a parable of sacrifice and forgiveness.

It is notable that this moment is underscored by classical music and not symphonic jazz or improvisation. While Mandel and Wise appear to be motivated by a more nuanced understanding of jazz music's potential in film, this scene demonstrates an ultimate reluctance to accompany a moment of real deliverance with music from the jazz realm. Indeed, while jazz elements do emerge throughout the symphonic score in connection with a variety of narrative themes, the unambiguous nature of the "crime jazz" cliché and a hesitance to fully detach improvisation from Graham's links to the underworld serves to perpetuate the jazz/deviance stereotype in *I Want to Live!* Lewis's music track to the 1957 film *Sait-on jamais* echoes the use of music in Wise's film in that it plays deviance triggers off more expansive jazz placement but can in turn be seen to go further, calling on improvisation in addition to jazz-imbued scoring as accompaniment to an array of themes that extend beyond the darker strains of the narrative.

Improvisation in Lewis's Score for *Sait-on jamais* (1957)

The path to Lewis's involvement in the *Sait-on jamais* project can at least partly be understood as stemming from his earlier creation and promotion of syncretic works within the French context. Lewis's recording of the album *Afternoon in Paris* following his 1956 tour of the Continent, for instance, demonstrated a willingness to juxtapose musical conventions seen by many to emerge from contrasting aesthetic realms. This compositional approach echoed French developments within the film noir genre during the same period. As Ginette Vincendeau (2007, 42) explains, in an attempt to expand film noir beyond clique status in France, French productions of the form between the late 1950s and early 1960s tended to cast its dark narrative strains against spectacular visual imagery, thus challenging standard noir conventions. She cites the Mediterranean setting of René Clément's *Plein soleil* (1960) as proof of this stylistic shift, although the Venetian landscape of the Roger Vadim film under scrutiny here, *Sait-on jamais*, serves as an equally pertinent case in point. Indeed, both films help illustrate Vincendeau's definition of a discrete French film noir style relying on a "paradoxical relationship between visual style and narrative ideology" (2007, 45). This approach to the form allowed the *policier* (French noir genre) to grow in appeal, attracting an audience outside the noir demographic through its use of spectacular visual imagery, eventually driving the genre to account for "a quarter of French film production" between the late 1950s and early 1970s (Guérif 1981, 75). Lewis's syncretic concept offered a sonic parallel to the paradox Vincendeau identifies, thus making him an ideal candidate for Vadim's noir project.

The plot of *Sait-on jamais* follows the character Sophie, portrayed by Françoise Arnoul, as she attempts to break free from her longtime caregiver, Baron Eric von Bergen, played by O. E. Hasse. The Baron, in addition to his role as Sophie's protector, is an expert forger with a staff of criminal accomplices. Early in the film Sophie meets Michel, a photojournalist, who impresses her with his honesty and legitimate income, and the two begin a romantic relationship. Distressed by Sophie's newfound love, the Baron confides to an underling named Sforzi that he has deposited millions of pounds into bank accounts across the Continent bearing Sophie's name. Sforzi seduces Sophie away from Michel in the hope of winning access to the hidden money. He then kills the Baron when told of his change of heart regarding Sophie and Michel's relationship along with his intent to transfer control of Sophie's assets to Michel. Michel suspects Sforzi of the Baron's murder, and after uncovering evidence to this effect in Sforzi's possession, the two are involved in a chase across rooftops that ends in Sforzi falling to his death.

Lewis's score for the film draws heavily on six different works: "The Golden Striker," "One Never Knows," "The Rose Truc," "Cortege," "Venice," and "Three Windows." Recordings of these pieces can be heard on the Atlantic album *No Sun in Venice*, released after the film in 1957. Both in the film and on the soundtrack recording (variations in arrangement and improvisation do exist between the two), the works are presented as the alternation of thematic head arrangements with improvisatory solos performed by Lewis, Jackson, and Heath. The composed themes, unsurprisingly, continue to evince Lewis's penchant for "masking" thematic material with European sonorities, most evident in the use of a fugal veneer on the work "Three Windows" (Owens 1976, 31).

The "Three Windows" theme is in turn deployed throughout the film as a deviance trigger along the lines Ford (2008) describes. Its opening four-note motive, typically played by the bass, is linked to appearances of the Sforzi character. As thematic stratification occurs through the introduction of the two other themes, Ford's "crime jazz" trope is activated, and it is this fully formed cue that is used to underscore scenes in which Sforzi's plans unfold (see appendix B). Lewis's intention to score the film in this way seems plain enough when comments he made in a 1962 interview with Ralph Gleason are considered. When asked by Gleason how he approached writing for film, Lewis replied, "For *No Sun in Venice* . . . I had to work from a script and a script that had time sequences, and from the script you had to get some idea of what you think the image and the sound should be going together." Expanding further, Lewis spoke about using the "old-fashioned Wagnerian technique [of] leitmotif" in connection with the "three main male characters in the picture" (J. Lewis [1962] 2006). Such comments are rather unambiguous and beg us to understand the placement of the "crime jazz" cliché as purposeful while in turn inviting us to read direct relationships between music and image during other moments in the film.

Along these lines, it is worth noting that Sophie's struggle toward liberation—a liberation at least tangentially connected to her burgeoning relationship with Michel—frequently unfolds in counterpoint to improvised material. The pairing of improvisation with this thematic strain begins diegetically in a club where Michel has brought Sophie on a date. The two discuss their feelings for each other while pointedly avoiding conversation about their problematic past relationships. There is the sense that while both share troubled pasts, their meeting indicates a new beginning. In the background, Milt Jackson improvises over the form of the "Three Windows" theme and is supported by bass, piano, and drums. This performance transitions to a new piece, "The Rose Truc," in which the theme is quickly followed by a vibraphone improvisation over the harmonic form. The following scene then sees Sophie convince Michel to come back to her room in the Baron's villa so that they can listen to music in a private setting. The camera cuts to Sophie's bedroom, where a vibraphone improvisation over a twelve-bar blues is used to underscore their flirtations. After a brief interlude in which Sophie tells the Baron of Michel's visit, Sophie returns to the room and appeals to Michel to rescue her from the Baron's control. Their subsequent tryst is accompanied by another vibraphone improvisation, played over "The Rose Truc" chord changes.

The use of improvisation to counterpoint Sophie's potential rescue in both the bar scene and these early bedroom scenes can be seen to mark a turn in film noir scoring toward increased improvisational presence. Cooke has made sense of this shift as part and parcel of the abstraction he hears occurring in the *Anatomy of a Murder* music track, referring to Lewis's score as "coolly detached" and grouping it with Miles Davis's improvisatory score to Louis Malle's *Ascenseur pour l'echafaud* (1957) as examples of "autonomous" scores that foreshadow "the non-specific use of music in many 1960s French films" (2009, 253). In other words, the break from specifically scored accompaniment seems to indicate, for Cooke, a break from the practice of purposefully placing particular musical material against specific narrative moments. Yet Lewis's comments seem to indicate that the presence of improvisation in these moments is meant to function in aid of the film narrative. Therefore, while it is difficult to articulate just what aspects of Sophie's liberation are being commented on through the use of improvisation in these moments, the ongoing presence of the crime jazz cliché might be seen as a tool used to purposefully cast these moments as being somehow oppositional to the darkest strains of the *Sait-on jamais* story.

This dynamic is perhaps made most clear in a subsequent scene in which the Baron informs Sforzi that he plans to transfer money out of Sophie's accounts and into Michel's control. The first part of their conversation, in which Sforzi tells the Baron that Sophie is beginning to remember signing papers setting up the accounts and that he intends to steal the money, is underscored by the crime jazz cliché in the form of the "Three Windows" theme. As the Baron produces a letter to the bank outlining his wishes, Jackson begins to improvise on the chord changes to "Cortege" and Sforzi articulates his distress that his plans to drain Sophie of her inheritance have been ruined. The music then abruptly stops as Sforzi tells the Baron that he has no choice but to kill him. The nondiegetic improvisation in this scene draws a distinction between the Baron's well-intentioned, if belated, support for Sophie and Sforzi's nefarious plans to strip Sophie of her millions. Importantly, the effect of this musical moment relies on the presence of the crime jazz cliché. That is to say, while it is difficult to unpack all the ways in which improvisation might play off the Baron's change of heart in this moment, we can be certain the convention is meant to mark distance from Sforzi's mind-set due to Lewis's placement of the crime jazz trope. In the context of this book, such an approach to scoring can be seen to provide further evidence of Lewis's penchant for placing hegemonic conventions at the center of projects aimed at moving forward musical boundaries, aligning it with the compositional approaches charted out in chapter 4.

Improvisation in Lewis's Score for *Odds against Tomorrow* (1959)

Lewis's subsequent film noir score for Robert Wise's *Odds against Tomorrow* evinces a further development of this compositional strategy. Butler (2009) was the first to identify the innovative treatment of improvisation in the work, tracing its connection with a variety of opposing thematic strains. Yet the manner in which the work continues to engage with specific noir conventions, such as the use of "dissonance and atonality . . . [and] the breakdown of traditional diegetic/nondiegetic distinctions" (Ness 2008, 52–53) begs for additional attention in relation to a discussion of Lewis's developing compositional practice. In particular, the use of a brass-heavy "twenty-three-piece orchestra" (Butler 2009, 231) that alternates with the sound of the MJQ and improvisations performed by Milt Jackson can be seen to once again frame the innovative (i.e., the more expansive use of improvisation) within the boundaries of the expected.

Even when music is left to the side, *Odds against Tomorrow* can be read as a film designed to break down barriers. It signified a series of "firsts" in Hollywood, among them the first film produced by an African American (Harry Belafonte) and the first film noir with an African American protagonist (also Belafonte).[5] The buzz surrounding these milestones was enhanced by Belafonte's refusal to play into African American stereotypes in the script, a resolve he articulated to the press months before the film's release as follows:

> The Negro always has played the same film part or a variation of the same part. Take my good friend Sidney Poitier; he always plays the role of the good and patient fellow who finally wins the understanding of his white brothers. Well, I think the audience is ready to go beyond even films like *The Defiant Ones*. I think they would be terrifically relieved to see on the screen the Negro as he really is and not as one side of a black-and-white sociological argument where brotherhood always wins in the end. (qtd. in Nason 1959, X7)

Such a desire for real human nuance contrasted with the "Freudian characterizations" of the noir genre, throwing into jeopardy conventional depictions of good and evil. Building on this concept, the emerging plot necessarily recast typical two-dimensional "heist" characters as three-dimensional battlers: struggling men navigating a complex range of racial prejudices, constructs of masculine loyalty, and the weight of familial responsibility.

The film plot follows the undoing of these men, each operating with varying degrees of hostility toward the law. Burke, played by Ed Begley, is an ex-cop forced to retire in the wake of an ethics hearing. He recruits Slater, played by Robert Ryan, and Johnny, played by Belafonte, to hold up a bank in the suburban town of Melton, New York. Slater, recently released from prison, agrees but becomes distressed once he finds out that Johnny is African American. Johnny, in contrast, is initially reluctant but relents when his gambling debts are called in. The three are then required to work together to plan the heist while mitigating Slater's prejudice, an ultimately futile act that ends with the death of all three.

The use of improvisation and scored material in the film is mapped in the soundscape that forms appendix C. The scored material largely derives from the theme played under the opening credits, consisting of both a four-note ascending scalic motive and a two-note ascending leap. As noted throughout appendix C, repetition of motives "a" (scalic) and "b" (leap) makes up the vast majority of composed material, and Lewis employs a variety of timbral and textural effects in order to imbue distinction upon these statements. Improvisatory material in *Odds* is similarly divided into two sets, one utilizing the electric guitar and one utilizing the vibraphone. Guitar improvisations employ pendular thirds and flat sevenths frequently while vibraphone improvisations take on the more chromatic elements of the bebop genre. The vibraphone in turn carries additional significance in *Odds* in that it is connected diegetically with Belafonte's character, Johnny (Butler 2009, 230).

Perhaps the most curious aspect of the score is the way in which the scored cues, many of which feature loud, dissonant chords orchestrated across the brass, seem to be placed in a somewhat abstracted relationship with the film image and narrative, while improvisation, at least in regard to the vibraphone, is frequently called on to give rise to the memory of Belafonte's character, Johnny. Lewis's towering chords do occasionally work to heighten specific moments of anxiety in the film, such as when they are used to underscore Slater and Burke's initial trip up to Melton or when Johnny sees the bank they have agreed to rob for the first time. Yet many times, the sort of anxiety they are meant to induce seems less clear, such as in the scene in which they sound in tandem with Johnny chauffeuring Burke downtown after initially rejecting his offer or the scene in which they are used to underscore Slater's arrival at Burke's apartment. Certainly a heavy pulse of anxiety connects these moments, yet the quality of the anxiety the audience is meant to experience is uncertain. That is to say, the scoring of dissonant brass chords does not function in *Odds against Tomorrow* the same way the "crime jazz" trope functions in *Sait-on jamais*. Their presence does color storytelling in the film at the macro level, but it clarifies little in relation to the undercurrents of specific scenes.

The use of vibraphone improvisation in the film, in contrast, plays a more direct storytelling role. The first moment of improvisation along these lines occurs diegetically in the jazz club scene I describe in the beginning of this chapter. As Butler remarks, use of the vibraphone as an echo of Johnny's character is then further explored during the longest section of nondiegetic improvisation in the score (2009, 230). This passage accompanies Johnny, Burke, and Slater's trip up to Melton on the eve of the robbery. Johnny travels by bus while Burke and Slater travel in separate cars, leaving one halfway between New York and Melton so that the group can split up after the robbery (Butler 2009, 230). Jackson begins improvising over a two-note ostinato figure as Slater tests the getaway car on a stretch of open road. According to Butler,

> What makes this sequence so striking is that Slater, a white racist, has his moment of emotional freedom accompanied by an improvised jazz solo played on the instrument diegetically associated with his colleague Johnny, the black jazz musician for whom he has nothing but contempt. Lewis underlines here, far more explicitly than anything in the script, the breakdown of the duality between Johnny and Slater. This point is of major significance—black jazz is employed to convey the innermost feelings of a white character. (2009, 230)

It seems that Butler's ideas of this moment's significance overlap with how it might be read in terms of a double-voiced analysis. The use of jazz vibraphone in connection with Slater, the darkest character in the film, harks back to stereotypical jazz deviance associations, providing an initial level of meaning. Yet the music is also the anthem of the most morally aware character in the film, Johnny, and its use highlights the fact that Slater, while inexcusably racist, is on some level still trying to do the right thing; he is tied up in the same financial and familial responsibilities as Johnny and is endeavoring, like Johnny, to claw his way out.

The echo of Johnny's morality in other moments of vibraphone improvisation further point to a purposeful deployment of these cues as a tool for enhancing scenes in specific ways. For instance, after finding out that Johnny is African American, a distressed Slater enters a bar. Polonsky's (1999, 70) script calls for an interior shot of this moment with a radio "humming old tunes," but in the released version of the film this requirement is replaced by the MJQ performing what would come to be known as "Cue #9" (1959) on the film soundtrack. The bar is populated by a young soldier, the soldier's girlfriend, and another male companion, and upon Slater's entrance the music grows louder, suggesting its diegetic role. As Slater sits and orders, the soldier demonstrates a self-defense move and inadvertently causes his male companion to collide with Slater. Jackson's improvisation and embellishments of the "Cue #9" theme underscore the altercation as Slater does his best to shake off the assault, embracing the moral qualities associated with Johnny. As the soldier continues his demonstration, this time with the girl as the model, Slater reaches his threshold of tolerance and the music cuts out in connection with the line "Honey, if you're goin' to throw that bum, throw him the other way" (Polonsky 1999, 73). This abrupt shift echoes Lewis's cue underscoring the Baron's murder in *Sait-on jamais*, requiring improvisation to conjure a certain emotional milieu before calling on its absence to articulate a narrative shift.

There is certainly a degree of collaboration that must be considered in this analysis of *Odds against Tomorrow*. The choice to locate improvisation diegetically in the jazz club sequence probably has more to do with the choices of Polonsky and Wise than those of Lewis. Yet the script itself would have made the symbolic nature of the vibraphone clear to Lewis, and it is therefore against this understanding that the presence of vibraphone improvisation in the film might best be read, especially given the attention to character Lewis paid in crafting his score for *Sait-on jamais*.

Of particular relevance to the arguments woven throughout this book is the fact that the effectiveness of such an approach relied on a rather conservative notion of how a film score might function. That is to say, in contrast to Cooke's argument about jazz scores enabling an abstraction to occur between image and film, Lewis can be seen to have used specific musical effects to enhance the narrative arc of the film projects with which he was involved. In turn, whether these effects related to the use of the "crime jazz" cliché in *Sait-on jamais*, the use of a brassy, dissonant, modernist backdrop in *Odds against Tomorrow*, or the use of a textural leitmotif in the shape of improvisation in both *Sait-on jamais* an *Odds against Tomorrow*, Lewis's aim to expand the presence of improvisation in these films was realized through dialogue with existing noir-scoring conventions. This strategy of engaging the familiar to deliver the unfamiliar links clearly with Lewis's projects outside the domain of film during the 1950s and allows us to understand in specific terms how his film scores might be seen to evince the continuation of an aesthetic practice forged in his earlier compositions.

6 • "Real" Black Music

As the 1950s drew to a close and frustration with the progress of the civil rights movement added fire to the "Black Nationalist" movement in the United States, the criticism Lewis faced took on a decidedly more militant feel. Leading the charge of this critical turn was a young writer named LeRoi Jones, who struck out against Third Stream artists and other Western art music appropriators in a 1961 essay for *Metronome* titled "The Jazz Avant-Garde." To be clear, in no way was Jones a "moldy fig"—a critic who believed jazz's best days were behind it, somewhere between Buddy Bolden and Duke Ellington. As he would write in the opening of his *Metronome* essay, "We are, all of us, *moderns*, whether we like it or not" (Jones [1961] 2010, 82). Yet at the same time Jones took exception to artists, like Lewis, who appeared to express their modernity uncritically—those who seemed to unquestionably engage with the hegemonic values and aesthetics of the dominant social class. For Jones, such an approach signaled the unforgivable sin of willful "indoctrination" and worked to undermine the real intellectual work achieved by those committed to stewarding what he believed to be the "roots" of African American music: the musical conventions of blues and bebop (Jones [1961] 2010, 82).

In an effort to clearly set out what a more appropriate approach to jazz modernism might look like, Jones's essay quickly pivoted to a discussion of the music produced by up and coming jazz saxophonist Ornette Coleman. Coleman had truly shaken up the jazz world two years prior with the release of his album *The Shape of Jazz to Come* (1959), a collection of six original compositions, each containing passages of non-chord-based improvisation. His follow-up album, *Change of the Century* (1959), was similarly conceived, and both have often been contextualized as prefiguring the "free jazz" movement of the 1960s. Yet the intrigue of these recordings lay for Jones not on their "free" aspects but on the fact that despite rejecting the use of an underlying harmonic structure, the tracks on these albums continued to articulate a very real connection to blues and bebop tropes—those musical elements Jones viewed as essential to authentic African American music production. In reference to Coleman's composition "Ramblin'", Jones wrote that "the very jaggedness and abruptness of the melodic fabric itself suggest[s] the boppers' seemingly endless need for deliberate and agitated rhythmical contrast" and that one simply needed to "whistle Ramblin', then any early Monk [piece]" for "the basic *physical* similarities of melodic lines . . . [to] be immediately apparent" ([1961] 2010, 87). Putting the same concept in more poetic terms, Jones argued that Coleman's modernist aesthetic might be best viewed as a project in which the innovations of beboppers like Charlie Parker were held up as a sort of "hypothesis" from which Coleman was then able to develop conclusions "separate and unique" ([1961] 2010, 85). Such an approach stood distinct in Jones's mind from the work of John Lewis, whose focus on Western art music principles set in place a very different core impulse—one that in Jones's mind "served to obscure the really valuable legacies of bop" ([1961] 2010, 88).

Given the intensity of Jones's critique, it is somewhat surprising to note that Lewis was in fact one of Coleman's strongest early supporters. Intrigued after witnessing performances of Coleman's group in 1958, Lewis encouraged Coleman to attend the Lenox School of Jazz in 1959 and facilitated his move to Atlantic Records in the same year, a career development that resulted not only in the albums *The Shape of Jazz to Come* and *Change of the Century* but also in Coleman's legendary album *Free Jazz* (1960) (Kaplan 2009, 204–5). Furthermore, throughout the early 1960s Lewis evinced a personal interest in the specifics of the young saxophonist's music, initiating double bills featuring the MJQ and Coleman's quartet at the Village Vanguard in 1960 and recording Coleman's original work "Lonely Woman" (1959) on the MJQ's 1962 album of the same name.

Of further curiosity is the fact that both Jones and Lewis appear to have been drawn into Coleman's "avant-garde" music in similar ways. In an interview published in the March 1960 issue of *Jazz Review*, Lewis reflected on the saxophonist's innovative use of bebop gestures in terms that neatly foreshadowed Jones's "hypothesis" model, stating,

> Ornette is, in a sense, an extension of Charlie Parker—the first I've ever heard. This is the real need I think [that] has to take place, to extend the basic ideas of Bird until they are not playing an imitation but actually something new. I think that they may have come up with something, not perfect yet, and it's still in the early stages, but nevertheless very fresh and interesting. (Qtd. in Thorne 1960, 7)

Yet despite the fact that both Jones and Lewis were able to discern a bebop echo in Coleman's music, the two would not articulate the significance of this echo the same way. For Lewis, extending the innovations of Charlie Parker fell neatly in line with the evolutionary narrative of jazz development endorsed by the Lenox School of Jazz and European modernists like André Hodeir. His praise of Coleman's group printed in Martin Williams's liner notes for *The Shape of Jazz to Come* is unambiguously made along these lines, highlighting the importance of forward movement in the genre through his comment that Coleman's music was "the only really new thing in jazz since the innovations in the mid-forties of Dizzy Gillespie, Charlie Parker and Thelonious Monk" (Williams 1959, 1). Jones, on the other hand, interpreted the significance of Coleman's innovations firmly along stewardship lines. He acknowledged that Coleman's method was undoubtedly shaped by the modern world but felt that its prioritization of certain bebop aesthetics activated or kept in play the "roots" of jazz music—musical "idea[s] we love, no matter what the subsequent disfigurement" (Jones [1961] 2010, 84).

The fact that both Jones and Lewis could hear in Coleman's music so much worth praising despite understanding its significance differently speaks volumes to the central idea of this book—that is, the very simple notion that one's understanding of musical significance is always unique. In other words, there is no empirical test through which we might be able to discern once and for all whether *The Shape of Jazz to Come* was an album focused primarily on the idea of vernacular stewardship or one focused primarily on the idea of breaking new ground—especially given the fact that the sonic result of the album can easily be interpreted through either paradigm of emphasis. Where one falls on the spectrum of interpretation rests instead on one's understanding of the historical energies surrounding the work. For Jones, the historical moment of *The Shape of Jazz to Come* was clearly charged with anxiety over the obliteration of the African American musical voice. His angry dismissal of "white middle-brow [critics] . . . enforc[ing] white middle-brow standards of excellence" (Jones 1963b, 17) in the pages of *Down Beat*, in connection with his critique of Cool and Third Stream artists in his "The Jazz Avant-Garde" essay, identify clearly those Jones viewed as responsible for the threat. Yet for Lewis, Coleman's album seemed to grow out of a different historical space. Shaped at the Lenox School of Jazz and supported by the same label that had supported Lewis's modernist projects, Coleman's work represented the fruits of (rather than a reaction against) a decade of progressive musical thought bent on challenging assumptions about what jazz music should, and should not, sound like.

Over the course of this book I have aimed to illuminate the myriad of forces behind why Lewis may have viewed such a challenge to be necessary as well as how such an ideology manifested aurally in his own musical works. This choice in storytelling began in my first chapter with a discussion of how the syncretic works surveyed in this book were conceived during a period of exceptional transition in the jazz market. During the 1940s, a shift in record company support from big bands to individual vocalists left an employment and audience hole in the jazz industry that several artists attempted to fill by designing works that utilized both Western art music and African American vernacular sonorities. While some of these artists discovered successful promotional models (Duke Ellington, for instance, stands out in this regard), most struggled to package their works in a manner that consistently enabled financial success. Fortunately, the modernist concept of jazz as a developing music advanced by Marshall Stearns and others at tertiary institutions during the late 1940s and early 1950s opened up a new type of venue primed specifically for the promotion of syncretic projects: the university campus. This advancement was of course not without its problems, with access to university venues initially limited to white syncretic jazz groups only. I therefore also discussed in this chapter how African American syncretic composers were forced to capitalize on increasing modernist interest by opening parallel "modern" music venues built on the foundation of established African American musical spaces. This shift in venue choice and aligned embrace of classical-jazz fusion techniques did indeed enable the recruitment of new supporters but, in the eyes of many, seemed to court alignment with Western art music to an uncomfortable extent.

Such unease appears largely linked to the historic essentialization of rhythm in African and African American musical discourse discussed in chapter 2. My discussion of Lewis's reception within this critical milieu aimed to illuminate the inevitable result of such a mind-set. Throughout the chapter I endeavored to show how ambiguous counterpoint and multi-movement formats utilized by the MJQ frequently pushed to the side rhythmic consideration in appraisals of the group's music made by the jazz press. Such criticism then worked to cast Lewis's music against established notions of "genuine" jazz. Furthermore, I set out the manner in which such criticism conjured an image of Lewis and the MJQ as abdicators of African American social norms. Specifically, I argued that the reception of Lewis's musical identity as "European" went hand in hand with ascriptions of conservative behavior and dress that were coded in the jazz press as "white," articulating a persistent stereotype about African American behavior and culture being the opposite: primitive and wild.

Yet for many African Americans, such assessments about what constituted "real" African American social and cultural norms missed the mark in more ways than one. In chapter 3 I looked at the history of challenges to African American behavioral and cultural stereotyping that took place in middle- and upper-class African American circles during the seventy years prior to Lewis's emergence in an effort to demonstrate both why African Americans saw power in a conservative cultural model that mirrored hegemonic values and how many African American artists sought to realize these values in musical terms. This discussion demonstrated that challenges to cultural stereotypes did indeed help many African Americans reassume the reigns of self-determination by effectively achieving behavioral parity within a society that overtly denied the basic facts of equality. I then put forth the argument that persistent segregation in the United States resulted in many members of this group viewing their maintenance of behavioral parity—most evident in the domains of "genteel behavior" and the celebration of Western art music—not as a shared cultural heritage with "white" America but as a discrete tradition.

The discussion of musical works that then took place in chapter 4 sought to graph how the legacy of this tradition impacted the exploration of new markets and Lewis's musical practice during his first decade of ensemble leadership. Immediately apparent in these analyses was the fact that Lewis frequently pursued contrapuntal ambiguity in his works—a compositional approach that engaged listeners in questions about where genre boundaries stood and whether the supposed rigidity of compositional realms was in fact something real. Such an approach required intimate knowledge of jazz-based improvisational practices as well as Western art music contrapuntal techniques (or processes) and quickly elevated Lewis's music to the forefront of a modernist jazz movement centered on the idea that jazz was an evolving, forward-looking music. The confidence Lewis gained from this acceptance—particularly in relation to the exponents of modernism abroad—seems to have in turn contributed to a deeper engagement with Western artistic ideas, most notable in his ongoing exploration of the commedia dell'arte theatrical form over the latter half of the 1950s. Yet the musical traditions of the African American middle and upper class discussed in chapter 3 allow us to view even these works as something other than outward-looking vehicles of appropriation. Indeed, whether or not one agrees entirely with the idea that works like "Colombine" and "Harlequin" should be ascribed the label of "real" black music, there is at the very least an historical basis for conceiving of these works as part of a bona fide African American music-making tradition based on the celebration and stewardship of Western artistic forms. Furthermore, Lewis's desire to expand the presence of improvisation in the realm of film scores, discussed in chapter 5, further confirms at least some level of involvement with a project aimed at reshaping ideas about African American music, aligning it with middle- and upper-class uplift strategy.

Beyond the Audible Black Voice

Interpreting Lewis's music in relation to this spectrum of cultural forces sets the stage for a discussion of the effects of sonic essentialism in African

American musical discourse more generally. For instance, in an examination of one of Lewis's contemporaries, bassist-composer Charles Mingus, Eric Porter rightly identifies a shift in the overtness of vernacular tropes following the scoring of Mingus's work "Revelations" (discussed in chapter 1) but couples this observation with the statement that "Mingus's music became, in a sense, 'blacker'" (2002, 117). On one hand, Porter is clearly right. The blues sonorities and rhythmic drive that permeate the 1959 albums *Blues and Roots* and *Mingus Ah Um* articulate a clear commitment to musical tropes from the folk realm. But pointing to the overt use of these tropes as the essence of what it means to produce "black" music marginalizes a history of African American music making concerned with the exploration of other sorts of musical phenomena. Porter uses quotation marks around the term "blacker" in an effort to denote that it is perceptions of blackness to which he is referring and so it is not his reading of Mingus's shift that directly requires revision. It is instead the enduring nature of essentialist perceptions of blackness that must be interrogated if we are to understand why audibility of blues sonorities continues to signal blackness to a greater extent than the sonic realization of a rhetorical trope like "revision with difference" or even the performance of certain works of Western art music—musical "traditions" that have at various times played equally central roles in African American musical experience.

Of course, one must not be naïve in regard to the danger of dismissing the many ways in which blues aesthetics have shaped significant aspects of African American culture. Indeed, the centrality of blues aesthetics to the vernacular theory texts of the 1960s and 1970s—of which Jones's/Baraka's *Blues People* (1963) and *Black Music* (1961) are a central part—can largely be understood as responding to the very real threat of cultural devaluation posed by those who would downplay the importance of blues sensibilities. The broad methodological trend in jazz discourse prior to the advent of vernacular theory typically involved tracing the evolution of structural elements in the genre through transcriptions and analytical techniques established for the study of Western art music. Evaluation in these investigations then revolved around a comparison of the structural elements of the jazz works studied with musical conventions typically found in the works of European composers. Winthrop Sargeant's *Jazz Hot and Hybrid* ([1938] 1975), published at the height of the swing era, provided the first book-length study oriented along these lines. As the incorporation of European elements into jazz became more pronounced following the 1940s, however, others would begin applying similar methodologies (Schuller 1958, 1968; Schmitz & de Lerma 1979). When viewed from a contemporary context, such assessments appear to evince Eurocentric bias. Were this to have become the dominant analytical trend in jazz discourse, it is conceivable that the genre's blues roots might have eventually become more or less a footnote in a broader discussion of a new style of syncretic American music.

Such an outcome was not desirable to those who understood and in many cases had participated in a system of creation that seemed distinct from Western creative practices. And whether or not this distinction was true in an absolute sense is beside the point.[1] Faced with marginalization, these authors understandably rejected descriptions of African American music that saw value in it only when it mirrored Western conventions and sought to illuminate innovative vernacular use whenever and wherever it occurred. While part of this involved the discussion of African American rhetorical tropes such as "revision with difference" and "double-voiced" constructs, sonic effects such as rhythmic syncopation, blues sonorities, pendular thirds, riffs, and all other facets derived from what Sterling Stuckey refers to as the "Ring Shout" (discussed in chapter 1) were in turn reasonably championed as valuable components of African American music making. Yet the way in which these authors prioritized this long list of sonorities associated with folk culture over sonorities developed in connection with cosmopolitan African American culture effectively drew a line in the sand for what might constitute "real" black music.

In a recent book titled *Racial Uplift and American Music: 1878–1943* (2012), Lawrence Schenbeck writes of being inspired by a question asked by one of his students in an introductory music class that appeared to grow out of this essentialist position: "Just what is black about the music of [orchestral] composer Florence Price (1888–1953)?" (2012, 3). Over the course of his monograph, Schenbeck answers this question by discussing the history of African American spirituals and orchestrated works through a framework similar to that used in chapter 3 of this book. Specifically, he focuses on how the "politics of respectability"—or what he refers to as "uplift ideology"—was used to redefine notions of African American identity throughout several historic periods of migration and community formation in the United

States. Writing about a shift toward more direct, community-oriented political activism at the end of the 1940s, Schenbeck then reaches the following conclusion:

> For better or worse black Americans' fight for civil rights and equal opportunity would no longer be waged in those concert halls and artist studios where the quiet demonstration of "civilized" behaviors had had to serve as the only weapon available for gaining basic respect and better treatment. Art as a survival strategy, as a marker of gentility, education, and potential for inclusion, would be supplanted in the coming decades by legal battles, protest marches and legislation. The privileges politely requested by the Talented Tenth would become rights demanded by all African Americans. And, linked to that sea change in attitudes, the stature of the Race's Nathaniel Detts, Carl Ditons, and Howard Swansons would be overtaken by its Duke Ellingtons, Dinah Washingtons, and Miles Davises. (2012, 242)

While I agree with the vast majority of Schenbeck's assertions, I do feel that the story I have told in this monograph paints a slightly different picture regarding the legacy of uplift ideology. In other words, I feel that Schenbeck's summary above has the potential to lead some readers to the idea that the sort of identities constructed through the uplift project were a means to a political end only and that as attitudes in the United States toward African Americans began to change, African Americans were allowed to slide back into their vernacular roots (or at the very least, to begin to lift the symphonic robes with which they had draped their blues sensibilities). Certainly there seems to be some truth in reading the situation that way. The acceptance of bebop and modern jazz in elite African American circles during the 1940s (discussed in chapter 3) shows absolutely how narratives regarding cultural evolution espoused by the New Negro movement were eventually used to elevate musical forms long associated with provincial folk elements—at least as soon as the white hegemony was also ready to embrace such forms as modern art.

Yet to suggest that this elevation was the only important outcome of the project seems to marginalize a group of people who had grown to think of their musical heritage in different terms. John Lewis's expansive view regarding the possibilities of modern music in particular seems to have grown out of a conception of musical practice that more often than not aimed to deny the audibility of folk elements and at other times went further, removing folk elements from the musical core of his works in order to make room for Western art concepts. The long history of utilizing "double-voiced" musical tropes in African American culture that I discuss in the opening of this book demonstrates one way in which we can see the former set of works as upholding African American cultural practice even as they produced content that challenged consensus surrounding what "real" black music should sound like. Contextualizing the latter group of works in similar terms is more difficult.

Still, before dismissing the latter group as somehow inauthentic, it is vitally important to consider Guthrie Ramsey's call to consider "what . . . modernity [was] to African Americans at the historical moment under consideration" (2003, 97) For many African Americans (although not nearly all), the 1950s were a moment of arrival. Decades of musical practice long undertaken separately from the white Western art music world were now bearing fruit in the form of interracial orchestral societies across the United States. Symphonic works by African American composers had in turn begun to infiltrate mainstream orchestral performance, and the segregation of traditionally white ensembles was beginning to slowly erode. These changes were not brought about apathetically. They resulted from nearly a hundred years' worth of struggle, training, and musical innovation within African American communities. To consider these advancements as somehow disconnected from the African American cultural world would therefore be to seriously misunderstand their significance.

Yet this is the attitude against which Lewis would struggle as he strove to promote his musical vision and the attitude against which his legacy would be assessed at the time of his death. It is worth keeping such a disconnect in mind as the historical particularities of jazz movements are parsed further—particularly as we continue to develop frameworks for understanding various conceptions of authenticity, a phenomenon experienced by many in very real terms but rarely agreed upon universally by those who lay claim to it. As we embrace this challenge, we must be prepared to nuance our long-held understandings about much-loved music, but the payoff of such a sacrifice is much greater than anything we might lose. Accepting the fact that multiple conceptions of "real" black music might exist at any one time allows the voices and stories of individuals, rather than the generalized voice of an imagined group, to gain critical weight. In this way we bring to the forefront of our musical discussions actual experiences of race and culture rather than imagined constructs of these terms and give power to individuals who for whatever reason have never fit easily into a single mold.

Appendixes

Appendix A
Formal Outlines of Selected Works

Table A. "All the Things You Are." Recorded December 22, 1952: Prestige LP7059.

M.	Section	Length (mm.)	Improvisation	Rhythmic features
1	Interplay between bass ostinato + cymbal/drum rolls.	7	X	Bass ostinato and cymbal/drum rolls.
7	"A" section of theme played by piano and vibraphone in unison at the octave twice with final two bars omitted.	14	X	Cont.
21	"A" section of the theme played by piano and vibraphone in unison at the octave. Theme evinces slight rhythmic alteration from lead sheet.	8	X	Drums switch to keeping swung time.
29	Second "A" section paraphrased in the piano, vibraphone improvisation played on top.	8	Vibraphone	Cont.
37	Piano improvisation over the chord changes of the "B" section.	8	Piano	Cont.
45	Piano and vibraphone play newly composed melody in unison over chord changes of the third "A" section (+ tag).	12	X	Cont.
57	Composed unison break followed by improvised vibraphone lick, which leads into the next improvisatory section.	4	X/vibraphone	Ensemble plays in rhythmic unison.
61	Vibraphone improvises over the thirty-six-bar form of the piece. Piano comps chords and bass plays changes.	36	Vibraphone	Drums keep swung time.
97	Piano improvises over a bridging section.	8	Piano	Cont.
105	Bass improvises over the chord changes of the "B" section and the first four bars of the third "A" section. Piano and vibraphone motifs derived from the melody provide harmonic support.	12	Bass	Cont.
117	Piano and vibraphone play melody from bar 49 with the final two bars omitted.	6	X	Cont.
123	First four bars of first "A" section played by the piano and vibraphone in unison at the octave. Bass ostinato and cymbal/drum rolls follow for four bars. Final bar is held on the tonic chord by the bass, vibes, and piano.	9	X	Bass ostinato and cymbal/drum rolls.

In relation to the discussion on p. 119, note the use of an asymmetrical introduction and the widespread use of improvisation in this work.

Table B. "Rose of the Rio Grande." Recorded December 22, 1952: Prestige LP7059.

M.	Section	Length (mm.)	Improvisation	Rhythmic features
1	Introductory call-and-response between vibes, piano, and bass.	4	X	Unison—drums begin playing with the ensemble on the piano entrance.
5	Theme composed of overlapping parts (vibraphone and piano) played for eight bars.	8	X	Drums (brushes) accent piano part.
13	Theme repeated.	8	X	Cont. In bar 18 drums proceed to play swung time and bass walks.
21	Vibraphone improvisation. Bar 21 contains quote of introductory call figure. Piano comps chords and short contrapuntal lines. Bass walks changes.	32	Vibraphone	Drums keep swung time.
53	Piano improvisation.	32	Piano	Cont.
85	Theme composed of overlapping parts (vibraphone and piano) played for eight bars.	8	X	Drums (brushes) accent piano part.
93	Theme repeated.	8	X	Cont. In bar 98 drums proceed to play swung time and bass walks.

In relation to the discussion on p. 119, note the contrapuntal interplay in the thematic statements as well as the widespread use of improvisation in this work.

Table C. "Vendome." Recorded December 22, 1952: Prestige LP7059.

M.	Section	Length (mm.)	Improvisation	Rhythmic features	
1	Fugal subject played by vibraphone in C minor.	3 + anacrusis	X	Drums (brushes) play swung time.	
4	Fugal answer played by piano in G minor. Vibraphone plays half-note-length harmonic support.	3	X	Cont.	
7	Fugal subject returns an octave higher in the vibraphone in C minor. Piano plays half notes in harmonic support and two bars of independent counterpoint.	3	X	Cont.	Exposition 1
10	Fugal answer played by bass in G minor while vibraphone and piano continue in independent counterpoint.	3	X	Cont.	
13	Vibraphone improvisation. Piano comps chords and occasionally independent contrapuntal lines. Over final bars ensemble modulates to F minor.	16	Vibraphone	Cont.	Episode 1
29	Fugal subject played by piano in F minor. Vibraphone plays answer while piano continues underneath in independent counterpoint.	7	X	Cont.	Exposition 2
38	Piano improvisation. Vibraphone plays whole-note-length harmonic support. Over final bars ensemble modulates to D major.	11	Piano	Cont.	Episode 2
49	Fugal subject played by vibraphone in D major.	4	X	Cont.	
53	Composed bridging passage involving vibes/piano and bass interplay.	13	X	Cont.	Exposition 3
66	Fugal subject played by piano in E minor.	5	X	Cont.	
71	Vibraphone improvisation. Modulation from E minor to G major. Piano comps chords and occasionally independent contrapuntal lines. Over final bars modulation back to C minor.	37	Vibraphone	Drums keep swung time (clearer accents on beats 2 and 4).	Episode 3
108	Overlapping statements of the fugal subject between the vibraphone and the piano played in C minor.	6.5 bars[1]	X	Cont.	Exposition 4
114.5	Composed coda for all instruments ending on Picardy third.	7	X	Cont.	Coda

[1]There appears to be a two-beat error (omission) in the performance around bar 113.

In relation to the discussion on p. 119, note how preplanned expositions alternate with improvised episodes in this work and how modulations that occur in the episodes enable expositions in a variety of tonalities.

Table D. "The Queen's Fancy." Recorded June 25, 1953: Prestige LP7057.

M.	Section	Length (mm.)	Improvisation	Rhythmic features
1	Opening fanfare.	5	X	Drum rolls on snare. Straight time.
6	Theme stated in the vibraphone.	8	X	Syncopated drum/piano/bass hits for first four bars, then on the beat hits for the remaining four bars. Straight time.
14	Theme played in the piano and offset in the vibraphone.	8	X	Drum rolls on snare; bass plays contrapuntal line for first five bars, then doubles the vibraphone in bar 19 and plays straight quarter notes in bars 20–21. Straight time.
22	Bass plays secondary theme and is accompanied by unison melodic interjections performed by the vibraphone and piano.	8	X	Drums keep swung time.
30	Repeat of opening fanfare with final bar omitted.	4	X	Drum rolls on snare. Straight time.
34	Vibraphone improvisation over AABA form.	32	Vibraphone	Drums keep swung time and bass walks changes. Piano comps chords.
66	Repeat of opening fanfare with final bar omitted.	4	X	Drum rolls on toms. Straight time.
70	Bridging passage in which the secondary theme is truncated into a motif played four times by the vibraphone and passed through a series of ii–V–I changes (beginning in F and ending in Db).	12	X	Drums keep swung time and bass walks changes.
82	Piano improvisation over AABA form.	32	Piano	Drums keep swung time and bass walks changes. Vibraphone comps a few melodic lines behind the improvisation.
114	Repeat of the eight-bar section beginning in bar 22.	8	X	Drums keep swung time.
122	Repeat of opening fanfare with final bar omitted.	4	X	Drum rolls on snare. Straight time.

In relation to the discussion on p. 121, note how straight-time and preplanned contrapuntal passages bracket improvisatory passages in this work.

Table E. "La Ronde." Recorded December 22, 1952: Prestige LP7059.

M.	Section	Length (mm.)	Improvisation	Rhythmic features
1	Composed introduction in which ensemble hits alternate with drum fills.	8	Drums	Improvised drum fills.
9	Theme played in unison at the octave by piano and vibraphone.	16	X	Drums keep swung time.
25	Theme repeated in unison at the octave by piano and vibraphone. Second half of the theme is modified melodically but continues to be played in unison.	16	X	Cont.
41	Composed bridging section.	8	X	Drums keep swung time.
49	Ensemble hits derived from the final eight bars of the theme alternate with drum fills.	16	Drums	Improvised drum fills.
65	Vibraphone improvisation over two twelve-bar blues forms. Piano comps chords and bass walks changes.	24	Vibraphone	Drums keep swung time.
89	Piano improvisation over one twelve-bar blues form. Bass walks changes.	12	Piano	Cont.
101	Composed bridging section. Piano plays in between ensemble breaks during bars 114–15. Drum fills alternate with ascending piano line in bars 117–20.	20	X/drums	Cont. Improvised drum fills in bars 117–20.
121	Theme played in unison at the octave by piano and vibraphone. Final two bars of form played as drum solo.	13	X/drums	Drums keep swung time.
134	Improvised drum solo for sixteen bars. Piano/vibes/bass play final chord in bar 150.	17	Drums	Improvised drum solo.

In relation to the discussion on p. 124, note the centrality of twelve-bar blues choruses embedded within a composed frame in this work.

Table F.1. "La Ronde Suite." Recorded January 9, 1955: Prestige LP7057. Part I (quarter note = 312 approx.) Tempo is not given in cut-time in order to facilitate comparison of form between the movements.

M.	Section	Length (mm.)	Improvisation	Rhythmic features
1	Composed introduction where ensemble hits alternate with piano fills.	8	X	Ensemble plays in rhythmic unison.
9	Theme played by the vibraphone while piano improvisation occurs simultaneously. Bass walks changes.	16	X/piano	Drums keep swung time.
25	Theme repeated in the vibraphone while piano improvisation continues. Bass walks changes.	16	X/piano	Cont.
41	Composed bridging section in which the bass and vibraphone play the melody while the piano improvises fills.	8	X/piano	Bass, drums, and vibraphone play in rhythmic unison.
49	Ensemble hits derived from the final eight bars of the theme alternate with piano fills.	16	X/piano	Ensemble plays hits in rhythmic unison.
65	Piano improvisation occurs over two twelve-bar blues forms. The vibraphone adds independent backing lines over the second chorus. Bass walks changes.	24	Piano	Drums keep swung time.
89	Composed bridging section; piano plays in between ensemble breaks in each bar.	8	X/piano	Bass, drums, and vibraphone play in rhythmic unison.
97	Theme played by the vibraphone while piano improvisation occurs simultaneously.	16	X/piano	Drums keep swung time.
113	Piano improvises unaccompanied coda.	20	Piano	Interpretation is swung but there is no percussion accompaniment.

Table F.2. "La Ronde Suite." Recorded January 9, 1955: Prestige LP7057. Part II (quarter note = 169 approx.)

M.	Section	Length (mm.)	Improvisation	Rhythmic features
1	Composed introduction where ensemble hits alternate with bass fills.	8	X	Ensemble plays in rhythmic unison.
9	Theme played by the piano and vibraphone while bass improvisation occurs simultaneously.	16	X/bass	Drums keep swung time.
25	Theme played by the piano and vibraphone while bass improvisation occurs simultaneously.	16	X/bass	Cont.
41	Composed bridging section in which the vibraphone and piano play the melody while the bass improvises fills.	8	X/bass	Cont.
49	Ensemble hits derived from the final eight bars of the theme alternate with bass fills.	16	X/bass	Cont.
65	Bass improvises over two twelve-bar blues forms while the vibraphone and piano play backing figures over both choruses.	24	Bass	Cont.
89	Composed bridging section; bass plays in between ensemble breaks in each bar.	8	X/bass	Drums hit on beat 1 of bars 89 and 91, then begin swung time in bar 93.
97	Theme played by the piano and vibraphone while bass improvisation occurs simultaneously.	16	X/bass	Drums keep swung time.
113	Bass improvises coda. Vibraphone and piano ostinato accompanies the first four bars, then the bass performs over swing time without vibraphone and piano backing until bar 123, where it plays unaccompanied.	12	Bass	Drums keep swung time until bar 123.

Table F.3. "La Ronde Suite." Recorded January 9, 1955: Prestige LP7057. Part III (quarter note = 260 approx.)

M.	Section	Length (mm.)	Improvisation	Rhythmic features
1	Composed introduction where ensemble hits alternate with vibraphone fills.	8	X	Piano and bass play in rhythmic unison. Drums keep swung time until bar 7, where they give a two-bar break.
9	Theme played by the piano while vibraphone improvisation occurs simultaneously. Bass walks changes.	16	X/vibraphone	Drums keep swung time.
25	Theme played by the piano while vibraphone improvisation occurs simultaneously. Bass walks changes.	16	X/vibraphone	Cont.
41	Composed bridging section in which the piano and bass play the melody while the vibraphone improvises fills.	8	X/vibraphone	Drums play in rhythmic unison with piano and bass.
49	Ensemble hits derived from the final eight bars of the theme alternate with vibraphone fills.	16	X/vibraphone	Drums keep swung time.
65	Vibraphone improvisation over two twelve-bar blues forms. Piano comps chords. Bass walks changes.	24	Vibraphone	Cont.
89	Composed bridging section; vibraphone plays in between ensemble breaks in each bar.	8	X/vibraphone	Drums hit on beat 1 of bars 89 and 91, then begin swung time in bar 93.
97	Theme played by the piano while vibraphone improvisation occurs simultaneously. Bass walks changes.	16	X/vibraphone	Drums keep swung time.
113	Vibraphone improvises coda. Piano and bass play hits over swung time until bar 123, when the vibraphone is left to play unaccompanied.	12	Bass	Drums keep swung time until bar 123.

Table F.4. "La Ronde Suite." Recorded January 9, 1955: Prestige LP7057. Part IV (quarter note = 192 approx.)

M.	Section	Length (mm.)	Improvisation	Rhythmic features
1	Composed introduction where ensemble hits alternate with drum fills.	8	Drums	Improvised drum fills.
9	Theme played in unison at the octave by piano and vibraphone. Bass plays on beat 1 of bars 9 and 13 before supporting the ensemble in rhythmic unison at bar 17.	16	X/drums	Cont.
25	Theme repeated in unison at the octave by piano and vibraphone. Bass plays on beat 1 of bars 25 and 29 before supporting the ensemble in rhythmic unison at bar 33.	16	X/drums	Cont.
41	Composed bridging section. Drums play fills in between ensemble breaks in each bar.	8	X/drums	Cont.
49	Ensemble hits derived from the final eight bars of the theme alternate with drum fills.	16	Drums	Cont.
65	Vibraphone and piano improvise over one twelve-bar blues form. Bass walks changes.	12	Vibraphone + piano	Drums keep swung time.
77	Vibraphone and piano play new chordal melody over twelve bars. Bass pedals on Db half notes.	12	X	Cont.
89	Composed bridging section. Drums play fills in between ensemble breaks in each bar.	8	X/drums	Improvised drum fills.
97	Theme played in unison at the octave by piano and vibraphone. Bass plays on beat 1 of bars 97 and 103 before supporting the ensemble in rhythmic unison at bar 107.	13	X/drums	Cont.
110	Drums play unaccompanied solo.	20 seconds	Drums	Drum solo.

In relation to the discussion on p. 124, note the centrality of the blues form in each movement of the suite.

Table G. "Fontessa." Recorded January 22, 1956: Atlantic LP1231.

M.	Time	Section	Length (mm.)	Improvisation	Rhythmic features
1	0:00	Colombine motif played by vibraphone and piano in straight-time counterpoint. Bass supports harmony with long, sustained notes.	21	X	Straight time. No percussion accompaniment until cymbal rolls with sticks in measures 15–19.
22	1:04	Harlequin theme played by the vibraphone and supported by chordal vamp in the piano. Bass supports using vamp rhythm.	8	X	Drums keep swung time.
30	1:23	Harlequin theme played by the vibraphone. Piano improvises contrapuntal lines with some blues sonorities behind vibraphone in the right hand while outlining vamp with the left. Bass supports using vamp rhythm.	8	X/piano	Cont.
38	1:42	Vibraphone and piano introduce a secondary melody in unison. Bass continues to support using vamp rhythm from bar 22.	8	X	Cont.
46	2:01	Harlequin theme is played in unison by the vibraphone and piano for one bar before being staggered between the two instruments. Bass continues to support using vamp rhythm from bar 22. The final two bars of this section consist solely of the drums keeping time.	8	X	Cont.
54	2:20	Vibraphone solos over the thirty-two-bar AABA form established between measures 22 and 53. Piano comps chords and bass alternates between playing vamp rhythm and walking. Piano plays independent contrapuntal line behind the vibraphone over the final "A" section.	32	Vibraphone/piano	Cont.
86	3:36	Bass plays supporting line from m. 22. Vibraphone improvises.	4	X/vibraphone	Cymbal rolls.
90	3:44	Harlequin theme repeated an octave higher in the vibraphone. Piano improvises contrapuntal lines behind vibraphone in the right hand while outlining vamp with the left. Bass supports using vamp rhythm.	8	X/piano	Drums keep swung time.
98	4:04	Vibraphone and piano play "B" section melody in unison. Bass continues to support using vamp rhythm from bar 22.	8	X	Cont.

Table G.—*continued*

106	4:24	Vibraphone plays Harlequin theme. Piano extracts rhythmic motif from secondary theme and plays a contrapuntal line. Bass continues to support using vamp rhythm.	7.5[2]	X	Cont.
114	4:39	Piano improvisation largely unaccompanied. Bass and vibes provide some chordal support in bars 121–25. Last two bars of solo repeat later in the work and appear to be preplanned.	Unclear	Piano/X	Straight time. Some drum hits, but minimal accompaniment.
	5:06	Piano improvises over new chord progression (Pierrot progression) while bass and vibes provide harmonic support.	6	Piano	Drums keep swung time.
	5:24	Piano plays material from bars 124–25	2	X	Swung time. No percussion accompaniment.
	5:30	Piano continues to improvise over chord progression from 5:06, which extends into the "filled" measures in this iteration.	8	Piano	Drums keep swung time.
	5:54	Unaccompanied piano solo.	Unclear	Piano	Straight time. No percussion accompaniment.
	6:21	Piano improvises over chord progression from 5:30 twice while bass and vibes provide harmonic support.	16	Piano	Drums keep swung time.
	7:00	Piano improvises over new eight-bar chord progression while bass and vibes provide harmonic support.	8	Piano	Cont.
	7:21	Ensemble returns to material and setting from 6:21.	8	Piano	Cont.
	7:42	Unaccompanied piano fill derived from the final measure of improvised material in the previous section.	Unclear	Piano	Swung time. No percussion accompaniment.
	7:46	Vibraphone and piano play new call-and-response riffs in cut-time.	8	X	Drums keep swung cut-time.
	7:57	Repeat of previous eight measures.	8	X	Cont.
	8:07	Unaccompanied piano solo. Vibraphone, drums, and bass play onbeat-offbeat hits between 8:15 and 8:20. Solo ends with piano material from mm. 124–25.	Unclear	Piano	Swung time. Percussion accompaniment accents onbeats during "hits" passage only.

[2]As the half measure of this section appears to be the result of an editing splice with the next section of the work, this schematic treats measures 106–12.5 as a full eight-measure block.

Tables G.—*continued*

8:27	Pantaloon section: Improvised bass solo with dissonant chord arpeggiation played by the vibraphone and piano. Drum fills on cymbals punctuate the solo.	Unclear	Bass	Swung time. Percussion accompaniment limited to the interjection of cymbal rolls during the solo.
9:11	Improvised drum solo with dissonant chord arpeggiation played by vibraphone, piano, and bass added at 9:40.	Unclear	Drums	Improvised drum solo.
10:09	Fontessa theme played again by vibraphone and piano in straight-time counterpoint. Bass supports harmony with long, sustained notes.	22	X	Straight time. No percussion accompaniment until cymbal rolls with sticks from 10:45 to 11:00.

In relation to the discussion on p. 129, note how preplanned thematic passages morph into improvised solos in this work. In relation to the discussion on pp. 142–45, note the different musical styles with which Lewis associates commedia dell'arte characters.

Table H. "Three Windows." Recorded February 20–21, 1958: RCA Victor LP1742.

M.	Section	Length (mm.)	Improvisation	Rhythmic features	
1	Drums play swung pattern on finger cymbals.	5	X	Swung time on finger cymbals.	
6	Fugal exposition. Violins state fugal subject, violas and violins state fugal answer while other violins play countersubject, low strings state subject once again while high strings play counterpoint. Exposition continues with a statement of the subject made by the flute while strings play in counterpoint behind followed by two more statements of the subject by the string sections of the orchestra.	12	X	Cont.	Exposition 1
18	Exposition continues with a statement of the subject by the flute accompanied by string counterpoint and two more statements of the subject by the string sections of the orchestra.	12	X	Cont.	
30	Improvised flute solo with melodic string countermelodies as backings over AAB chord progression (eight measures per section).	24	Flute	Cont. with the incorporation of other cymbals.	Episode 1
54	Improvised flute solo with pizzicato string backings over another "A" section.	8	Flute	Swung time on finger cymbals.	
62	Flute improvisation plays subject motifs while bass plays countersubject.	4	Flute	Cont.	
66	Violins play fugal subject. Flute continues to improvise.	4	Flute	Cont.	Exposition 2
70	Two statements of the fugal subject. Flute joins the ensemble.	8	X	Cont.	

Table H.—*continued*

M.	Section	Length (mm.)	Improvisation	Rhythmic features	
78	Flute introduces new composed melody. Strings echo in call-response.	8	X	Cont.	
86	Melodic turns in the flute and pizz. hits from measures 81–82 are repeated.	4	X	Cont.	
90	Another new theme is played by the saxophone over the first four measures and echoed in the strings over the second four measures.	8	X	Cont.	Episode 2
98	Strings continue to play melodic material derived from saxophone theme.	6	X	Cont.	
104	Ensemble breaks with fills by the flute and saxophone derived from the fugal subject.	10	X	Cont.	
114	Fugal subject stated in the saxophone. Answer and countersubject performed by strings.	8	X	Cont.	Exposition 3
122	Exposition continues with two more statements of the subject by the string sections of the orchestra.	8	X	Cont.	
130	Improvised saxophone solo with melodic string countermelodies as backings over AABA chord progression.	32	Saxophone	Cont.	Episode 3
162	Saxophone continues to improvise while bass plays countersubject.	4	Saxophone	Cont.	
166	Violins play fugal subject. Saxophone continues to improvise.	4	Saxophone	Cont.	Exposition 4
170	Two more statements of the subject occur in the strings alone.	8	X	Cont.	
178	First two measures of the fugal subject are repeated in harmonic sequence by the strings. Final measure of the work sustains on a Picardy third.	9	X	Cont.	Coda

In relation to the discussion on p. 149, note the use of improvised subject motifs in the flute solo beginning in bar 62 and the improvised counterpoint juxtaposed against the fugal subject beginning in bar 66.

Appendix B
Sait-on jamais (1957) Soundscape

Appendix B. *Sait-on jamais* (1957) soundscape

Time	Diegetic/ nondiegetic	Sound source	Scene description	Music description
1:07–1:18	Nondiegetic	N/A	Sophie is watching a cartoon in a cinema. The cartoon character is kidnapped by a flying saucer.	Orchestral accompaniment.
1:52–2:04	Nondiegetic	N/A	Aliens speaking in "jive" describe the good-looking girls on the alien planet.	Blues-based trumpet melody played over drum ostinato.
2:12–2:15	Nondiegetic	N/A	Cartoon character is introduced to alien king.	Trumpet fanfare.
4:12–4:15	Nondiegetic/ Diegetic	Cinema speakers	Sophie leaves the cinema.	Trumpet fanfare plays as part of the cartoon.
5:12–6:35	Nondiegetic	N/A	Michel introduces himself to Sophie outside of the cinema. They walk through the streets of Venice.	"Golden Striker" theme "One Never Knows" theme (MJQ).
6:36–7:50	Nondiegetic	N/A	Sforzi sees Michel and Sophie speaking outside a bar.	"Crime jazz" cliché "Three Windows" theme (MJQ).
7:51–8:13	Nondiegetic/ Diegetic	Live jazz quartet	Michel and Sophie enter bar.	"Three Windows" theme continues (MJQ).
8:14–9:50	Nondiegetic/ Diegetic	Live jazz quartet	Michel and Sophie flirt while avoiding discussion of past relationships.	Vibraphone **improvisation** over "Three Windows" form (MJQ).
9:51–10:37	Nondiegetic/ Diegetic	Live jazz quartet	Sforzi enters bar to confront Sophie.	"The Rose Truc" theme (MJQ).
10:38–11:40	Nondiegetic	N/A	Sforzi takes Sophie over to empty bandstand to warn her against seeing Michel.	Vibraphone **improvisation** over "The Rose Truc" form (MJQ).
11:41–12:52	Diegetic	Live jazz quartet	Sophie and Michel eat dinner while a jazz combo plays in the background. Sophie invites Michel back to her villa.	"Venice" theme (MJQ).
13:43–14:32	Nondiegetic/ Diegetic	Record player	Michel and Sophie discuss their relationship in Sophie's bedroom.	Vibraphone **improvisation** over major twelve-bar blues.
15:38–16:02	Diegetic	Live piano	Michel stumbles on Bernard playing piano.	Unidentified rag.
17:35–19:43	Nondiegetic/ Diegetic	Record player	Sophie tells Michel of how the Baron rescued her from poverty.	"Venice" theme Vibraphone **improvisation** over "Venice" form "The Rose Truc" theme (MJQ).

Appendix B.—*continued*

Time	Diegetic/ nondiegetic	Sound source	Scene description	Music description
19:44–19:52	Diegetic	Live piano	Bernard plays ragtime on the piano. The Baron, frustrated by Michel's presence, enters and tells him to stop.	Unidentified rag.
22:17–22:58	Diegetic	Record player	Sophie tells Michel she loves him the morning after their tryst.	Piano **improvisation** over major twelve-bar blues.
22:59–24:38	Nondiegetic	N/A	Michel bets on racing mice with Bernard and Sforzi.	Piano **improvisation** continues, transitions to vibraphone improvisation.
26:12–29:09	Nondiegetic	N/A	Michel plays chess with the Baron. The Baron offers a different version of how he and Sophie met then the one Sophie offered the previous night.	"Three Windows" theme "One Never Knows" theme (MJQ).
32:22–33:15	Nondiegetic	N/A	Michel enters the Baron's study, where the Baron is either restoring or forging a painting.	"Three Windows" theme (MJQ).
33:16–34:40	Nondiegetic	N/A	Michel tells the Baron he is taking Sophie away.	Piano **improvisation** over "Three Windows" form (MJQ).
34:40–34:55	Nondiegetic	N/A	Sophie goes to say good-bye to the Baron.	"Three Windows" theme (MJQ).
38:22–38:42	Nondiegetic	N/A	Sforzi enters the Baron's villa and finds a man hanging by a noose.	"Cortege" theme (MJQ).
38:43–38:57	Nondiegetic	N/A	Sforzi pulls the hand of the man and it comes off, revealing it to be a dummy constructed by the servants as a practical joke.	Piano **improvisation** over "Three Windows" form (MJQ).
45:32–47:20	Nondiegetic	N/A	Sforzi interrupts Michel and Sophie at their hotel. He attempts to seduce Sophie in an effort to bring her back to the Baron.	Chopin, Piano Sonata No. 2 in Bb Minor, op. 35
48:30–49:46	Diegetic	Live jazz quartet	Michel and Sophie have dinner at a Venice club.	Unidentified calypso (MJQ).
49:47–51:22	Diegetic	Live jazz quartet	Sophie is confronted by Sforzi in a back room of the club. He hits her and declares his love for her.	"Venice" theme (MJQ).

Appendix B.—*continued*

Time	Diegetic/ nondiegetic	Sound source	Scene description	Music description
51:23–52:57	Diegetic	Live jazz quartet	Sophie returns to Michel and asks to leave. Sforzi meets the detective investigating the Baron at the bar. The detective tells Sforzi he has blood on his shirt.	Vibraphone **improvisation** over "Venice" form Piano **improvisation** over "Venice" form (MJQ).
53:07–54:22	Nondiegetic	N/A	Sforzi meets Sophie on her way home from the shops. He gives her a rose and convinces her to leave Michel.	"Crime jazz" cliché "Three Windows" theme (MJQ).
1:01:39–1:02:05	Nondiegetic	N/A	Sforzi enters the Baron's study and tells the Baron that Sophie remembers where to find the hidden money.	"Three Windows" theme "Cortege" theme (MJQ).
1:02:06–1:02:30	Nondiegetic	N/A	The Baron shows Sforzi a letter he has written to Michel transferring access to the funds.	Vibraphone **improvisation** over "Cortege" form (MJQ).
1:03:03–1:04:05	Diegetic	Piano in far room	Sforzi explains to the Baron why he needs to kill him.	Chopin, *Grande Walse Brillante*, op. 34, no. 2.
1:04:45–1:05:00	Nondiegetic	N/A	The Baron tells Sforzi he doesn't believe he has the courage to commit murder.	"The Rose Truc" them (MJQ).
1:05:01–1:05:31	Nondiegetic	N/A	Sforzi stabs the Baron.	Cymbal roll, ascending vibes/piano/bass melody.
1:11:45–1:12:52	Nondiegetic/ Diegetic	Record player	The detective interviews Michel about his relationship with Sophie and Sforzi in Michel's hotel room.	Guitar melody.
1:14:05–1:15:32	Nondiegetic	N/A	Funeral procession through canals.	"Cortege" theme (MJQ).
1:15:33–1:16:25	Nondiegetic	N/A	Michel pulls up to Sophie's gondola and kisses her hand.	Vibraphone **improvisation** Piano **improvisation** over "Cortege" form (MJQ).
1:16:26–1:17:18	Nondiegetic	N/A	An angry Sforzi hits Sophie. Sophie tells the gondolier to let her out.	"Cortege" theme (MJQ).
1:22:26–1:24:11	Nondiegetic	N/A	Sophie waits with Sforzi in his apartment. She secretly lets Michel in to find the letter the Baron wrote giving Michel control over his estate.	"Crime jazz" cliché "Three Windows" theme Piano **improvisation** over form (MJQ).

Appendix B.—*continued*

Time	Diegetic/ nondiegetic	Sound source	Scene description	Music description
1:29:30–1:29:43	Nondiegetic	N/A	Sforzi leaps a gap between buildings while chasing Michel across the rooftops of Venice.	Cymbal roll, ascending vibes/piano/bass melody (same as scene where the Baron is stabbed).
1:31:12–1:33:44	Nondiegetic	N/A	Police pull Sforzi's body from the canal after he has fallen to his death.	"Three Windows" theme "One Never Knows" theme (MJQ).

Appendix C
Odds against Tomorrow (1959) Soundscape

Appendix C. *Odds against Tomorrow* (1959) soundscape

Time	Diegetic/ Nondiegetic	Sound source	Scene description	Music description
0:00-0:14	Nondiegetic	N/A	Universal logo.	Universal theme music.
0:15–1:57	Nondiegetic	N/A	Opening credits.	Introductory theme in which motive "a" and motive "b" are paired and orchestrated for the full ensemble.
2:05–2:35	Nondiegetic	N/A	Slater walks down a New York street on the way to Burke's apartment.	Motive "b" is stated by the guitar and transitions to motive "a."
2:36–2:43	Nondiegetic	N/A	Cont.	Solo trumpet interlude (not obviously improvised).
2:44–2:50	Nondiegetic	N/A	Cont.	Motive "a" performed by solo guitar.
2:51–3:07	Nondiegetic	N/A	Slater careens into an African American child playing outside the apartment building. He refers to her as a "pickininny."	Motive "a" continues in the guitar and is paired with motive "b" in the trumpet. An additional trombone line adds dissonance.
3:08–3:22	Nondiegetic	N/A	Slater enters Burke's apartment building and pounds on the manager's desk.	Motive "b" orchestrated into dissonant brass chords.
7:37–8:08	Nondiegetic	N/A	Slater confronts Burke about the assumption that he is a criminal.	Drums play on toms and are paired with bass. Horn plays motive "b," trumpets enter with the same motive.
8:09–8:14	Nondiegetic	N/A	Burke tries to convince Slater to do the robbery.	Drums and bass play a syncopated riff utilizing octaves and a flat seventh.
8:15–9:10	Nondiegetic	N/A	Johnny drives up to the front of Slater's apartment building, exits his car, and enters.	Brass chords to the rhythm of motive "b" transition to a flute solo over quartet backing. While the solo is not obviously improvised, it evinces a good deal of syncopation and it is swung.

Appendix C.—*continued*

Time	Diegetic/ Nondiegetic	Sound source	Scene description	Music description
12:58–13:57	Nondiegetic	N/A	Johnny gives Burke a ride downtown.	Layering of horn and trombone melodies set a tritone apart give way to variations of motive "a" played by the vibraphone and set against a sustained low brass pedal. Dissonant brass chords played to the rhythm of motive "b" are used to signal the end of the scene as Burke exists Johnny's car.
17:27–18:47	Nondiegetic	N/A	Slater's girlfriend loans Slater money for the trip to Melton.	Motive "b," played by a solo guitar, transitions to a doubling of the motive in the guitar and bass. Motive "a" is then played by the guitar and supported by dissonant brass chords before being paired solely with flute trills.
19:04–19:51	Nondiegetic	N/A	Slater and Burke drive to Melton.	Motive "b" orchestrated into dissonant brass chords.
19:52–20:26	Nondiegetic	N/A	Slater and Burke arrive in Melton.	Layering of motive "b," beginning in the tuba and then incorporating the French horn and trumpets.
20:44–22:25	Nondiegetic	N/A	Slater and Burke watch a waiter deliver food to the bank after hours. Burke describes the robbery plan.	Tympani plays motive "b" and these statements are interspersed with snare rolls.
22:30–24:41	Diegetic	Live band	Johnny sings and plays the vibraphone at a jazz club.	"My Baby's Not Around" (1959), written by Belafonte and performed by the MJQ with Belafonte as vocalist. Milt Jackson **improvises** over a discussion between Johnny and one of his creditors. Apart from Belafonte, the other musicians on stage pantomime their parts.
24:55–28:50	Diegetic	Live band	Johnny runs into his ex-girlfriend and has his debt called in by the local crime boss.	Bebop-style improvisation beginning in the piano is followed by bass and saxophone **improvisation**.
29:28–30:22	Diegetic	Live band	Johnny drunkenly accompanies another singer at the jazz club.	"All Men Are Evil" (1959), an R&B-style song written by Belafonte and performed by Mae Barnes. The song ends with a frantic vibraphone **improvisation** pantomimed by Belafonte.

Appendix C.—*continued*

Time	Diegetic/ Nondiegetic	Sound source	Scene description	Music description
33:18–33:42	Nondiegetic	N/A	Johnny kisses his wife good-bye when picking up his daughter.	Motive "a" performed by the vibraphone, underscored by string pedal.
33:44–35:22	Diegetic/Nondiegetic	Merry-go-round	Johnny's daughter rides the merry-go-round. Johnny sees that he is being followed by the gangsters he owes money to.	Carnival-style organ music transitions to motive "b," played by the trumpets.
35:23–36:30	Diegetic	Skating rink speakers	Johnny calls Burke from a pay phone to confirm his involvement in the robbery.	"Skating in Central Park" (1959), orchestrated.
40:48–42:20	Diegetic/Nondiegetic	N/A	Slater enters a bar and confronts a young army cadet.	Vibraphone **improvisation** over the form of "Cue #9" (1959). Music stops abruptly at the time of confrontation, effectively confirming a nondiegetic sound source.
43:38–44:27	Nondiegetic	N/A	Slater explains to the bartender that he didn't mean to hurt the cadet.	Guitar and brass perform a variation of motive "a," which transitions to chordal brass statements of motive "b" and then solo guitar statements of motive "b."
44:28–47:35	Nondiegetic	N/A	Burke's girlfriend attempts to console him.	Motive "b" in the guitar transitions to swing ostinato doubled in the bass. An **improvised** guitar solo utilizing blues tropes follows. Dissonant brass chords to the rhythm of motive "b" accompany Slater's girlfriend's exit and his call to Burke confirming his participation.
48:00–51:22	Nondiegetic	N/A	Johnny and his wife flirt. She then asks him to leave the apartment for the sake of their child.	Motive "a" begins in the guitar and is doubled by the vibraphone. A bass ostinato and vibraphone solo follows (not obviously improvised). Motive "a" then returns in the harp accompanied by a flute melody.

Time	Diegetic/ Nondiegetic	Sound source	Scene description	Music description
51:27–55:17	Nondiegetic	N/A	Slater's next-door neighbor comes over to complain about her husband. She asks Slater about the man he killed before he went to prison. Their flirtations lead to sex.	Bass and drum ostinato gives way to cascading piano lines and brass chords played to the rhythm of motive "b." This passage in turn gives way to the quartet performance of "No Happiness for Slater"(1959), during which Lewis **improvises**.
59:01–59:40	Nondiegetic	N/A	Burke praises Johnny for his idea on how to get the bank guards to open the door after hours.	Ensemble trumpet passage ending with motive "b."
59:41–1:01:00	Nondiegetic	N/A	Slater's girlfriend apologizes for their fight.	Swung guitar performance of motive "b" with high hat and flute accompaniment.
1:02:05–1:04:45	Nondiegetic	N/A	Burke, Johnny, and Slater travel up to Melton.	Ostinato first stated in the vibraphone and then in the bass accompanied by drums. As the tempo of the score increases, the ostinato reduces from four notes to two and an extended vibraphone **improvisation** can be heard over the top. This passage is punctuated by dissonant brass chords played to the rhythm of motive "b."
1:05:58–1:07:54	Nondiegetic	N/A	Burke and Slater discuss the hiring of Johnny. During the conversation, the bus Johnny is taking to Melton passes them on the highway.	Motive "b" in the brass is followed by motive "a" in the harp before returning to motive "b" in the brass. This passage then transitions back to the four-note ostinato of the previous scene.
1:10:03–1:10:16	Nondiegetic	N/A	Johnny sees the bank for the first time.	Dissonant layering of motive "b" in the brass.
1:13:01–1:17:53	Nondiegetic	N/A	The three independently explore Melton before the robbery.	Tympani rolls paired with motive "a" in the guitar and motive "b" in the flute. This passage is followed by a return to the four-note and then two-note ostinato figure accompanied by a vibraphone melody with added trills and gliss embellishments. The vibraphone melody gives way to an **improvised** guitar melody utilizing blues tropes. The passage ends with a brass fanfare.

Appendix C.—*continued*

Time	Diegetic/ Nondiegetic	Sound source	Scene description	Music description
1:22:58–1:23:53	Non-Diegetic	N/A	Johnny approaches the bank dressed as the waiter.	Tympani plays motive "b" and these statements are interspersed with snare rolls.
1:25:09–1:26:56	Non-Diegetic	N/A	Johnny, Slater, and Burke enter the bank.	Motive "a" is played at a fast tempo while the brass repeat a countermelody in unison. Dissonant brass chords played to the rhythm of motive "b" are then added to the passage.
1:27:08–1:28:24	Non-Diegetic	N/A	Slater pulls the real waiter inside the bank to avoid his calling the police.	Unison trumpet melody utilizing blues third and blues seventh alternates with dissonant brass chords. Toward the middle of this passage, lip trills are added to the brass chords.
1:32:29–1:34:08	Non-Diegetic	N/A	Johnny chases Slater into a gas plant.	Tympani plays motive "b" and these statements are interspersed with both snare and cymbal hits. Cymbal hits evolve to a constant cymbal roll, the ending of which corresponds to the plant explosion.
1:34:46–1:36:01|	Non-Diegetic	N/A	Johnny's and Slater's corpses are revealed to the police investigators.	Exit theme combining elements of motive "a" and motive "b" transitions to "No Happiness for Slater" (1959), performed by the MJQ underneath the ending credits.

Notes

Introduction

1. The words *Signifyin(g)* or *Signifies* will appear without quotation marks from this point forward. I have adopted Gates's spelling in an effort to clarify usage between the English-language term *signifying*, in which there can be only one meaning for something that is signified, and the rhetorical trope of the "double-voiced" described here.

2. Still, for instance, is shown to mask his use of twelve-bar blues by integrating it into "a sonata-allegro format" in his *Afro-American Symphony* (1930) (Floyd 1995, 253).

3. Wolfram Knauer's overview of the Modern Jazz Quartet's reception in Europe, for instance, holds that even though some on the Continent felt these musical fusions stifled improvisation, Lewis's musical approach was generally effective in building an audience of "educated middle class" patrons who were "accustomed to classical music" (1990, 58). In turn, in an assessment of the German context, Andrew Hurley has pointed to the way in which the MJQ's use of European sonorities fit neatly into legitimization paradigms developed by Joachim-Ernst Berendt that sought to build acceptance for the music in the postwar era (2009, 24–25).

4. Feature articles in the *Chicago Defender* throughout the 1920s and 1930s frequently worked to tell this story. For instance, W. S. Turner's 1927 *Social Forces* article "Has the Negro Arrived?" was reprinted in the *Defender* in the same year under the heading "Writer Says There Is No Such Thing as 'New Negro.'" Turner's argument held that while on the surface there appear to be differences in achievement between the races in the United States, most of these could be explained away through an analysis of institutionalized racism; once such a force was accounted for, intellectual parity was evident. Other notable articles that provide additional evidence of this type of argument include Carter Wilson's "Dr. Woodson Raps Race 'Tear-Down' Tendencies" published in the *Defender* on January 21, 1933, and Jesse Thomas's "The History of Race Relations," published on May 4, 1935.

5. The original text in French reads, "En définitive, ces concerts marquerent une importante victoire du 'modern sound' dans notre pays et les amateurs français purent constater de visu que le jazz ne s'est jamais mieux porté."

6. This is not to suggest that the French reception of the Modern Jazz Quartet was without detractors. Indeed, at the end of the very same *Jazz Magazine* article that wel-

comed Lewis to the Continent we are presented with a collection of interviews under the heading "We posed the question to 10 jazzmen that was on everyone's lips . . . is the Modern Jazz Quartet jazz?" ("Sous le signe du 'Birdland'" 1956, 19), in which the musicians Ralph Schecroun and Martial Solal take Lewis to task for abandoning what they view as the essential rhythmic drive of the music.

7. The original text in German reads, "Die Verbindung von Jazz und europäischer Musik, an der zahllose weiß Musiker in Amerika seit Jahren experimentieren, wurde von John Lewis—ohne ein Stadium des Experimentes—in seinem Modern Jazz Quartet."

Chapter 1

1. Polo's first improvisatory chorus is accompanied by bass, piano, and drums. The brass then enter with backings during the second chorus and Folus can be heard to play in counterpoint to Polo's improvisation. The third chorus, led by Folus, involves constant reiterations, or echoes by Polo, uniting the two in improvisatory dialogue.

2. On the September 4 broadcast Davis trades fours with drummer Max Roach over his last two choruses. On the September 18 broadcast this trading occurs only during the first half of the third chorus, at which point Roach plays the chorus out.

3. Dizzy Gillespie's 1947 performance at Cornell University stands in contrast to this trend. His premiere at Carnegie Hall in the same year and Stearns's creation of the Rhythm Club at Cornell should be taken into account in viewing this event in the overall context of venue access.

4. The MJQ's entirely African American racial composition stands in contrast to the trend identified above and will be contextualized as part of a perception of "whiteness" discussed in chapter 2.

5. In a clear indication of the important role college audiences played in Brubeck's success, *Down Beat* would subsequently report, "Dave Brubeck's quartet will henceforth play only a limited number of club dates in the east. . . . [His] main concentration . . . will be on college and other concerts because of unprecedented demand for his quartet on campuses throughout the country, and also because Brubeck feels that the college audience has been vitally important in his popularity" ("Brubeck Dave" 1954, 1).

6. According to Davis (1989, 143), Lewis left early on the recording date for *Miles Davis and Horns*, leaving Davis to play most of the piano tracks himself.

7. Floyd sets out his understanding of Stuckey's research as follows:

> Stuckey regards the Negro spiritual as central to the ring and foundational to all subsequent Afro-American music-making. He noticed in descriptions of the shout that, in the ring, musical practices from throughout black culture converged in the spiritual. These included elements of the calls, cries, and hollers; call-and-response devices; additive rhythms and polyrhythms; heterophony, pendular thirds, blue notes, bent notes, and elisions; hums, moan, grunts, vocables, and other rhythmic-oral declamations, interjections, and punctuations; off-beat melodic phrasings and parallel intervals and chords; constant repetition of rhythmic and melodic figures and phrases (from which riffs and vamps would be derived); timbral distortions of various kinds; musical individuality within collectivity; game rivalry; hand-

> clapping, foot patting, and approximations thereof; and the metronomic foundational pulse that underlies all Afro-American music. Consequently, since all of the defining elements of black music are present in the ring, Stuckey's formulation can be seen as a frame in which all black-music analysis and interpretation can take place—a formulation that can confirm the importance of the performance practices crucial to black music expression. (1991/1999, 267–68)

Chapter 2

1. There exists, of course, the possibility that *blood* serves as a metaphor for culture in the statement, yet I would argue that based on Radano's (2003) study, if the term is being used as a metaphor, the choice of comparison is indebted to a history of biological predisposition discourse and that essentialist connotations remain.

2. Machito was born Francisco Raúl Gutiérrez Grillo in Havana, Cuba, on February 16, 1908 (Child 1998, 801).

3. The work was written by George Russell for the Gillespie ensemble in 1947, although Monson notes in her discussion of the work that "the idea for the project came from Gillespie" (1998, 165).

Chapter 3

1. In purely archival terms, David Music has pointed out that "African-American spirituals . . . made little impact on mainline congregational song collections (whether white or black) until after World War II" (2001, 8).

2. This phenomenon is explored in considerable detail throughout Paul Lopes's *Rise of a Jazz Art World* (2002). See in particular pp. 215–16.

3. A striking example can be seen in a 1946 article about the potential use of bebop in symphony orchestras written by Elaine Greenidge for the *Pittsburgh Courier*. Greenidge presents quotes by Teddy Wilson, Tadd Dameron, and Edgar Sampson about the suitability of the style within the orchestral context that utilize the language of evolution. Dameron, for instance, claims, "Bebop will hold a high place in the classical world of tomorrow. In bebop, instead of jumping from one chord to another, you find various ways of getting to each chord. This allows for more originality and feeling in arrangements" (qtd. in Greenidge 1946, 21). Similar endorsements of bebop as a new, "intelligent" form of jazz in the African American press can be found in Dan Burley's (1948, 25) assessment of Thelonious Monk's "genius" published in the *New York Amsterdam News* and the *Chicago Defender*'s framing of the music as linked to an expansion of tertiary music training ("Lionel Hampton Writes of Bebop" 1948, 8).

4. I am not attempting to dilute or belittle the very real "pioneering" work these composers undertook in the service of jazz music. For an extensive discussion of these contributions, see John Howland's *Ellington Uptown: Duke Ellington, James P. Johnson, and the Birth of Concert Jazz* (2009). My intent here is to simply point out that a wider array of precedent existed in relation to their work than was normally acknowledged in the trade press.

Chapter 4

1. The group disbanded for the first time in 1974. It then reformed in 1981 and performed in a variety of contexts until the death of Connie Kay in 1994.

2. Short introductions were often included before bebop heads (see Dizzy Gillespie's "Bebop" [1945] and Charlie Parker's "Yardbird Suite" [1946]), and the general structure of the head-solos-head format remained in Lewis's arrangements, with improvisation continuing to permeate the standards. Indeed, sections of open improvisation occur in over 57 percent of the bars that make up "All the Things You Are" and over 64 percent of the bars that make up "Rose of the Rio Grande" (see tables A and B in appendix A).

3. As Paul Walker notes in his definition of *episode* in *Oxford Music Online*: "A fugue is generally laid out as an opening Exposition followed by alternation between episodes and groups of thematic statements" (2010, ¶1).

4. Wolfram Knauer's analysis of the work touches on this phenomenon in his observation that Lewis delivers an improvised solo "integrated fully into the compositional frame" (1990, 126).

5. The album *Modern Jazz Quartet with Milt Jackson* contains all the tracks recorded on December 22, 1952, and June 25, 1953.

6. As Thomas Owens (1965, 12) rightly points out in his 1965 MA thesis, describing the improvised side of this equation as "collective improvisation"—which some critics were prone to do—was somewhat of an overstatement. Lewis's improvised contrapuntal lines were far more compact than what might result from a simultaneous solo. Yet this, in fact, seemed largely the point of the approach. Despite their improvisatory genesis, these interjections mirrored closely the contrapuntal subjects or motifs Lewis would use in the opening and closing sections of his works.

7. The name *The Modern Jazz Quartet* does appear below the word *Concorde* on the album cover, but it is less prominent, and as it refers to a group rather than an individual, it is less focused on individuality.

8. In Thomas Owens's view, such ambiguity was heightened by the fact that Lewis often composed thematic material in a style similar to the melodic lines he would improvise. In relation to the fugal work "Three Windows" (1957), discussed in chapter five, Owens writes, "Lewis obtains further unity by composing the thematic material completely in the style of his own improvisational style. Each of the subjects and countersubjects sounds as if it had been improvised on the spur of the moment, yet each fits with the others in an obviously preplanned way" (1965, 79).

9. The original text in German reads, "Es wird damit deutlich, wie vieles, was in der Musik des MJQ als eindeutig 'europäisch' erscheint, unterbewußt improvisiert wurde von Musikern, die—außer John Lewis selbst—sich allein der Jazz-Tradition verpflichtet fühlen und in keinem Augenblick ahnen, daß irgend etwas, was sie spielen, 'europäisch' sein könnte."

10. Use of the same arrangement can be discerned by comparing the SDR recording with the recording of the Modern Jazz Society concert released on Verve Records 823 089–1.

11. The original text in French reads, "Nous avons posé à 10 jazzmen la question qui était sur toutes les lèvres . . . le M.J.A. fait-il du jazz?"

12. The original text in French reads, "S'agit-il d'une formule intéressante et valuable en elle-même, mais qui n'aura pas d'incidence sur l'evolution du jazz, comme par exemple le quintette à cordes de Django Reinhardt?"

13. The musicians interviewed by *Jazz Magazine* were Don Byas, Kenny Clarke, Sacha Distel, Raymond Fol, Mac Kac, Henri Renaud, Ralph Checroun, Martial Solal, Benny Vasseur, and Barney Wilen.

14. These three works were released in connection with recordings of "Dear Old Stockholm" (retitled "Warmland") and the Lewis original "The Bad and the Beautiful" (1956), recorded in the summer of 1956, along with the Rogers and Hart song "Little Girl Blue" (1935) and the Lewis original "D&E" (1955), recorded in February 1957 for the label.

Chapter 5

1. Authorship of these songs is attributed to Lewis in Michelle Best's (1999) discussion of the *Odds* score, but copyright registered to Belafonte and Okun credits the pair for words and music. Copyright for "My Baby's Not Around" was first issued on March 5, 1959, and caries U.S. Copyright Office (USCO) registration number EU0000565275. It was renewed on December 18, 1987, with USCO registration number RE0000360706. Copyright for "All Men are Evil" was first issued on March 5, 1959, with USCO registration number EU0000565274. It was renewed September 9, 1987, with USCO registration number RE0000349661.

2. This discussion relies on Mervyn Cooke's (2009, 255) definition of *symphonic* film music as music that is both "pre-composed" and "orchestral."

3. Ford's analysis is linked to the released 1958 version of the film. The 1998 director's cut, informed by editing instructions from Welles to Universal Studios, replaces Mancini's opening with a series of diegetic cues (Eagan 2010, 545).

4. Ford (2008, 117) points to the term's use by "collectors of obscure vinyl" and in the recently collated *Crime Jazz: Music in the First Degree* (Rhino 72912) and *Crime Jazz: Music in the Second Degree* (Rhino 72913) when sourcing its origin.

5. In addition to the politics of race, Belafonte sought to wage a quieter political battle in the film's production by enlisting the blacklisted writer Abraham Polonsky to write the script (Schultheiss 1999, 137). Polonsky won recognition in Hollywood as an exceptional scriptwriter following his 1948 noir classic *Force of Evil* but was blacklisted for his leftist sympathies during the congressional hearings of Senator Joseph McCarthy in 1951. Polonsky continued to work as a television writer in New York during the 1950s but was forced to use other writers' names as "fronts" and to tone down the leftist sympathies that had brought about his blacklisting (Schultheiss 1996, 148–49).

Chapter 6

1. As I have noted previously; "Amy Fenstermaker views the Signifyin(g) act as closely related to what Linda Hutcheon (1989) refers to as 'complicitous critique,' a device through which an author 'draws on a historical figure or event and simultaneously undermines the historical accuracy of that representation' in an effort to highlight 'the ideology behind that representation.' She goes on to assert that 'whether one calls the artistic process "complicitous critique" or Signifyin(g), the term one uses is, to some extent, dependent upon the author's race' (Fenstermaker 2008, 1)" (Coady 2011, p. 7).

Bibliography

Abbott, R. S. (1934, March 10). Refinement Sadly Lacking in Modern Youth, Says Editor. *Chicago Defender*, p. 11.

Abbott, R. S. (1935, March 2). Education, Culture Should Keep Apace Says R. S. Abbott. *Chicago Defender*, p.11.

Agawu, K. (1995). The Invention of "African Rhythm." *Journal of the American Musicological Society*, 48(3), 380–95.

Angel City Symphony Plans Second Concert. (1958, July 31). *Los Angeles Sentinel*, p. A12.

Another Race Barrier Falls. (1944, December 23). *Chicago Defender*, p. 12.

Applaud Duo Featured in Two-Piano Recital. (1954, April 17). *Chicago Defender*, p. 14.

The Arts and the MJQ. (1959, March 19). *Down Beat*, p. 10.

Atlantic Records Names John Lewis A&R Man. (1962, October 6). *New York Amsterdam News*, p. 22.

Avakian, G. (1957). The Brass Ensemble of the Jazz and Classical Music Society. In *Music for Brass* [LP liner notes] (p. 1). Columbia Records.

Baker, H. (1984). *Blues, Ideology and Afro-American Literature: A Vernacular Theory*. Chicago: University of Chicago Press.

Baker, H. (1987). *Modernism and the Harlem Renaissance*. Chicago: University of Chicago Press.

Baldwin, D. (2007). *Chicago's New Negroes: Modernity, the Great Migration and Black Urban Life*. Chapel Hill: University of North Carolina Press.

Balliett, W. (1971). *Ecstasy at the Onion*. New York: Bobbs-Merrill.

Be-Bop, Be-Bopped. (1946, March 25). *Time*, p. 52.

Bebop to Carnegie Hall. (1947, September 24). *Down Beat*, 14(20), 5.

Berendt, J. (1955). John Lewis—König des Cool Jazz. *Melos*, 22(1), 348–50.

Berg, C. M. (1978). Cinema Sings the Blues. *Cinema Journal*, 17(2), 1–12.

Berlack-Boozer, T. (1938, June 11). Bledsoe Gives Rare Treat at Town Hall. *New York Amsterdam News*, p. 10.

Best, M. (1999). John Lewis and the Film Score for "Odds against Tomorrow." Pt. II. In J. Schultheiss (Ed.), *"Odds against Tomorrow": The Critical Edition* (pp. 309–13). Northridge: California State University.

Bethune, M. (1950, February 4). Lionel Hampton Beats Out New Rhythm for Civil Rights Fight. *Chicago Defender*, p. 6.

Blesh, R. (1946). *Shining Trumpets: A History of Jazz*. New York: Alfred A. Knopf.

Bosman, W. (1705/1814). New and Accurate Description of the Coast of Guinea. In J. Pinkerton (Ed.), *A General Collection of the Best and Most Interesting Voyages and Travels of All Parts of the World* (pp. 337–547). London: Private publisher. Digitized by Google Books.

Bouchard, F. (2001). John Lewis: 1920–2001. *Down Beat*, 68(6), 22.

Bouchard, F. (2002). John Lewis: Hall of Fame. *Down Beat*, 69(8), 26–28.

Bourne, M. (1992). Bop Baroque The Blues. *Down Beat*, 59(1), 24–27.

Brackett, D. (1992). James Brown's "Superbad" and the Double-Voiced Utterance. *Popular Music*, 11(3), 309–24.

Brandeis Arts Festival Will Feature Jazz. (1952, May 21). *Down Beat*, p. 5.

Brooks, T. (2004). *Lost Sounds: Blacks and the Birth of the Recording Industry, 1890–1919*. Urbana: University of Illinois Press.

Brown, R. (1997). Price, Florence Beatrice. In S. Floyd (Ed.), *International Dictionary of Black Composers (pp. 937–45)*. Chicago: Fitzroy Dearborn.

Brubeck, D. (1950). Jazz' Evolution as an Art Form. *Down Beat*, 17(3), 13,18.

Brubeck Dave Is Campus Fave. (1954, October 20). *Down Beat*, p. 1.

Burley, D. (1948, Feb 21). Thelonious Monk and His Bebop. *New York Amsterdam News*, p. 25.

Burrows, G. (2007). Black, Brown and Beige and the Politics of Signifyin(g). *Jazz Research Journal*, 1(1), 45–71.

Butler, D. (2002). *Jazz Noir: Listening to Music from "Phantom Lady" to "The Last Seduction."* Westport, Conn.: Praeger.

Butler, D. (2009). "No Brotherly Love": Hollywood Jazz, Racial Prejudice, and John Lewis's Score for *Odds against Tomorrow*. In G. Lock & D. Murray (Eds.), *Thriving on a Riff: Jazz & Blues Influences in African American Literature and Film* (pp. 221–39). New York: Oxford University Press.

Campbell, W. (1948, May 29). Buffalo. *Chicago Defender*, p. 18.

Child, J. (1998). Machito. In D. Clarke (Ed.) *The Penguin Encyclopedia of Popular Music* (2nd ed., pp. 743–44). New York: Penguin Putnam.

Clar, M. (1964, September 28). Modern Jazz Group Opens UCLA Series. *Los Angeles Times*, p. C15.

Claude Thornhill to Disband Ork. (1948, June 2). *Down Beat*, p. 1.

Coady, C. (2011). From Gospel to Gates: Modal Blending in African-American Music Discourse Before *The Signifyin(g) Monkey. PORTAL Journal of Multidisciplinary International Studies*, 8(1), 1–17.

Cohen, H. (2004). The Marketing of Duke Ellington: Setting the Strategy for an African American Maestro. *Journal of African American History*, 89(4), 291–315.

Contralto Here in Recital. (1946, November 9). *Chicago Defender*, p. 19C.

Cooke, M. (2009). Anatomy of a Movie: Duke Ellington and 1950s Film Scoring. In G. Lock & D. Murray (Eds.), *Thriving on a Riff: Jazz & Blues Influences in African American Literature and Film* (pp. 240–62). New York: Oxford University Press.

Coss, B. (1956). Jazz Society at Town Hall. *Metronome*, 72(1), 50.

Covering Concerts. (1945, December 1). *New York Amsterdam News*, p. 6.

Crease, S. (2002). *Gil Evans: Out of the Cool, His Life and Music*. Chicago: Chicago Review Press.

Crosby, I. (1971). Prophet without Honor. *Jazz Journal*, 24, 9.

Daniel, V. (1944). Negro Classes and Life in the Church. *Journal of Negro Education*, 13(1), 19–29.

Davis, F. (1983). The Art of Fugue. *Village Voice*, 28, 70, 80.

Davis, M. (1989). *Miles the Autobiography/Miles with Quincy Trope*. New York: Touchstone.

Dean Dixon Back in Concert Series. (1946, November 9). *Chicago Defender*, p. 10.

Dean Dixon to Conduct Stockholm Symphony Orchestra. (1953, February 13). *Wichita Post-Observer*, p. 4.

Delage, M. (1926, April). Le musique de jazz. *Revue Pleyel*, pp. 18–20.

De Micheal, D. (1961). Jackson of the MJQ. *Down Beat*, 28(14), 18–21.

De Micheal, D., & Welding, P. (1964). Jazz Basics: The Concluding Part of a History of Jazz on Record. *Down Beat*, 31(22), 25.

DeVeaux, S. (1991). Constructing the Jazz Tradition: Jazz Historiography. *Black American Literature Forum*, 25(3), 525–60.

DeVeaux, S. (1997). *The Birth of Bebop*. Berkeley: University of California Press.

Dinerstein, J. (2008). "Emergent Noir": Film Noir and the Great Depression in *High Sierra* (1941) and *This Gun for Hire* (1942). *Journal of American Studies*, 42(3), 415–48.

Diton, C. (1955, April 14). Interracial Concert Held at Town Hall in New York. *Atlanta Daily World*, p. 5.

Dixon, F. (1928, March 21). Hal Johnson Negro Choir in Concert. *New York Amsterdam News*, p. 9.

Du Bois, W. E. B. (1946, February 23). The Winds of Time. *Chicago Defender*, p. 15.

Du Bois, W. E. B. (2007). *The Souls of Black Folk*. New York: Oxford University Press. Originally published 1903.

Durgnat, R. (1970). Paint It Black: The Family Tree of Film Noir. *Cinema*, 6(7), 49–56.

Eagan, D. (2010). *America's Film Legacy: The Authoritative Guide to the Landmark Movies in the National Film Registry*. New York: Continuum.

Ellington, D. (1943). Spoken introduction. *Black, Brown and Beige: The Duke Ellington Carnegie Hall Concerts, January 1943*. Prestige CD 2PCD-34004-2.

Ellsworth, R. (1957). Classic Modern. *Down Beat*, 24(14), 34.

Epstein, D. (1977). *Sinful Tunes and Spirituals: Black Folk Music to the Civil War*. Urbana: University of Illinois Press.

Eva Vorhies, Pianist Pays Harlem a Visit. (1942, November 14). *Chicago Defender*, p. 21.

Everett Lee to Conduct Symphony. (1948, May 8). *Pittsburgh Courier*, p. 16.

Everett Lee to Present Mixed Symphony Group. (1947, October 25). *New York Amsterdam News*, p. 6.

Fauser, A. (2006). Aaron Copland, Nadia Boulanger, and the Making of an "American" Composer. *Musical Quarterly*, 89(4), 524–54.

Fenstermaker, A. (2008). *Bridging the Gap between (White) Metafiction and (Black) Self Reflexivity*. Doctoral dissertation, University of Rochester.

Finkelstein, S. (1948). *Jazz: A People's Music*. New York: Citadel Press.

Floyd, S. (1991/1999). Ring Shout! Literary Studies, Historical Studies, and Black Music Inquiry. In G. D. Caponi (Ed.), *Signifyin(g), Sanctifin', & Slam Dunking: A Reader in African-American Expressive Culture* (pp. 309–30). Amherst: University of Massachusetts Press.

Floyd, S. (1995). *The Power of Black Music: Interpreting Its History from Africa to the United States*. New York: Oxford University Press.

Ford, P. (2008). Jazz Exotica and the Naked City. *Journal of Musicological Research*, 27(2), 113–33.

46 Get Rosenwald Fund Fellowship Awards. (1945, May 26). *Chicago Defender*, p. 2.

Fraterrigo, E. (2009). *Playboy and the Making of the Good Life in Modern America*. New York: Oxford University Press.

Frazier, E. F. (1957). *Black Bourgeoisie*. Glencoe, Ill.: Free Press.

Frazier, E. F. (1964). *The Negro Church in America*. Liverpool: Liverpool University Press.

Fuller, A. B. (2007). *Chaplain Fuller: Being a Life Sketch of a New England Clergyman and Army Chaplain*. Boston: Walker, Wise. Digitized by NYPL Research Libraries. Originally published 1863.

Garcia, A. J. (2001). Dave Brubeck: His Music Keeps Us Here. *Jazz Education Journal*, 34(3), 38–41, 43–45.

Gates, H. L. (1988). *The Signifying Monkey: A Theory of African-American Literary Criticism*. New York: Oxford University Press.

Gennari, J. (2006). *Blowin' Hot and Cool: Jazz and Its Critics*. Chicago: University of Chicago Press.

Giddins, G. (1988). *Satchmo*. New York: Doubleday.

Giddins, G. (1998). *Visions of Jazz*. New York: Oxford University Press.

Giddins, G., & Armstrong, L. (1986). *Satchmo: My Life in New Orleans*. New York: Da Capo Press.

Gillespie, D. (1979). *To Be, or Not . . . to Bop: Memoirs*. With Al Fraser. New York: Doubleday.

Gioia, T. (1989). Jazz and the Primitivist Myth. *Musical Quarterly*, 73(1), 130–43.

Gioia, T. (1992). *West Coast Jazz: Modern Jazz in California, 1945–1960*. New York: Oxford University Press.

Givan, B. (2010). *The Music of Django Reinhardt*. Ann Arbor: University of Michigan Press.

Gleason, R. (1951). Charlie Mingus: A Thinking Musician. *Down Beat*, 18(9), 7.

Gleason, R. (1956). Perspectives. *Down Beat*, 23(8), 18.

Goffin, R. (1944). *Jazz from the Congo to the Metropolitan*. New York: Doubleday.

Goldberg, J. (2002). Jazz: 50 Years (More or Less) of the Modern Jazz Quartet. *Billboard*, 114(23), 26–27.

Goldmark, D. (2005). Jungle Jive: Race, Jazz and Cartoons. *Institute for Studies in American Music Newsletter*, 34(2), 1–3.

Goodman-Armstrong Team in 1st Jazz Concert. (1953, April 11). *New York Age*, p. 12.

Gottlieb, W. (1947a). Rhumba Bands May Cut Hot Orks. *Down Beat*, 14(16), 10.

Gottlieb, W. (1947b). Thelonious Monk—Genius of Bop. *Down Beat*, 14(20), 2.

Granger, L. (1948, December 25). Manhattan & Beyond. *New York Amsterdam News*, p. 11.

Granz' "JATP" Swings toward Foreign Stages. (1953, August 22). *New York Age*, p. 19.

Greenidge, E. (1946, October 5). Teddy Wilson Sees Bebop in Symphonies. *Pittsburgh Courier*, p. 21.

Guérif, F. (1981). *Le cinéma policier français*. Paris: Veyrier.

Haggerty, M., & Clarke, K. (1985). Under Paris Skies. *Black Perspective in Music*, 13(2), 195–221.

Haines, H. (1984). Black Radicalization and the Funding of Civil Rights: 1957–1970. *Social Problems*, 32(1), 31–43.

Handy, D. A. (1981). *Black Women in American Bands & Orchestras*. Metuchen, N. J.: Scarecrow Press.
Hare, N. (1965). *The Black Anglo Saxons*. New York: Marzani & Munsell.
Harris, M. (1992). *The Rise of Gospel Blues: The Music of Thomas Andrew Dorsey in the Urban Church*. New York: Oxford University Press.
Hartman, C. (1948, December 5). Bop: Skee, Re or Be, "It's Still Got to Swing." *New York Times*, p. X13.
Hentoff, N. (1953a). Counterpoint. *Down Beat*, 20(26), 8.
Hentoff, N. (1953b). Jazz Reviews: Modern Jazz Quartet. *Down Beat*, 20(22), p. 16.
Hentoff, N. (1954a). Caught in the Act: Modern Jazz Quartet: Birdland, New York. *Down Beat*, 21(20), 32.
Hentoff, N. (1954b). Counterpoint. *Down Beat*, 21(1), 6, 27.
Hentoff, N. (1954c). Jazz Fills Role of Classical Composition, Brubeck Learns. *Down Beat*, 21(11), 2.
Hentoff, N. (1955a). Initial Modern Jazz Society Concert Marks Some Firsts. *Down Beat*, 22(26), 8.
Hentoff, N. (1955b). Modern Jazz Quartet Sparks Rewarding Town Hall Concert. *Down Beat*, 22(26), 14.
Hentoff, N. (1957a). The Birth of the Cool. *Down Beat*, 24(9), 15–16.
Hentoff, N. (1957b). John Lewis. *Down Beat*, 24(4), 15–16.
Hentoff, N. (1958). European Windows: John Lewis. In *European Windows* [LP liner notes] (p. 1). RCA Victor.
Hersch, C. (1996, Winter). "Let Freedom Ring!": Free Jazz and African-American Politics. *Cultural Critique*, 32, 97–123.
Higginbotham, E. B. (1993). *Righteous Discontent: The Women's Movement in the Black Baptist Church, 1880–1920*. Cambridge, Mass.: Harvard University Press.
Hodeir, A. (1956a). *Jazz: Its Evolution and Essence*. New York: Grove Press.
Hodeir, A. (1956b). Les mérites du Modern Jazz Quartet. *Jazz Hot*, 22(116), 34.
Hoefer, G. (1948). "Jax" Bringing Jazz to Carleton College, Minn. *Down Beat*, 15(19), 11.
Hoefer, G. (1959). Modern Jazz Quartet , Beaux-Arts String Quartet. *Down Beat*, 26(23), 46.
Holley, E. (2000). Farewell to the Quartet. *Down Beat*, 67(4), 38–41, 43.
Holt, N. (1944, December 23). Music-Liberty Hand in Hand Dixon Proves. *New York Amsterdam News*, p. 6.
How Deaf Can You Get? (1948, May 17). *Time*, p. 74.
Howland, J. (2009). *Ellington Uptown: Duke Ellington, James P. Johnson, and the Birth of Concert Jazz*. Ann Arbor: University of Michigan Press.
Hughes, L. (1954, October 16). Simple Says Jazz, Jive and Jam Could Help Integration Along. *Chicago Defender*, p. 9.
Hunter, B. (1962, October 8). MJQ Leader Milt Jackson Stresses Culture in Jazz. *Chicago Daily Defender*, p. 16.
Hurley, A. (2009). *The Return of Jazz: Joachim-Ernst Berendt and West German Cultural Change*. New York: Berghahn Books.
Hutcheon, L. (1989). *The Politics of Postmodernism*. New York: Routledge.
Jackson, J. (2002). Making Jazz French: The Reception of Jazz Music in Paris, 1927–1934. *French Historical Studies*, 25(1), 149–70.
Jazz Bitterly Opposed in Germany. (1928, March 11). *New York Times*, p. 10.

Jazz, Classical Music Society to Hold First Concert Oct. 19. (1956, October 3). *Down Beat*, p.11.

Jazz Composers Workshop. (1954, March 10). *Down Beat*, p. 21.

Jazz Course at NYU. (1950, October 20). *Down Beat*, p. 1.

Jazz Experiment. (1952, May 21). *Down Beat*, p. 8.

Jazz in Films. (1959, November 12). *Down Beat*, pp. 16–17.

Jazz Is Barred from Campus by U. of Kentucky Educators. (1951, April 6). *Down Beat*, p. 16.

Jazz School's First Session Set at Lenox. (1957, March 6). *Down Beat*, p. 13.

Jazz Society Spots MJQ in Concert. (1955, November 30). *Down Beat*, p. 52.

Jazz und Alte Musik. (1957). (LP). Telefunken LA6193.

Jones, L. (1963a). *Blues People*. New York: Morrow.

Jones, L. (1963b). Jazz and the White Critic. *Down Beat*, 30(23), 16–17, 34.

Jones, L. (2010). The Jazz Avant-Garde. In L. Jones (Ed.), *Black Music* (pp. 69–80). Renegade Reprint Series. New York: Akashi Books. Originally published 1961.

Jordan, M. (2010). *Le Jazz: Jazz and French Cultural Identity*. Urbana: University of Illinois Press.

Jordan, M. (2011). The French Connection: Mythologies of *La Nouvelle Orléans* in French Discourse on Jazz. *European Journal of Cultural Studies*, 14(5), 507–25.

Joyner, D. (2000). Analyzing Third Stream. *Contemporary Music Review*, 19(1), 63–87.

Junior Choir in Annual Spring Recital. (1942, April 25). *Chicago Defender*, p. 17.

Kaplan, F. (2009). *1959: The Year Everything Changed*. Hoboken, N.J.: John Wiley and Sons.

Keepnews, P. (2001, March 31). John Lewis, 80, Pianist, Composer and Creator of the Modern Jazz Quartet, Dies. *New York Times*, p. B9.

Keith, H. (1958, June 21). Data 'Bout Discs: "The Golden Strike." *Pittsburgh Courier*, p. 16.

Kenton Lecture on Jazz. (1951, March 9). *Down Beat*, p. 7.

Kernfeld, B. (2002). Soul Jazz. In *New Grove Dictionary of Jazz*. (Vol. 3, pp. 635–36). New York: New Grove's Dictionaries.

Knauer, W. (1990). *Zwischen Bebop und Free Jazz: Komposition und Improvisation des Modern Jazz Quartet*. Mainz: Schott Musikwissenschaft.

Knauer, W. (1997). Lewis, John Aaron. In S. Floyd (Ed.), *International Dictionary of Black Composers* (pp. 730–38). Chicago: Fitzroy Dearborn.

Korrol, S. (1983). *From Colonia to Community: The History of Puerto Ricans in New York City, 1917–1948*. Westport, Conn.: Greenwood Press.

Kramer, G. (1960). Golden Striker. In *The Golden Striker* [LP liner notes] (p. 1). New York: Atlantic.

Kramer, G. (1962). The Comedy/The Modern Jazz Quartet. In *The Comedy* [LP liner notes] (p. 1). New York: Atlantic.

Lalo, T. (1991). *John Lewis*. Paris: Éditions du Limon.

Laubenstein, P. F. (1929). Jazz—Debit and Credit. *Musical Quarterly*, 15(4), 606–24.

Leonard, Herman. (2010). *Jazz*. London: Atlantic Books.

Leroy Hurte Directs Choirs for Gala "Jubilee Festival." (1960, October 6). *Los Angeles Sentinel*, p. C2.

Levin, M. (1947). Despite Bad Acoustics, Gillespie Concert Offers Some Excellent Music. *Down Beat*, 14(22), 1.

Levine, L. (1989) Jazz and American Culture. *Journal of American Folklore*, 102(403), 6–22.

Lewis, G. (2008). *A Power Stronger Than Itself: The AACM and American Experimental Music*. Chicago: University of Chicago Press.

Lewis, J. (1956). Fontessa. In *Fontessa* [LP liner notes] (p. 1). Atlantic Records.

Lewis, J. (1960). Excerpts from *The Comedy* [Score]. New York: MJQ Music.

Lewis, J. (2006). *The Complete Jazz Casual Series* [DVD]. Rhino Records. Originally released 1962.

"Life" Points Out Northern Bias Areas. (1957, March 15). *Crusader*, p. 2.

Lionel Hampton Writes of Bebop, the New Movement in Swing Music. (1948, July 17). *Chicago Defender*, p. 8.

Locke, A. (1939). The Negro's Contribution to American Culture. *Journal of Negro Education*, 8(3), 521–9.

Lopes, P. (2002). *The Rise of a Jazz Art World*. Cambridge: Cambridge University Press.

Lopes, P. (2005). Signifying Deviance and Transgression: Jazz in the Popular Imagination. *American Behavioral Scientist*, 48(11), 1468–81.

Lyons, L. (1983). *The Great Jazz Pianists Speaking of their Lives and Music*. New York: Da Capo Press.

Magee, J. (2007). Kinds of Blue: Miles Davis, Afro Modernism, and the Blues. *Jazz Perspectives*, 1(1), 5–27.

Mead, A. (1994). *An Introduction to the Music of Milton Babbitt*. Princeton, N.J.: Princeton University Press.

Meadows, E. (2003). *Bebop to Cool*. Westport, Conn.: Praeger.

Mingus, C. (1976). *Revelations* [score]. New York: Margun Music.

MJQ to Storyville. (1955, February 23). *Down Beat*, p. 6.

MJQ Views. (1987, September). *Crescendo International*, p. 28

Modern Jazz Quartet Here Saturday Night. (1959, April 14). *Atlanta Daily World*, p. 3.

Modern Jazz Quartet Top Unit to Emerge from 1940 "Bop" Era. (1963, April 25). *Chicago Daily Defender*, p. 29.

Modern Jazz Quartet Wins Acclaim in Paris. (1960, June 13). *Chicago Defender*, p. A17.

Monson, I. (1995). The Problem with White Hipness: Race, Gender, and Cultural Conceptions in Jazz Historical Discourse. *Journal of the American Musicological Society*, 48(3), 396–422.

Monson, I. (1998). Oh Freedom: George Russell, John Coltrane, and Modal Jazz. In B. Nettle & M. Russell (Eds.), *In the Course of Performance: Studies in the World of Musical Improvisation* (pp. 149–68). Chicago: University of Chicago Press.

Moreno, J. (2004). Bauzá—Gillespie—Latin/Jazz: Difference, Modernity and the Black Caribbean. *South Atlantic Quarterly*, 103(1), 81–99.

Mulligan, G. (1995). *I Hear America Singing*. Retrieved January 5, 2005, from http://lcweb2.loc.gov/diglib/ihas/html/mulligan/gm-hom.html.

Murphy, J. (1990). Jazz Improvisation: The Joy of Influence. *Black Perspective in Music*, 18(1/2), 7–19.

Music, D. (2001). *Christian Hymnody in Twentieth-Century Britain and America*. Westport, Conn.: Greenwood Press.

Music for Moderns in Second Concert. (1957, May 11). *New York Amsterdam News*, p. 13.

Myers, D. G. (1990, February). Signifying Nothing. *New Criterion*, 8, 61–64.

Myrdal, G. (1971). The Negro Church: Its Weakness, Trends and Outlook. In H. Nelson,

R. Yokley, & A. Nelson (Eds.), *The Black Church in America* (pp. 256–64). New York: Basic Books. Originally published 1944.

Naremore, J. (1998). *More Than Night: Film Noir in its Contexts*. Berkeley: University of California Press.

Nason, R.W. (1959, March 15). Evaluating the "Odds": Harry Belafonte Tries Broad Racial Approach in Locally Made Feature. *New York Times*, p. X7.

Negro Maestro Makes Bow with Opera Company. (1955, April 22). *Kansas Whip*, p. 1.

Ness, R. (2008). A Lotta Night Music: The Sound of *Film Noir*. *Cinema Journal*, 47(2), 52–73.

A New Approach to Jazz Concerts. (1954, December 15). *Down Beat*, p. 12.

New Series Explores Jazz Developments. (1955, January 12). *Down Beat*, p. 16.

New York Orchestral Society Embodies Cross-Section of Harlem's Talent. (1953, June 6). *New York Age*, 7.

Nicoll, A. (1963). *The World of Harlequin: A Critical Study of the Commedia Dell'Arte*. Cambridge: Cambridge University Press.

Norrell, R. (2009). *Up from History: The Life of Booker T. Washington*. Cambridge, Mass.: Harvard University Press.

Northern, C. (1948, June 5). 26-Year-Old Symphony Conductor Makes Debut. *Chicago Defender*, p. 13.

Noss, L. (1948). Stan Kenton: Progressive Jazz Series; The Original Recording Arrangements Used by the Stan Kenton Orchestra. *Music Library Association Notes*, 5(3), 414–15.

NYU to Conduct Jazz Course. (1950, February 10). *Down Beat*, p. 1.

O'Connor, N. J. (1957). Jazz at Brandeis. *Down Beat*, 24(15), 18.

Ohio. (1946, January 26). *Chicago Defender*, p. 11.

Omi, M., & Winant, H. (1994). *Racial Formation in the United States from the 1960s to the 1990s*. New York: Routledge.

Overton, C. (1934, November 24). Dawson's Symphony Played at Carnegie. *New York Amsterdam News*, p. 4.

Owens, T. (1965). *Improvisation Techniques of the Modern Jazz Quartet*. Master's thesis, University of California, Los Angeles, 1965.

Owens, T. (1976). The Fugal Pieces of the Modern Jazz Quartet. *Journal of Jazz Studies*, iv, 22–33.

Panassié, H. (1936). *Hot Jazz*. New York: M. Witmark & Sons.

Pautrot. J. (2006). *The André Hodeir Jazz Reader*. Ann Arbor: University of Michigan Press.

Payne, D. A. (2001). *Recollections of Seventy Years*. Nashville: Publishing House of the A.M.E. Sunday School Union. Digitized by the University of North Carolina at Chapel Hill. Originally published 1891.

Perchard, T. (2011). Tradition, Modernity and the Supernatural Swing: Re-reading "Primitivism" in Hugues Panassié's Writing on Jazz. *Popular Music*, 30(1), 24–45.

Pfeil, F. (1993). Home Fires Burning: Family Noir in *Blue Velvet* and *Terminator 2*. In J. Copjec (Ed.), *Shades of Noir* (pp. 227–61). London: Verso.

Polonsky, A. (1999). Screenplay to *Odds against Tomorrow*. In J. Schultheiss (Ed.), *"Odds against Tomorrow": The Critical Edition* (pp. 7–136). Northridge: California State University.

Porter, E. (2002). *What Is This Thing Called Jazz?*. Berkeley: University of California Press.

Praise Goes to Town Hall Pianist, New York "Cinderella." (1955, April 6). *Atlanta Daily World*, p. 8.

A "Precious Asset" for John Lewis. (1960, July 7). *Down Beat*, p. 9.

Priestley, B. (1982). *Mingus: A Critical Biography*. New York: Da Capo.

Pulley, H. (1960). So They Say. *Daily Defender*, May 18, A17.

Race Symphony Is Played in N.Y.C. (1935, November 30). *Chicago Defender*, p. 5.

Radano, R. (2003). *Lying up a Nation: Race and Black Music*. Chicago: University of Chicago Press.

Ramsey, G. (2001). Who Hears Here? Black Music, Critical Bias, and the Musicological Skin Trade. *Musical Quarterly*, 85(1), 1–52.

Ramsey, G. (2003). *Race Music: Black Cultures from Bebop to Hip-Hop*. Berkeley: University of California Press.

Record Review: Miles Davis. (1949a, April 22). *Down Beat*, p. 14.

Record Review: Miles Davis. (1949b, May 20). *Down Beat*, p. 14.

Record Review: Miles Davis. (1949c, October 21). *Down Beat*, p. 15.

Roland Hayes in 1st Concert at Town Hall. (1937, September 25). *New York Amsterdam News*, p. 20.

Ronan, E. (1947). Concerts Keep Cats in Cakes! Musicians Turn to Halls to Tide Them Over Dance Biz Lull. *Down Beat*, 14(8), 1.

Russell, G. (1959). *The Lydian Chromatic Concept of Tonal Organization for Improvisation*. Cambridge, Mass.: Concept. Originally published 1953.

Ryder, G. (1997). Dett, R(obert) Nathaniel. In S. Floyd (Ed.), *International Dictionary of Black Composers* (pp. 365–72). Chicago: Fitzroy Dearborn.

Sachs, E. (1959). John Lewis, Man and Musician. *Down Beat*, 26(3), 18.

Salamone, F. (2005). Jazz and Its Impact on European Classical Music. *Journal of Popular Culture*, 38(4), 732–43.

Sargeant, W. (1975). *Jazz Hot and Hybrid* (3rd ed.). New York: Da Capo Press. Originally published 1938.

Saul, S. (2003). *Freedom Is, Freedom Ain't: Jazz and the Making of the Sixties*. Cambridge, Mass.: Harvard University Press.

Schenbeck, L. (2012). *Racial Uplift and American Music: 1878–1943*. Jackson: University of Mississippi Press.

Schiff, D. (1997). *Gershwin, Rhapsody in Blue*. Cambridge: Cambridge University Press.

Schmitz, H., & de Lerma, R. (1979). Baroque Music and Jazz. *Black Perspective in Music*, 7(1), 75–80.

School Dance Contest Opens. (1953, February 11). *Down Beat*, p. 1.

The School of Jazz. (1957, October 3). *Down Beat*, pp. 23, 48.

Schrader, P. (1972). Notes on Film Noir. *Film Comment*, 8(1), 155–91.

Schuller, G. (1957). The Brass Ensemble of the Jazz and Classical Music Society. In *Music for Brass* [LP liner notes] (p. 1). Columbia Records.

Schuller, G. (1958). Sonny Rollins and the Challenge of Thematic Improvisation. *Jazz Review*, 1(1), 6.

Schuller, G. (1968). *Early Jazz: Its Roots and Musical Development*. New York: Oxford University Press.

Schuller, G. (1986). *Musings: The Musical Worlds of Gunther Schuller*. New York: Oxford University Press.

Schultheiss, J. (1996, April). A Season of Fear: The Blacklisted Teleplays by Abraham Polonsky. *Literature/Film Quarterly* 24(2), 148–64.
Schultheiss, J. (1999). Annotations to the Screenplay. In J. Schultheiss (Ed.) *Odds Against Tomorrow: The Critical Edition* (137–64). Northridge: California State University.
Scott, L. (1949, January 15). Lillian Cannon Is Dynamo of Symphony. *Chicago Defender*, p. 13.
Shim, E. (2007). *Lennie Tristano: His Life in Music*. Ann Arbor: University of Michigan Press.
Silver, A., & Ward, E. (Eds.). (1992). *Film Noir: An Encyclopedic Reference to the American Style*. New York: Overlook.
Singer Thrills Tucson Crowd. (1944, July 8). *Chicago Defender*, p. 17A.
Six Works of Jazz Commissioned by Brandeis University. (1957, April 7). *Down Beat*, p. 11.
The Slipped Disc. (1957, December). *Esquire*, p. 12.
Smith, C. (1959). 25 Years of Jazz. *Down Beat*, 26(16), 37–39.
Smith, I. (1938, April 9). Marian Thrills at Town Hall Concert. *Pittsburgh Courier*, p. 19.
Snyder, J. (1997). Burleigh, Harry [Henry] T(hacker). In S. Floyd (Ed.), *International Dictionary of Black Composers* (pp. 182–93). Chicago: Fitzroy Dearborn.
Snyder, J. (2004). Harry T. Burleigh, “One of Erie’s Most Popular Church Singers.” *Black Music Research Journal*, 24(2), 195–225.
Sous le signe du ‘Birdland’: Paris a accuilli l’élite du jazz moderne. (1956, December 22). *Jazz Magazine*, p. 18–21.
Spotlight Review. (1960, December 8). *Down Beat*, p. 36.
Stearns Starts Club on Cornell Campus. (1947, March 26). *Down Beat*, p. 4.
Stephenson, S. (2009). *The Jazz Loft Project: Photographs and Tapes of W. Eugene Smith from 921 Sixth Avenue, 1957–1965*. New York: Alfred A. Knopf.
Still’s Symphony to Be Presented Here. (1936, February 29). *Pittsburgh Courier*, p. 8.
Stovall, T. (1996). *Paris Noir: African Americans in the City of Light*. New York: Houghton Mifflin.
Stowe, D. (1994). *Swing Changes: Big-Band Jazz in New Deal America*. Cambridge, Mass.: Harvard University Press.
Strong, W. (1997). Dawson, William Levi. In S. Floyd (Ed.) *International Dictionary of Black Composers* (pp. 354–59). Chicago: Fitzroy Dearborn.
Stuckey, S. (1987). *Slave Culture: Nationalist Theory and the Foundations of Black America*. New York: Oxford University Press.
Tarrytown. (1947, January 4). *Chicago Defender*, p. 17.
Taubman, H. (1956, April 22). An Even Break: Preparing for Columbia University’s Obeisance to Mozart. *New York Times*, p. X9.
These Two Leave Worthy Heritage. (1953, June 27). *New York Age*, p. 10.
Thompson, R. (1932). The Contemporary Scene in American Music. *Musical Quarterly*, 18(1), 9–17.
Thorne, F. (1960). An Afternoon with John Lewis. *Jazz Review*, 3(3), 6–9.
Thornhill Ork on 3-Week Vacation, Budget Cut for Glen Island Job. (1947, March 12). *Down Beat*, p. 1.
Tomlinson, G. (1991). Cultural Dialogics and Jazz: A White Historian Signifies. *Black Music Research Journal*, 11(2), 229–64.

Tompkins, G. (1941, February 22). Frankie Fambro Scores Triumph in Loop Recital. *Chicago Defender*, p. 18.
Top Jazz Musicians Join 1958 Faculty of the School of Jazz. (1958, June 14). *Pittsburgh Courier*, p. 15.
Tristano Returns to Chi in Blue Note Two-Weeker. (1951, April 20). *Down Beat*, p. 6.
Tucker, M. (1993). *The Duke Ellington Reader*. New York: Oxford University Press.
Twin Brothers Are Honored at Recital. (1950, August 26). *Chicago Defender*, p. 24.
Ulanov, B. (1952). *A History of Jazz in America*. New York: Viking Press.
Ulanov, B. (1975). *Duke Ellington*. New York: Da Capo Press. Originally published 1946.
Valentine, G. (1935, March 23). Morehouse and Fisk Groups Pleasing. *Atlanta Daily World*, p. 1.
Van de Leur, W. (2001). The American Impressionists and the Birth of the Cool. *Tijdshrift voor Muziektheorie* 6(1), 18–26.
Van de Leur, W. (2002). *Something to Live For: The Music of Billy Strayhorn*. New York: Oxford University Press.
Vernet, M. (1993). Film Noir: On the Edge of Doom. In J. Copjec (Ed.), *Shades of Noir* (pp. 1–31). London: Verso.
Vincendeau, G. (2007). French Film Noir. In A. Spicer (Ed.), *European Film Noir* (pp. 23–54). Manchester: Manchester University Press.
Walker, P. (2010). Episode. *Oxford Music Online*. Retrieved December 15, 2010, from www.oxfordmusiconline.com.
Walser, R. (1993). Out of Notes: Signification, Interpretation, and the Problem of Miles Davis. *Musical Quarterly*, 77(2), 343–65.
Washington, B. T. (2010). *Up from Slavery: An Autobiography*. New York: Doubleday. Originally published 1901.
Williams, M. (1970). *The Jazz Tradition*. New York: Oxford University Press.
Wilson, J. S. (1956, September 16). Jazz Workshop to Grow Next Year. *New York Times*, p. X9.
Wilson, J. S. (1957, June 2). Written Jazz. *New York Times*, p. 97.
Wilson, J. S. (1958a, April 6). Homecoming Jazzmen: Striped Pants of the Modern Quartet Astounded a British Enthusiast. *New York Times*, p. X9.
Wilson, J. S. (1958b, November 2). Serious or Jazz? *New York Times*, p. X12.
Wilson, J. S. (1958c, November 15). Modern Jazz Quartet Is Heard in Concert at Nonagon Gallery. *New York Times*, p. 18.
Wilson, J. S. (1959, May 25). Jazz Concert Given at Carnegie Hall. *New York Times*, p. 33.
Wilson, J. S. (1960, November 3). Extremes of Jazz Meet Nightly. *New York Times*, p. 47.
Wilson, J. S. (1961, April 2). Duke Ellington Still the Pioneer. *New York Times*, p. X16.
Wintle, C. (1976). Milton Babbitt's Semi-simple Variations. *Perspectives of New Music*, 14(2), 111–54.
Work, J. (1998). *American Negro Songs: 230 Folk Songs and Spirituals, Religious and Secular*. New York: Dover. Originally published 1940.
Yanow, S. (2004). *Jazz on Film*. San Francisco: Backbeat Books.

Scores

Bauer, B., & Sher, C. (1991). *New Real Book*. Vol. 2. Petaluma, CA: Sher Music.
Lewis, J. (1954). *Concorde* [Score]. New York: MJQ Music.
Lewis, J. (1957). *Three Little Feelings* [Score]. New York: MJQ Music.
Lewis, J. (1959). *Sketch for Double Quartet* [Score]. New York: MJQ Music.
Lewis, J. (1960). *Excerpts from "The Comedy"* [Score]. New York: MJQ Music.
Lewis, J. (1987). *Three Windows* [Score]. New York: MJQ Music.
Mingus, C. (1976). *Revelations* [Score]. New York: Margun Music.

Filmography

Ascenseur pour l'echafaud. (1957). Louis Malle (director). DVD. Paris: Nouvelles Editions de Films, 2002.
Cab Calloway's Hi-De-Ho. (1934). Fred Waller (director). In *The Best of Jazz and Blues.* Hollywood Rhythm, vol. 1. DVD. New York: Kino International, 2001.
I Want to Live!. (1958). Robert Wise (director). DVD. Los Angeles: MGM, 2002.
Odds against Tomorrow. (1959). Robert Wise (director). DVD. Los Angeles: MGM, 2003.
Sait-on jamais. (1957). Roger Vadim (director). DVD. Paris: René Chateau, 2005.
Touch of Evil. (1958). Orson Welles (director). DVD. New York: Universal Pictures, 2000.

Index